For ~~~~

You improved this book in 2012 and you've enriched my life since 1981!

Devotedly,

Bob

May 2014

Paul Diederich and the Progressive American High School

A Volume in
Readings in Educational Thought

Series Editor:
Wesley Null, *Baylor University*

Readings in Educational Thought
Wesley Null, Series Editor

*Readings in American Educational Thought:
From Puritanism to Progressivism* (2004)
edited by Andrew J. Milson, Chara Haeussler Bohan,
Perry L. Glanzer, and J. Wesley Null

*Forgotten Heroes of American Education:
The Great Tradition of Teaching Teachers* (2006)
edited by J. Wesley Null and Diane Ravitch

*American Educational Thought:
Essays from 1640-1940—2nd Ed.* (2010)
edited by edited by Andrew J. Milson, Chara Haeussler Bohan,
Perry L. Glanzer, and J. Wesley Null

*Clinical Teacher Education:
Reflections From an Urban Professional Development School Network* (2011)
edited by Chara Haeussler Bohan and Joyce E. Many

Paul Diederich and the Progressive American High School (2014)
by Robert L. Hampel

To Arthur G. Powell and to the memory of
Theodore R. Sizer (1932-2009)

Paul Diederich and the Progressive American High School

by
Robert L. Hampel
School of Education, University of Delaware

INFORMATION AGE PUBLISHING, INC.
Charlotte, NC • www.infoagepub.com

Library of Congress Cataloging-in-Publication Data

CIP data for this book can be found on the Library of Congress website http://www.loc.gov/index.html

ISBNs: Paperback: 978-1-62396-577-8
       Hardcover: 978-1-62396-578-5
       eBook: 978-1-62396-579-2

Copyright © 2014 IAP–Information Age Publishing, Inc.

All rights reserved. No part of this publication may be reproduced, stored in a retrieval system, or transmitted in any form or by any electronic or mechanical means, or by photocopying, microfilming, recording or otherwise without written permission from the publisher.

Printed in the United States of America

CONTENTS

Acknowledgments ix

Introduction xi

PART I: LESSONS LEARNED FROM THE EIGHT YEAR STUDY

1. Eighteen Shortcomings of American Education (1942) 3
2. Running Away (1942) 39
3. Free Reading (1942) 43

PART II: THE SPIRIT AND SUBSTANCE OF A PROGRESSIVE HIGH SCHOOL

—*Educate for the sake of a just society and a good life*

4. What Kind of Society Do We Want? (1936) 65
5. Philosophy for Teenagers (1940) 71
6. The Virtues Schools Should Cultivate (1945) 77

viii   CONTENTS

—Make the curriculum less onerous

7. Latin Grammar Without Tears (1939) 89
8. A Monstrous Schedule of Cramped Inactivity (1959) 101

—Provide more individual attention

9. "Progress Toward Complete Living": Guidance and
    Counseling in High School (1949) 109
10. Waiting Without Giving Up (1969) 129

—Restructure

11. When Should High School Begin And End? (1954) 137
12. A Seamless Eight Year Liberal Arts Education (1958) 145
13. Cutting Class Size by Half (1960) 155
14. Reorganizing the Educational Testing Service (1970) 163

Epilogue: Remembering (October 3, 1996) 179

More Diederich 181

About the Author 183

Index 185

ACKNOWLEDGMENTS

My interest in Paul Diederich began in 1982 at the archives of the Educational Testing Service (ETS). As I read correspondence between ETS President Henry Chauncey and former Harvard University President James Conant, I saw Diederich's critique of Conant's prescriptions for secondary education. Diederich's misgivings impressed me, and I quoted him in my book, *The Last Little Citadel: American High Schools since 1940* (Houghton Mifflin, 1986). In 1988, I returned to the ETS archives for research on the history of testing, and in the Ben Wood Papers I found the long essay that is now the first chapter in this book. When I later considered editing that essay by itself, I learned that ETS had a large collection of Diederich materials: over one hundred published and unpublished articles, nine research reports, and several dozen memoranda.

Elsewhere I was fortunate to find other indispensable sources. A trip to the University of Chicago unearthed more Diederich letters, several unpublished essays, and correspondence with Morris Finder, one of Ralph Tyler's biographers. At Harvard University, the student files for Diederich contain valuable biographical information. The I.A. Richards Papers at Harvard lack Diederich letters, but the Rockefeller Archives Center in Tarrytown, New York has several items about Richards and Diederich, and its files on the Eight Year Study are extensive. A crucial collection was in the basement of Diederich's daughter, Anne Groom, who saved the copies of hundreds of letters Paul wrote in his retirement (his earlier papers were destroyed when his house burnt to the ground in 1972). Most of those letters were sent to his best friend and former University of Chicago colleague Siegmund Levarie, whom I interviewed in New York City on September

Paul Diederich and the Progressive American High School, pp. ix–x
Copyright © 2014 by Information Age Publishing
All rights of reproduction in any form reserved.

28, 2008. To understand the places where Paul worked, I relied on dozens of articles and books on the Ohio State University campus school, the Eight Year Study, Harvard University, the University of Chicago, and ETS. Biographies of Ralph Tyler, I.A. Richards, Robert Hutchins, and Henry Chauncey were also helpful. I learned more about Ohio State University through conversations with Robert Butche and Mary Tolbert, former students at the OSU school; Professor Craig Kridel, the coauthor of an excellent history of the Eight Year Study; and Professor James Raths, whose father worked for Tyler and with Diederich. At ETS, I spoke with Sydell Carlton, one of Paul's closest collaborators, and 12 other ETS veterans I interviewed in 2004 for a different project. Professor Norbert Elliot (New Jersey Institute of Technology) shared his extensive knowledge of ETS. I am indebted to Paul's children Anne Groom and Bob Diederich, whom I interviewed repeatedly, and Len Groom, Anne's husband.

I am also indebted to the ETS archivists. In the 1980s, Gary Saretzky guided me through the voluminous Ben Wood Papers and other collections at ETS. For my recent work, Jason Wagner helped make each trip to Princeton enjoyable and productive.

I thank David Blacker (University of Delaware) and Craig Kridel (University of South Carolina) for their cogent comments on an earlier version of this anthology. Andy Milson (University of Texas at Arlington) gave the final draft a careful review. I am especially grateful to Arthur G. Powell for his painstaking critique of the first draft. He and Theodore R. Sizer changed my life in the early 1980s, persuading me to leave 19th century political history for the 20th century history of education. The dedication of this book to Art and to the memory of Ted barely conveys how much they have meant to me.

INTRODUCTION

No one cleared the table after a meal in the Diederichs' apartment in Chicago. Each glass, dish, and piece of silverware was attached to five long boards that pivoted sideways to be sprayed by a hose. The hardest work was emptying the water that funneled to a large bucket on the dining room floor.

Paul Diederich built the table because his wife despised housework, but he was a lifelong craftsman. As a child in Kansas he made his own toys in the workshop of his grandfather, a carpenter born in Germany. As an adult he created lap-size chalkboards for first grade students, an electronic keyboard for elementary school music classes, and a "teaching machine" inspired by the work of psychologist B.F. Skinner. For his two children, Diederich built music stands, a bed that folded into a desk, and a square boat; for his wife, a biologist, he hung warrens from the basement joists to hold the guinea pigs for her genetics experiments. No wonder his retirement gift in 1976 was a new saw.[1]

Throughout his career, Diederich's knack for making ingenious shortcuts served him well. What he enjoyed doing with his hands also engaged his mind—designing efficient structures and procedures for American schools. Not every project he undertook featured shortcuts, but every stage in his professional life yielded them. For his Columbia University dissertation, he developed a simple method of learning Latin grammar. Over 90% of the words students learned, he claimed, could be understood by knowing only 18 common endings and eight rules for variable endings. In contrast, mastery of the typical Latin textbook required the memorization of more than 1,500 items. Diederich used his streamlined approach

---

Paul Diederich and the Progressive American High School, pp. xi–xviii
Copyright © 2014 by Information Age Publishing
All rights of reproduction in any form reserved.

in his first job—he was hired in 1932 to teach Latin at the Ohio State University campus school for 7th to 12th grade students.

Three years later, Ohio State Professor Ralph Tyler convinced him to join the evaluation staff of the "Eight Year Study," a coalition to reconfigure the college preparatory curriculum in several dozen public and private high schools. What Diederich saw and heard in those schools shaped his proposal to trim the daily schedule to four periods. For the 1940/41 academic year Tyler lent him to Harvard, where he worked with literary critic I.A. Richards on "Basic English," a barebones version of the language. "With 850 words you can run the planet," Richards boasted, and with one thousand words he translated Plato's *Republic*, occasionally asking Diederich for advice.[2]

In 1942, Diederich became the "Examiner" for English at the University of Chicago, where Tyler chaired the Department of Education and directed the staff that wrote and read comprehensive exams. As in many European colleges, Chicago undergraduates could earn their degree whenever they passed examinations (eight for high school graduates, 14 for younger admits). Most students stayed for the customary four years but with the creation of the Board of Examiners in 1931 Chicago had set aside the traditional American graduation requirements—course credits and grade point averages.[3] Furthermore, Chicago's President Robert Hutchins questioned the longstanding break between secondary and higher education after grade 12, and in several essays Diederich showed how to merge the second half of high school with the first half of college. During his 27 years (1949-1976) as a researcher at the Educational Testing Service (ETS), he wrote several plans to minimize repetition in 11th to 14th as well as 7th to 10th grades.

Restructuring secondary education was not a priority for ETS, but several other changes Diederich oversaw there were successful. In one project, schools in 16 urban districts recruited college-educated housewives to read and correct English papers, a blessing for any high school teacher facing the prose of 150 students. The good work of those part-time "lay readers" Diederich considered his greatest achievement at ETS, although he helped even more students with another accomplishment: from his adjunct college teaching in the 1950s he wrote *Short-Cut Statistics for Teacher-Made Tests*, a pamphlet so popular that ETS distributed over a half million copies.

In a field afflicted with amnesia, educators too often forget the enduring insights of previous generations, especially the ideas generated by the junior varsity—the men and women who worked for famous educators. Because Diederich never led an organization, he was not as well known as his mentors, trailblazers who ran small new organizations dedicated to transforming American schools—a university lab school, a foundation-funded project to overhaul the high school curriculum, an institute to revamp English language instruction, a university's Board of Examiners to assess college students, and a nonprofit consortium to improve testing. Diederich's writing therefore sheds light not just on school improvement writ large but on five important chapters in the history of reform.

It also sheds light on a frame of mind that is rare in school reform today. Alongside his bent for the practical—the side of education that calls for learning through doing--Diederich was a lifelong philosopher—a person who learned through abstractions, for whom doing is thinking. "I revel in detailed specifications and will uncork them at a moment's notice," he told a University of Chicago colleague in 1947, but he was also "digging down to bedrock for basic principles."[4] The geological metaphor is revealing—he saw philosophy not as ornamental but as foundational. It is no wonder that his two heroes in American history were Benjamin Franklin and Thomas Jefferson. Like them, he loved the world of theory as much as the world of technical detail. He combined a passion for utopian speculation and a fascination with practical problems.

His own education equipped him to undertake moral and social philosophy. He was exceptionally well read. Valedictorian of his Waterbury, Connecticut high school class of 400, Diederich graduated with honors from Harvard in 1928, majoring in classics. Professor Francis Spaulding in the Harvard Graduate School of Education, where Diederich earned his masters degree in 1930, called him "one of the most brilliant students we have had for some time" and Henry Holmes, the Dean, used the same word—brilliant—to describe him.[5] Proficient in five languages, Diederich read quickly—for one seminar he finished the Iliad in Greek in six days and the Odyssey in five. The scope of his adult interests spanned the humanities—in addition to his mastery of classical languages, Diederich read widely in philosophy, religion, history, literature, and music (he was an excellent violinist). His relentless curiosity generated a collection of 2,000 books by the time he was 65.

The readers of this book will see how keenly Diederich believed that the essential elements of a good life must permeate the curriculum. In his opinion, the five elements were health, love, work, beauty and truth (his utopia, in other words, was far broader than a world centered on manual dexterity or technical prowess—he did not place woodwork or other "shops" at the heart of the curriculum, an option that would have yoked his love of theory and his love of tinkering). Education had to encourage students to strive for those goals. Teachers should not avoid them for fear that parents might disagree on what the elements meant or how they should be formed.

Parts of Diederich's vision of the good life, especially his left-to-far-left politics, would have irritated conservative parents (including his own father, a middle class salesman and lifelong Republican). His ideas went beyond the New Deal reforms of the 1930s. For example, he supported free medical care and full employment through well-paid 20 hour work weeks. Curious about Communism, he briefly joined a New York City cell to discuss Lenin's writings (which he soon abhorred). To Diederich, capitalism was full of snares. Too many people craved wealth and status rather than embracing work as service. The economy would collapse again after World War II, he predicted, and politicians would respond badly because most of them were incompetent or corrupt. Demoralization was bound to increase because fewer and fewer Americans shared the intense religious convictions of their parents and grandparents. "We have lost the old faith without finding a new one," he wrote in 1945.[6]

By then, Diederich had shed his own intensely religious upbringing, relocating the quest for redemption from the church to the schoolhouse. Like so many early to mid-20th century educators, he glorified education as a holy cause that would help students find and follow the path to a virtuous life.[7] In his youth, the Catholic church shaped his moral development (his mother went to mass every morning), but after two years at Holy Cross College, he transferred to Harvard. Thomas Aquinas' doctrines constrained the Holy Cross curriculum and the faculty was humorless: the lines "Take back my soul/I'll be a troll" in a poem Paul wrote prompted the professor to send him to confession for blasphemy. At 24 he no longer believed in life after death, and the Catholic ban on contraception convinced him to leave the church at 30. In retirement he wrote incessantly about religion; his quarrel with Catholic doctrine was lifelong (he even calculated that Christ was born five years later than everyone assumed). He justified his notions of virtuous conduct by explaining why he rejected tenets such as salvation by faith (rather than hard work and good deeds) and belief in miracles (like those held by test takers who wrote JMJ—Jesus, Mary and Joseph—at the top of their SAT answer sheets). With his characteristic simplification, he pared religion to "awe, wonder, and delight in the spectacle of the universe" made by an unknowable supreme creator. In place of formal services, an apt form of worship would resemble the bird calls at the feeder he built outside his kitchen window.

Many other early to mid-20th century educators shared Diederich's retreat from religion, but he stands apart from most "administrative progressives" by virtue of his sharp criticisms of American values. Historians usually describe the administrative progressives as efficient managers who reinforced rather than challenged the prevailing attitudes and beliefs in American society. When they sought change, they envisioned gradual progress through rational planning, educational research, and leadership by credentialed experts rather than uninformed voters. Racial, class and gender disparities were not very troublesome, and lightly regulated capitalism was wholly admirable. In contrast, Diederich (who was enamored of research, science, and rational planning) was more radical, closer to the "social reconstructionists" who exhorted educators to support sweeping economic and social changes on behalf of the disenfranchised. The boxes in which historians place individuals like Diederich may be too small to accommodate the scope of their world views.[8]

There is another distinctive feature of Diederich's writings that sets him apart and justifies the resurrection of his work. His blunt and jargon-free prose style is remarkable. Do you want to know what's wrong with gym classes in high school? He will tell you. From Diederich we get clear and pungent descriptions of life in schools. At times he will exaggerate (and he knows it). His son-in-law recalled that he enjoyed being an *agent provocateur*, a gadfly who could speak freely because he was not the leader, an *infant terrible* with a messianic confidence that the stakes were high, time was short, and his favorite solutions were right.

Were his solutions right? Right in the sense of anticipating what happened later? The record is mixed. Most high schools avoided strong stands on the components of a good life—an avoidance that became an endorsement of tolerance, variety, and choice.[9] Aside from some private schools, American high schools preferred neutrality on the big issues Diederich raised. The greatest gains in regard to social justice inside the schools derived from landmark court cases (on civil rights, disabilities, and gender equity) rather than visionary educators. In contrast to the 1930s and 1940s, reform proposals since the 1980s shied away from social engineering. Economic gains have eclipsed ethical benefits as the primary rationale for school improvement, even if the persistent interest in homeschooling, private education, and charter schools indicates that values and morals are priorities for many families.

Diederich's specific proposals came closer to adoption. He addressed topics that constantly preoccupied schools—the daily schedule, connections with colleges, guidance, new core courses, and instructional methods. His own recommendations usually went beyond what most American high schools tried. But the underlying spirit of his various recommendations certainly took hold, especially in the late 1960s and early 1970s. What he wrote in defense of a more relevant curriculum, a less stressful school climate, and better counseling were taken seriously in those years when progressive ideas enjoyed a resurgence.

Was Diederich right in the sense of making feasible proposals, whether or not they were ever adopted? To be fully persuaded by Diederich requires a leap of faith with respect to teachers, students, and politics. His notions hinge on three assumptions some readers will consider suitably optimistic and others might find naive.

Like most progressives, he set forth ambitious goals that presupposed a very talented teaching force. Consider one important theme in his work: in each classroom there is a wide range of ability and ambition. Even if all students need the essential elements of the good life, they still differ. The current talk of everyone reaching common standards would have struck Diederich as quixotic. As a teacher he could not alter raw intelligence, and motivation was almost as hard to change as IQ. What he could do was enable all students to move ahead, but at varying rates. In his own classes, Diederich supplied lively materials, interesting assignments, and the flexibility for students to learn as much as they could. Working alone and in small groups, the pupils would occasionally seek his advice—what he called "elbow teaching"—rather than hear daily lectures. The key was to offer options *within* each classroom, even if the school used "homogeneous grouping" to sort students among different sections.

To be thorough, individual attention required detailed information about every student. The scope of the dossiers would go beyond academic achievements to describe habits, attitudes, and interpersonal relations. Diederich cast teachers as counselors rather than assign guidance to specialized staff and administrators. He had seen the teacher-as-counselor approach used in the Ohio State lab school, and at ETS he proposed an elaborate system of data gathering. He stopped short of the psychiatric diagnoses that several colleagues on the Eight Year Study endorsed; even so, he wanted to monitor the students' minds and characters.

To be an elbow teacher who also counseled: no small order! The traditional structure of most high schools made that job exhausting if not impossible. Even in a school redesigned along the lines sketched throughout this book, it would take an unusually skillful teacher to carry out Diederich's proposals. One can imagine his favorite new course—a wide-ranging exploration of how people get the things they need—mangled by an instructor without deep knowledge of the social sciences (and a tactful personality). Diederich rarely discussed teacher preparation—how would talented rookies be recruited and trained?—and his comments on worthwhile professional development for experienced teachers praised what was beyond the reach of nearly everyone—full time immersion in six weeks of summer workshops.

What would make a diligent teacher's job a bit easier was a second major Diederich assumption: the innate goodness of youth. He thought the vast majority of high school students would relish his "how we get what we need" course—they were eager to understand the world around them. As he wrote in one essay, adolescents are "keenly alive to the spectacle of the universe," his way of saying that they loved the outdoors and would learn more science there than sitting at a desk. He occasionally called teenagers "healthy young animals" who matured fast enough to marry and hold a job by the time they were 21. When they misbehaved, they were simply tired or tense. When Diederich saw well behaved students who were not especially curious or motivated, he blamed the traditional routine of the schools rather than abandon his faith in the nobility of youth.

A third assumption running throughout his career was the power of good ideas to carry the day. Diederich wrote almost nothing about educational politics. Local school boards, state departments of education, courts, and other sources of policy held little interest. Identifying the constituencies for his reforms, thinking about how to mobilize support, figuring out where to get funding: we rarely see him address those nitty-gritty issues. He did not acknowledge that private schools would probably be more likely to adopt his ideas, especially his eagerness to teach students to strive for the essential elements of a good life. He thought his notions should take hold across the public schools, yet he paid little attention to the political headwinds he would have faced, including the growing resentment of ETS as elitist, arrogant, and omnipotent.

Whether you find Diederich utterly naïve or admirably idealistic, I think you will see in these essays a series of bold and provocative ideas. As his high school principal wrote, "he will have his say and take his chances of being boiled in oil afterwards ... he will fight with all the devils—yes, with all the angels—if they differed with him."[10] Diederich raises major questions about the purpose of education and the structure of schools. In contrast, the reach of current school reform seems modest. Are we wise for rejecting his radicalism, or are we timid for not thinking as boldly as he did?

Before you start: I wrote the notes in each of the following chapters. I did not omit Diederich's own footnotes; he never used them. To highlight the central point of each chapter, I created the titles, with Diederich's original heading and the location of the paper in the endnotes. In the introductions to the papers, I provide contextual as well as biographical information. I selected essays that do not presuppose familiarity with American education from the 1930s through the 1970s; in fact, I picked pieces that can introduce the reader to the era. For readers with deeper background knowledge, eight of the 14 essays here have never been published, and my introductions draw on various archives rather than repeat familiar secondary sources. There are dozens of other Diederich articles; my footnotes include only a sliver of what he wrote. I have not included his technical research on tests (much of that work is available in an anthology of his work on English composition).[11] This anthology features his reflections on high schools, the segment of American education he knew best. Anyone interested in more Diederich will find him readily accessible through electronic databases or interlibrary loan.

ENDNOTES

1. The biographical information in this introduction comes from interviews with Diederich's children, Anne Groom and Bob Diederich, as well as the letters Paul wrote (and xeroxed) in retirement.
2. *The New York Times,* September 8, 1979.
3. *The Idea and Practice of General Education* (Chicago: University of Chicago Press, 1950), 25-102, 273-324.
4. Diederich to F.C. Ward, July 30, 1947 in Dean's Records, Box 15, Folder 10, University of Chicago Archives.
5. Sheldon Fellowship application in "Diederich, Paul Bernard" folder, UAV 350.284, Box 160, Harvard University Archives. Introduced in 1924 and scaled back in 1942, the full time, two year Ed.M. program at Harvard sought bright young liberal arts graduates rather than part-time mid-career educators. The curriculum featured "fundamental principles" rather than "tools of the trade" and was designed, like the Harvard MBA, to be the highest degree any practitioner would need. Arthur G. Powell, *The Uncertain Profession: Harvard and the Search for Educational Authority* (Cambridge: Harvard University Press, 1980), Ch. 7.
6. "General Objectives of Education" in *The Elementary School Journal*, April 1945, 440. Later in life he muted his criticism of capitalism, but he never admired (or sought) wealth as an end in itself (he never bought stocks or bonds, for instance).
7. The best work on this important theme is David Tyack and Elizabeth Hansot, *Managers of Virtue: Public School Leadership in America, 1820-1980* (New York: Basic Books, 1982).
8. One of Tyack's student made this point for an earlier era: David A. Gamson, "District Progressivism: Rethinking Reform in Urban School Systems, 1900-1928" in *Pedagogica Historica*, v39, n4, August 2003, 417-434. For a recent overview of how various historians define progressive education, see William J. Reese, "In search of American progressives and teachers" in *History of Education*, v42, n3, 2013, 320-334.
9. Arthur G. Powell, Eleanor Farrar, and David K. Cohen, *The Shopping Mall High School: Winners and Losers in the Educational Marketplace* (Boston: Houghton Mifflin, 1985), Ch. 1.
10. Letter of recommendation for a Harvard scholarship (1926) in UA 111.15.88.10, 1890-1968, Box 1190, Harvard University Archives
11. Paul B. Diederich, *Measuring Growth in English* (Urbana IL: National Council of Teachers of English, 1974).

PART I

LESSONS LEARNED FROM THE EIGHT YEAR STUDY

Paul Diederich cannot be understood apart from the Eight Year Study. His first job was in a school that belonged to the Study, and his next job was on the staff of the Study. His commitment to innovation reflects what he did and saw as a teacher at the Ohio State campus school (1932-1935) and as a curriculum and evaluation coach (1935-1940) with the Study, which historians of education consider an unusually broad reconsideration of what high schools could accomplish.[1]

Diederich was hired in 1935 because the pace of change had been slow. The schools had the freedom to alter the traditional college preparatory curriculum: several hundred colleges had promised to modify their course requirements for applicants from the Study schools, so the pioneers could experiment without penalizing their students. For decades high schools had complained about the constraints imposed by college admissions. What would secondary school coursework become if teachers could recast it? That was the key question that gave rise to this undertaking. Each school could answer that question as it saw fit; there was no model to adopt, no mandates to follow, and no expulsions for deviating from a party line. What Diederich and his colleagues offered the participants was information and advice. They helped schools clarify their objectives and decide how they could determine if their students achieved those goals.

Not every Eight Year school teacher wanted to experiment. Perhaps the leaders did—in 28 of the 30 initial schools the principal wrote the proposal to join—but many teachers felt proud of what they had always done, and all 30 schools had excellent reputations.[2] Often the innovators were a little platoon inside what today we would call a "pilot project" or a "school within a school." Elsewhere the curricular modifications, especially the enthusiasm for "core courses" that merged previously separate fields, altered *what* was taught more than it transformed *how* teachers taught. The pace and extent of change varied from school to school (the Ohio State lab school went farther and faster than most, as Chapter 7 will show). In his travels to each site Diederich began to form his own opinions of where schools fell short and what they should do to move forward.

In 1942, three papers set forth Diederich's reflections on the crucial issues he felt schools needed to face but too often avoided. After editing a large book of case studies of the Eight Year Study schools, Diederich was deferred from the war because of his poor eyesight. While considering several job options in the spring, he wrote two long essays and also published a much shorter third article. They all shed light on the history of the Eight Year Study as well as expressing the major themes that mark his other ruminations on American high schools. The subtitles that organize the rest of this anthology convey those themes: educate for the sake of a good life and a just society, make the curriculum less onerous, provide more individual attention, and restructure schools.

The papers of 1942 also display the characteristic Diederich prose—direct, unpretentious, serious but playful. Unlike the gnarled words of John Dewey and many other reformers, Diederich's writing leaves no doubts about what he believes. The style never masks the radicalism of his proposals. Yet the simple language also casts him as a clear-headed man of common sense who questions traditional practices that are not logical, and as a result many readers might conclude that his proposals are not at all revolutionary.

ENDNOTES

1. For a thorough account of the Eight Year Study, see Craig Kridel and Robert V. Bullough, Jr., *Stories of the Eight-Year Study: Reexamining Secondary Education in America* (Albany NY: State University of New York Press, 2007). For a contemporary account, see Wilford M. Aikin, *The Story of the Eight-Year Study* (New York: Harper and Brothers, 1942).
2. Ralph Tyler to Morris Finder, May 17, 1991 (Finder Papers, Box 1, University of Chicago Archives).

CHAPTER 1

EIGHTEEN SHORTCOMINGS OF AMERICAN SCHOOLS

(1942)[1]

Diederich thought high schools should have only four periods—a core course, outdoor play, shop, and free reading. The core course would focus on how people get what they need in life, everything from food and shelter to beauty and justice. Outdoor play would include competitive sports, unsupervised games, and nature study. Third period encompassed science, industrial arts, fine arts, home economics, music, and theater, thus transforming the usual connotations of the word shop. Free reading would alter something else—the school library—as students read, watched films, heard records, and discussed their choices in groups and with teachers.

Diederich published a short version of that schedule in 1945, but this essay is a fuller account of what he liked and disliked in American schools.[2] In this feisty and occasionally hyperbolic paper, Diederich dreams of schools shaped by teachers' judgments of their students rather than graduation and college entrance requirements. He wants to do away with artificial measures of progress. In place of an accumulation of grades and credits, teachers and counselors would know all students with a thoroughness rarely found in American schools. What Diederich proposes in this paper goes beyond the scope of the changes he had seen at any Eight Year Study school by 1940. Halfway measures held little interest for him, and he paraphrased the Book of Revelations for his opinion of piecemeal change: "Thou art neither hot nor cold; I spit thee out."[3]

Paul Diederich and the Progressive American High School, pp. 3–38
Copyright © 2014 by Information Age Publishing
All rights of reproduction in any form reserved.

4   Eighteen Shortcomings of American Schools (1942)

This essay frequently mentions child psychology because Diederich wrote it for Daniel Prescott, a University of Chicago professor who faulted schools for slighting the emotional health of both students and teachers.[4] The paper can be read as a contribution to the debate within the Eight Year Study on the feasibility of linking the curriculum to the psychological wellness of youth. Several "commissions" within the Study explored the complexities of adolescence. Seminar discussions led by psychoanalyst Caroline Zachry included future superstars like Benjamin Spock, Margaret Mead, Karen Horney, Erik Erikson, and Ruth Benedict, which sparked one angry letter about "a group of Austrian Jews [who] feel that its job is to shove Freud down the throats of school people."[5] Diederich did not share Zachry's enthusiasm for linking curriculum and instruction with child psychiatry. His notion of "needs" (a widely used word at the time) was more sociological and philosophical than psychological.

Eighteen Shortcomings of American Schools (1942)

1. **Marks:** Don't we know enough to say that the whole system of marks in courses is bad, and to hell with it? It is the social duty of child psychologists to quit being tentative on this point and to come out decisively against it. The system may be innocuous or even helpful in a few cases, but on the average throughout the country it is bad for children, for education, and for the future of our society. The objections I see are the following:

   a. Practically all children—even the brightest—worry about marks a great deal.
   b. They are one of the most fertile sources of tensions with parents, and one of the places where parents put the most unjustified pressure on children.
   c. There is an electric tension around any school while [grade] reports are being made out, and a terrific let-down afterwards.
   d. Marks substitute a symbol for reality. They enable a school to impose perfectly meaningless tasks on children and make them work for the sake of marks.
   e. They probably inhibit real thinking. Once in my youth I set up a competitive system in my Latin class in which I assigned "credit" for the number of lines of Latin read multiplied by test scores on these lines. Children read an astonishing lot, but when I finally woke up and abolished the system, I found (1) that nobody wanted to read any more, and (2) that nobody knew how to read Latin. It was incredible how little they had learned from plow-

ing through all that material with their eyes on just one goal: the marks in my record book. I found later that reading even half as much, with the motive of wanting to learn something, resulted in much more learning than twice as much activity with the motive of wanting to beat somebody. I concluded that we learn *what we are attending to* in the course of an activity. If we are attending only to marks, practically all the learning involved in getting them may slough off with miraculous rapidity once they have been earned.

f. They are outrageously competitive. Both my wife and I were spoiled darlings of the marking system. We now cannot find joy in any activity if we cannot excel in it. We know that it would add considerably to our well-being to engage in certain activities for their own sake, but in fact we never get around to them because we aren't good at them. My wife won't even do her housework because she is a dub at it, and it offers no chance for her particular talents to excel.

g. They don't tell anything about the important aspects of children's development. An A in English may mean anything. It doesn't even stand uniformly for excellence in the subject-matter commonly taught in English. It may stand for sheer brightness, or reward for effort, or reward for good behavior, or some special excellence such as in spelling. Marks are notoriously invalid and unreliable, and not at all standardized from one school or class to another. Yet by filling our reporting systems they obstruct the development of records of growth that really mean something, and that might be useful in guidance. Probably the basic motive for giving marks is disciplinary. They force children through the tasks which teachers set for them. Yet teachers won't accept the idea of giving up marks and making all of a child's work in school meaningful and important because they don't yet know how to make all school work meaningful and important. They have to have some coercive power to tide over the periods when, frankly, they aren't as good teachers as they would like to be. Hence they will reject any proposal to give up marks and be perfect teachers as utopian. They know they aren't that good. What is important to tell them, in order to give them the security they need to abolish marks, is that there are other ways of putting the fear of God into kids. This may sound crude, but in this imperfect world I am prepared to accept the fact that even I (proud of my teaching ability as I am) will occasionally have to bawl out a pupil simply because

I haven't been good enough, consistently, to get along without this disciplinary power.

We must give plenty of reassurance on this point—it sustains the system of giving marks in spite of all the disadvantages, grief, and toil it causes teachers. They just don't feel sure that they would be good enough teachers to get kids to go along with them without this crutch. Let's cite the experience of schools which have given no marks for years. None of them has experienced the expected slump in work and in decent behavior. Lacking this artificial way of giving hell, they reverted to the primordial human way of doing it: simply pitching into a brat when you can think of nothing better to do. We may have theoretical objections to hell giving, but granting its imperfection, it is better than the refined, postponed, forever-in-the-record torture of marks. When all else fails, I say, go ahead and blow up if you have to. You'll find that it does everything marks were supposed to do, and does it better, and leaves some scars, but not such deep and serious scars as marks.

2. **Failure:** Everything said about marks goes double for academic failure—the repetition of courses or the failure to earn credit toward graduation, hence sometimes an extra year to graduate. I am told that it has been proved that children learn more when arbitrarily passed along with their class than when forced to repeat a course. The emotional scars of failing a course and having to repeat it, while losing face and losing contact with all one's friends in that group, must be terrific. This is an unnecessary coercive measure, and in this case doubly ineffective because the punishment is postponed until the very end of the year. Its only wallop is that it is the nastiest thing that could happen to anyone: hence it is the most powerful threat to hold over the head of the wayward pupil. But whole school systems have proved that they can get along without this threat, and once it is gone, nobody misses its support. Only a few of the many fields of study are cumulative.

One can perfectly well learn medieval history after failing to learn anything about ancient history. In the cumulative fields, in most cases failure to learn enough the first year to enable one to go on with the group indicates that one should not go in that field at all. The best answer, but one which teachers will have to learn to work out (and it is not a problem to be sniffed at), is that they must make more drastic and fundamental provision for individual differences than they now dream of. They must expect that under optimum conditions the fastest pupil may learn twenty times as much of the content and skills of a given field as the slowest pupil. That is no exaggeration. Even in my Latin classes under anything but ideal conditions the fastest pupil read *fourteen times* as much as the slowest. To get the best out of both these pupils I had to arrange conditions so they could go at these widely varying rates. When provisions like that are made, the whole concept of "being ready for second year Latin" as though it were the same thing for all pupils just doesn't mean anything. In the second year some pupils will be reading Tacitus while others while still be reading about Julia and the Sailor. This can be done, and when it is done, we no longer will have to fail some pupils in order to drive a class in harness. Some teachers and parents argue that because failure occurs in real life, pupils should not be artificially protected from it. Here is a semantic blunder of the first order. Because two things have the same name is no guarantee that they represent the same thing. Academic failure bears practically no relationship to any sort of failure which occurs in life. If we fail in a job, we get bounced out; we aren't required or even allowed to "repeat" it. If we fail in marriage, we get divorced or suffer torment; we don't "repeat." And so on. If the academic concept of "failure" were eradicated, there would still be plenty of failure in school of the sort which occurs in life: failure to get things done, failure to make friends, etc. I don't say this is a good thing, but in so far as some failure of human purposes is inevitable, it will occur in school as elsewhere, and can be made just as educative or miseducative as we are smart enough to make it.

3. **Credit:** In 1905 the famous Carnegie Commission crystallized our high school curriculum in its present form by its recommendation that pupils take not more than four courses a year in specified academic subjects, each of which would earn one unit of "credit" toward graduation and college entrance.[6] Subjects and activities outside this list were given half credit or none at all—which hamstrung the development of work in the arts, vocational and practical courses, and extracurricular activities (they were extra-curricular largely because they could not be granted "credit"). Pupils were allowed to fail in one of these sixteen units, so that only fifteen were required for graduation, and this has subsequently been reduced to twelve in many places. This recommendation is still the basis of the requirements for admission printed in most college catalogues; up to 1941 it was the basis of the College Entrance Board examinations, and it is the effective basis for the secondary school curriculum today. The Eight Year Study was at bottom simply an effort to have a fresh look at the recommendations of the Committee of Ten.[7] In its time this was a progressive, liberalizing educational program. Eugene Randolph Smith told me that in his youth he had to offer something like 17 different courses in mathematics to meet the capricious demands

of the various colleges which his pupils planned to enter.[8] After this Carnegie pronouncement, he had to offer only one program, vastly more sensible and substantial, and he devoutly thanked God for having given life and wealth to Andrew Carnegie. The same happened in every other field of study. Life became simpler and better. But now that we are ready to say that colleges have no business to prescribe the program of secondary education and can get the hell out, the Carnegie unit and the idea of credit which it brought in are barriers to further educational progress. Specifically, they deny credit to some of our most educative school activities: theatre, vocational and practical courses, work on school publications, the practice of any of the arts (although learning *about* the arts out of a book is OK), school government work, etc. They require all educative activities during adolescence to be chopped into sixteen stove-length "units" each meeting five times a week for a period of not less than forty-five minutes. If any experience should properly occupy one period a week for 12 weeks, that is all right if you don't want credit, but just too bad if you want to graduate and get into college. If it should take all of a pupil's time for three weeks and then stop, it can't possibly be reconciled with academic bookkeeping. Even the schools which have stuck out their necks to the mild extent of setting up core courses have had to balance the books by giving them one unit of credit in English and one in Social Studies—and then there is hell to pay if they don't teach the usual content of English and Social Studies.

Some previously mentioned objections apply here too: credit substitutes a symbol for reality, probably inhibits real learning, constitutes half the sting of failure (the other half being the threat of having to repeat the course), and helps schools to get away with meaningless tasks. And the whole thing is sheer fiction, just a word that got a hold on our imagination: Credit! Let's simply eradicate the concept of credit. Above all, let's not extend credit to all worthy school activities; let's not give credit to *any* school course or activity. Let's simply drop the whole idea, substitute absolutely nothing for it—and everyone will be better off.

4. **Semester promotions:** Of all the devices of the devil that unaccountably got loose in education, this is one of the worst. Look at Des Moines [Iowa]—a grand school system, led by some of our ablest educators, full of wildly frustrated but very competent and devoted teachers, doing more fundamental thinking about the curriculum than 95% of our favored private schools. And what happens? Every four months every teacher in that school system meets upwards of 200 pupils whose faces he has never seen before. By the time he loses them he still does not know some of their names. Everybody

in Des Moines seems to admit that this is a bad thing, but while they retain semester promotions, not one is smart enough to figure out a schedule which will keep any group of pupils together for more than a semester. Why not drop semester promotions, we ask? Because parents are afraid their children may possibly "lose" half a year in school (a queer sense of lose—it means that they might have to be in school half a year longer). Think what this does not only to teacher-pupil relations but to relations among pupils. Never once in their six years of secondary education are they with the same group of pupils more than four and one-half months. If any adolescent in Des Moines has any lasting friendships, it is done in spite of the schools. The way out here is obvious if any of the previous recommendations are followed. There won't be any promotions, semester or otherwise. Pupils will just automatically go forward with their age-group and keep together as long as possible.

5. **Age-grouping:** If there are no promotions and no failures, how shall we group children? We should put children of the same chronological age together, and keep them together with the same group of teachers, as long as possible. When they enter new schools and larger groups, we might try to keep together neighborhood groups as long as possible. When there is any doubt or choice, I should rest the matter almost entirely upon friendships. The basic principle I would follow is that a pupil should work in the groups from which he draws his friends—or where he has the best chance of making friends. What do the psychologists have to say about that?

6. **Graduation:** The idea of making graduation from any unit of our public school "mean something"—in the sense of meaning the attainment of any given standard of scholarship, behavior, or general intelligence—seems to me just a pipe-dream. It couldn't be so, even if it were desirable. With any reasonable provision for individual differences, some pupils are bound to come out knowing hundreds of times more than others, and begin markedly superior or inferior to others in various aspects of character and personality. Let's not say better or worse; just different. No customer of a school can expect a uniform product. The only point in graduation seems to me to be a ritual marking some growth and some assumption of adult status, responsibilities, and privileges. Pupils should graduate whenever they come to the end of the term of years cared for by their school, and the ceremony should do everything in our power to give them a sense of inalienable membership in a society that will never let them down, no matter what they do, but which expects their best efforts for the good of all. And what we then say about them to colleges or prospective employers will naturally differ for each individual.

7. **The elective system:** I look upon the elective system as another device of the devil which got loose in education to meet a need which can now be cared for on a different basis. President Eliot of Harvard [in the 1870s and 1880s] had as much to do with this system as any man, and he promoted it to smash the narrow classical curriculum of the colleges of his day.[9] That was good—but the idea of dividing everything that is known into an indefinite number of courses of uniform length, and inviting children to select any sixteen of these fragments and call it a high school education—that just does not add up to a proper education for adolescents. You do not cater properly to individual differences by allowing one child to take French while another child takes German. Probably neither of those courses is appropriate for either child. And when you get to the college level and they have to choose French Literature from 1790 to 1810, or the Spectrum Analysis of the sodium vapors, or fourteen other such courses, and call it a college education—then it reaches the wildest heights of absurdity. No individual differences among children call for such alternatives as those; there is absolutely no way to assemble a rich and full educative experience out of specialized fragments of irrelevant information. We can do all that we need to do to care for individual differences within *one* good modern course based on needs and interests, and run by a teacher who knows his pupils and cares about their all-around development. I shall indicate more of the sort of curriculum I approve of as I proceed, but I don't want any possible disagreement with my proposals to obscure the fact that the elective system as it now operates is *not* good for children. Anyone who claims that it is based on the scientific lore of individual differences should have his ears batted down. Can we agree on that much as a start?

8. **The school day:** In the University of Chicago Laboratory Schools [which Diederich's son and daughter attended] children get to the fourth grade before they meet something like ten different teachers in the course of a week. In the high school they carry as many as eight different courses or activities daily, going from one totally different activity to another at intervals of 40 minutes or so all day long. Is there any doubt that all this hectic activity is confusing and disintegrating? That so many teachers, each zealous to get as much of his subject as possible into students, constitute altogether too many competing high powered stimuli? That pupils cannot possibly assimilate what they "learn" under such pressure? That most of it *must* be forgotten? That added to the increasing tempo of life outside of school—radio, movies, sports, comic strips, freer social intercourse, automobile riding, etc.—it leaves pupils literally no time whatever to think?

Unless powerful contrary forces are set in motion, this crowding of the curriculum is going to get worse.[10] Each major subject field is now smitten with the idea of "continuous contact" with pupils. To leave out science or art or social studies or mathematics or English or a foreign language or vocational courses or a wide range of student activities seems an irreparable injury. All these fields are well organized and are putting pressure at all the right places to get their fields into the school day of every pupil. The net result is going to be chaos unless the people interested primarily in children call a halt.

Every faculty annually deplores this situation and sets out to do something about it in the school schedule. But then someone always rises to object that the schedule is an "administrative matter," and must wait until educational issues have been settled. While those issues ought to include the rhythm and unity of the school day, in practice they come down to settling the competing claims of the various subjects. Simplifying the school day means leaving something out, and no one wants to be left out. It means bread and butter to him to get as much time for his subject as he can. This issue will probably never be settled until someone recognizes that the schedule is itself an educational problem, and a very fundamental one. I would rather first plan a school day that would be good for children and then fit the available activities into it rather than vice versa.

9. **More activity needed:** In spite of protestations to the contrary, secondary education still consists largely of sitting on hard chairs five or six hours a day listening to other people talk. This is obviously hard on healthy animals, yet when you begin to howl for more activity, supposedly bright people get you to admit that much activity may go on (in the top part of the head) while sitting still; therefore the school provides enough activity! Another hurrah for semantics! Let's make it plain we mean that the healthy animal wants to stand up and move around and do things with its muscles. Even the lions in a cage get a better break than most children in school.

10. **A chance to talk with friends:** One of the most valuable assets a person could have would be conversational ability: a pleasant speaking voice, the ability to refrain from using it occasionally, and the ability to amuse and entertain friends. Yet this is the one activity which is forbidden during 98% of the school day. Children may get a moment to chat while classes are passing in noisy corridors, another moment during a hurried and noisy lunch, and on the way to and from school. Yet they desperately need and want to talk a great deal with one another during adolescence. For this reason I would expect the principal activity of any school recreational period to be conversation. Just open a few of the largest and most attractive classrooms

for this purpose and let kids talk to one another. If they have no such opportunity, they will do it in the middle of my Latin class and annoy me to no end. The schools which have daily recreational periods report that the "social rooms" are the major answer to their problem of what to do with the pupils. They require almost no equipment, are fairly easy to manage, and obviously fill a great and pressing need. All that we could do about conversation in speech classes would not come within gunshot of what pupils could teach one another in this way.

11. **Rest** While we are on this point, let me call attention to the fact that *rest* was also listed among the recreational activities provided by some schools. Some pupils simply won't do it, but others obviously need it and can be persuaded to go to quiet, darkened rooms and lie down for a nap. No school that I know has proper facilities for such purposes. Another possible application: progressive teachers never know what to do when a child grossly misbehaves in class. Almost every punishment except a dirty look and "social pressure" is taboo for one reason or another. It is my hunch that children in school, just like children at home, often misbehave simply because they are tired and tense. The best thing we could do for them would be to suggest, very quietly, that they lie down and think things over for a few minutes. If the school had facilities for rest and a procedure for snaking kids into it when they became obstreperous, this would solve an awful lot of tense situations in class. At present there is nothing whatever that one can do with these wrought-up children except smack them down in one way or another or send them to the office, where what they get often just makes their condition worse. Exclusion from the group in order to rest would in itself constitute a mild punishment—a gentle warning not to do it again if one could help it—but that side of it should not be emphasized at all. Just say something like, "John, you're not yourself just now, and I think I know why. Just go up to Room 310 for a few minutes, and come back when you feel better." After all, every parent uses this method with the little fellows, and it seems to be what they need. Why shouldn't it work in school? Even if it had not the physiological basis I think it has, it would be the smoothest, most graceful exit from a lot of difficult classroom situations I can think of.

12. **The Arts:** In 1936 or 1937, I put together the figures on enrollment in the arts from the biennial reports of the United States Office of Education, and concluded that on the average pupils spend about 6 percent of their time in the senior high school in all of the arts put together: fine and industrial arts, music, dancing, home economics. Only theatre arts were excluded from this calculation; no figures

were available because this—probably the most sure-fire educative activity there is—is never listed as a regular subject. I doubt that my figures would be altered much if I had been able to include the theatre, since time for rehearsals is almost universally scheduled outside the regular school day. Compare this with 13 to 20 percent of the time (depending on the section of the country) devoted to the study of foreign languages. This figure means that the average student gets one semester of one of the arts in the senior high school—and remember that "average" means that half of the students get less than this.[11]

Causes? One very obvious and immediate cause is that the Carnegie Commission of 1905 did not assign "credit" toward graduation or college entrance for the *practice* of the arts, assuming that only dumb-bunnies would do this, and college catalogues have followed suit ever since. Some have grown liberal enough to assign half credit for work in music or fine arts, but shop activity that might have vocational significance is still not kosher. So if you want to spend an extra year in high school earning enough credits to graduate or to get into college, you can get some work in the arts, but if you want to get ahead fast, you had better not.

Moreover, you still incur the suspicion of being unable to carry academic work if you load up your program with art courses. When I went to high school and saw all the beautiful shops there, I wanted so badly to get into them that I could have wept. I signed up for a course that included a lot of shop work, and all my teachers at once ganged up on me. They explained as tactfully as they could that only the dumbbells elected that curriculum, and if I did, not only would I have a horrible time getting into college but I would also be corrupted by associating with that gang. The bright boys who knew what was good for them took the regular college preparatory course. So the program card I filled out so hopefully was quietly thrown into the waste basket. I watched it go down like a ship sinking, and then was handed a pen and made to fill out a new card under the watchful eye of the teacher who had my best interests at heart. And if I hadn't been the apple of her eye, she would not have bothered.

How often do you suppose this is still done in high schools? My guess is that there are not a hundred schools in the country even today in which this is not the regular practice. At least this much is true even in our "Thirty Schools" [in the Eight Year Study]: If a child fills out a program card and includes no foreign language, or no math, or does not allow time for a course or two in science, there is hell to pay. The chances of his getting away with it are almost nil. But if there is no art of any kind in his program, the adviser does not even raise his eyebrows. He checks off Latin, algebra, physics, English, ancient history, etc., and says OK. Until we can get advisers to raise their eyebrows and say, "What, no art?" the arts are not going to get an even break in the program. And this eyebrow-raising is a cultural change. You could change the Constitution easier than you could change that.[12]

Let's figure it this way. You can have sixteen courses in high school. Four of them have to be English; in more and more schools now four more have to be social studies. Then anyone who is more than a half-wit is still practically required to take at least two years of one foreign language and three of another. That is the modal expectation for college-going students; conservative schools still expect four years of one language and three of another. Even at the smaller figure, however, that means 13 out of 16 courses gone. Then just try to get away without at least two years of mathematics. That leaves one course open, and you have to have at least that much science. If you cut down anywhere else, they will insist on two years of science. The only way to explain how any student can get in any of the arts is that the median high school program still does not include four years of social studies, but it is rapidly moving in that direction. Another opening but a disreputable one is that the dumb-bunnies get away with only two years of one foreign language, and then are summarily dumped into the arts. So practically the only pupils who get a decent program in the arts are those who can't do foreign languages, or who are in schools which do not have a strong social studies program.

Just try to leave any of these things out, and powerful lobbying organizations swing into action. I once made a very mild statement which was construed as prejudicial to the present position of foreign languages in the curriculum, and within a week I received a very sharp letter from the vigilante committee of the American Classical League, asking me to explain and apologize.

The only vulnerable spot in this line-up that I think would yield to about a thousand tons of dynamite is that first foreign language which is pursued for two years in the 9th and 10th grade and then forgotten more completely than any other terrestrial experience. It is probably the most useless thing in the world. Not a vestige of it remains even at graduation from high school; it could not possibly be used in college or in foreign travel; and it makes pupils hate foreign languages. Not to mention the fact that it costs the country directly in teachers' salaries at least $100,000,000 a year. With enough pressure by all hands in the right places I think we might establish the convention that no pupil may study more than one foreign language in high school. The program I am whooping for now, as the only practicable next step, is three years of one foreign language for properly qualified students, beginning in the 10th grade. That last item is important; otherwise the initial stages of language-learning straddle the break between junior and senior high school. Very few other things in the curriculum make so much bad blood and lost motion. The 10th grade language teacher is universally convinced that preparation in the junior high school is inadequate, so she makes the junior teacher's life a burden to her and makes the pupils practically repeat the work of the first year, which is always the most distasteful part of language work. Even such a conservative and influential school as Horace Mann in New York has swung over to the standard of no language below the 10th grade. We can use such precedents.

My only interest in knocking out that first language is that it frees two courses for the arts—provided we get our foot in the door. Otherwise the gap will be instantly closed by more work in science, mathematics, and other academic subjects. Hence pressure on the first foreign language must be accompanied by a powerful drive toward getting at least two units of practice in the arts into the program of every pupil.

What has this to do with child development? Among other things, just this: I once visited a large public high school on the West coast which was proud of its long progressive tradition. I finished one interview at 11:20 and had nothing to do until 11:45, so I started tramping up and down the corridors and peeking into classrooms. What I saw interested me, so I made a quick tour of the whole building. In every academic classroom, without a single exception, the teacher was in front of the room talking and the pupils were sitting on their tails listening. In the arts, the science laboratories, and the gym pupils were standing up and moving around. The answer to me is practically as simple as that. Anything we can do to diminish the wear and tear on the buttocks in secondary education is a good thing for normal development. I know that teachers will say that they can make provision for large-muscle activity in any of the academic subjects, but the proven fact is that they won't.

Of course I am using this only as a symbol for everything else that this picture implies. The sort of education which consists almost exclusively of sitting on hard chairs six hours a day listening to teachers talk (and it does—no matter what we say) is not good for adolescents, and I am out to scuttle it. But this can't be done just by condemning it. We have to find a vulnerable spot in the academic line-up and push before we can free even two courses for the arts. Then these two arts courses won't be any good, but they will be there, and will have a chance to improve. That much change is enough to occupy one lifetime profitably.

13. **Vocational education as a part of general education:** One of the most pernicious dichotomies in schools is that between general education and vocational education. General education teaches you how to think and how to live, is the story; vocational education teaches you only how to make money. The most approved current doctrine is that you should keep on in general education as long as possible; then it is all right to have brief, intensive training for a specific job. And most jobs, we point out, require only a few weeks' training or none at all. Whatever training is needed can be provided most efficiently on the job. That leaves general education, now purified of vocational elements, in command of the field. In strict theory it excludes vocational education altogether, but we retain a little of it because the more sinister of our pupils would otherwise tear the schools apart. So it is admitted grudgingly, mainly as a dumping ground.

   That theory is complete nonsense, and absolutely poisonous to normal development through adolescence. In America of all places, where our lives and our values center around our jobs more than anywhere else, why we should leave the job out of any scheme of education for living is a mystery. So long as work is a part of living, and a very central part for most of us, it is a legitimate and necessary element in general education. Why shouldn't we make a similar distinction between general education and health education, or general education and education for family living, or general education and education for leisure time? On the ground that general education should be the same for all, but vocational education should be specialized? That is a stock argument, and it is moonshine. I deny both the first and the second parts of it. General education should not be and is not the same for all; it includes some common elements and some unique elements for every individual. So should vocational education. It becomes highly specialized only when you think of those last few weeks of training for a specific job—which I agree may better be given on the job—but in my view those few weeks should be preceded by 12 years of education in which a study of the work of our society is a very central element, possibly the chief unifying factor.

   Many of these years (I really think all of them) could well be spent in a core course for all pupils, with only the provision for varied interests and individual differences which we make in any good core course. I believe that in the years to come one of the most important series of units in the core will be those on the topic I have discussed ad nauseam [in conversation, not in this paper]: what things do we all need, and how do we propose to get them? There will be units on bread, milk, meat-packing, canning, frosted foods, clothing and textiles, housing, building, community planning, fuel, power, tools, manufacturing, transportation, communication, recreation, education, health services, money, credit, exchange, insurance, taxation, government, freedom, justice, security, etc. We shall study how we get these things now, and how each rising generation could do a better job. This study will provide 12 years of intimate contact with many lines of work, with the challenge of their unsolved problems. It will provide a better basis for a wise vocational choice than anything we now dream of, and it will give a bird's eye view of how the work of the country is laid out that will be useful as background in any line of work. It will be especially useful, I think, to girls, who cannot anticipate the future occupation of their future husbands, so they need a general acquaintance with the lay-out of the work of our society in order to be intelligent about the work of their soul-mate.[13]

Kids are so interested in the work they see going on around them, and so eager to understand it and to find their place in it that it wrings my heart to think how sternly we prevent their thinking about it. I once had to coach a class of boys who were falling behind in geometry and hating it like poison. One day I asked idly how they would like it if we simply dropped geometry and devoted the class time to a study of the work of the town. As soon as they understood what I meant, the boys were on their feet in a flash. "Gosh! Do you think we really could? Would they let us?" I shook my head sadly, and they were as crestfallen a group of boys as I have ever seen. I hope and trust that revolt smolders in them and will in time blow the lid off many an academic sepulcher. Granted that they have not my adult interest in social amelioration; that is something that has to grow. But if we could just have stepped outside the school and studied how trains run, how the factories are operated, how we make the various things we need, how we sell them, and who gets the money, that would have interested them in a way which geometry can never hope to interest them, no matter how skillfully it is taught. I could have got in a crumb or two of this live interest if I could have thought of a way to make it appear that I was teaching geometry via garage mechanics, etc., but isn't that silly? Why should geometry have priority? Not one of these kids is going to use any trace of his conflict with geometry ever again once he discharges his obligations to that superlatively useless subject, but he is going to work and think about his work every day of his life. The more social vision, technical understanding, ability to work with people, and high purpose we can drum up in support of that future job, the better it will be for each individual and for all of us.

One more thought: we develop our philosophies, our methods of thinking, and our social vision in one compartment labeled "general education" and then take on a vocation in another compartment where business is business. Until we get those two together, the philosophy, the scientific spirit, and the social vision are not going to operate in the sphere of living where they will do the most good. For heaven's sake, let's develop our philosophies in connection with the work we plan to do, and see its relation to social betterment and all the rest of it. Otherwise ideals will forever be one thing and business another.

The specific relation of this to child development is somewhat as follows. About my junior year in college [Harvard], I got so fed up with piddling lazy academic work that I could have screamed. I was grown up, ready and eager to do a man's work, to get married, and to find my place in the world, and they kept me doing a hundred lines of Dante a night and a lot of similar trifles that absorbed a fraction of my energy and brains. It was schoolboy stuff, and I was sick unto death with it. And I had the advantage that I was good at this tripe, and saw far more sense in it than the average boy. I suspect that what happened to me happens to most boys at least four years earlier. I knew my bright and brilliant future rested upon my continuing this piddling until I got a degree, so I stuck it out, but I coasted. God, how I coasted! All the work I did during my last two years in college could easily have been done in a month if I had worked as a man works. I literally did about a half hour of honest work a day on the average, and spent the balance of the time learning to be lazy and to acquire the gentlemanly vices.

May there not come a time when a boy suddenly and decisively feels himself to be full grown, and compulsively puts away childish things? We may hope that we can make school work hard enough and important enough to enlist his full energies, but may we not be kidding ourselves? It is conceivable that no school work, however compelling, that does not constitute a man's work with a genuine economic basis—pulling one's own weight in the boat—can satisfy a boy beyond this point. I think that it is entirely possible that the optimum length of schooling may terminate at some point varying from the age of 14 to the age of 21, and once the breaking point is past, any further schooling prior to a job is going to be largely a waste of time. If this is biologically true, we may have to rearrange our institutions, put people to work earlier, and continue their education in a variety of ways during adulthood. This is a point which I wish the child-study people would investigate. I know that nothing could be done about it for some time to come, but I should at least like to throw a brick through the complacent assurance of the schoolteacher that he is going to grab a larger and larger share of the span of a lifetime until in the best of all possible worlds no one will go to work before the age of 30. I have a hunch that in the best of all possible worlds almost everyone should have a position and a home established before the age of 21, and that we had better make our educational plans accordingly.

If this is true, it has a bearing on my earlier remarks about graduation. It would remain true that, at all the intermediate divisions of the school system, graduation would still occur whenever the child had completed the usual span of years, but the final exodus from the system might properly occur when the pupil murdered his French teacher. That would mark full growth and the natural terminus of adolescent patience with academic trivialities. For Quakers and other sects with a prejudice against blood-letting, we might substitute rape (preferably of a teacher) as a graduation requirement. Then the school system would really be attuned to the growth cycle.

14. **The Outdoor Program:** In all the interest questionnaires we circulated during the Eight Year Study, interests in outdoor sports and games so far exceeded interests in any other activity connected with schools that they messed up our statistics. A representative sample of activities offered by physical education departments would not discriminate among students; practically all students said they liked all of them. In order to discover different levels of interest in sport and games we finally had to cut out every normal interest like baseball and football and include nothing less recondite than lacrosse. Even so, scores on sports and games remained consistently high.

When we also consider how much students learn on the playground, and how it is the primary duty of every young animal to grow up healthy and strong, and how much easier children are to live with in the classroom and at home if we run the pants off them first, it all adds up to the fact that we ought to let them play outdoors just as much as we can get away with. It is probably the cheapest, the most easily managed, the most natural, and the most sure-fire education there is. The Greeks assumed as a matter of course that half the school day should be spent in sports and games, and considering their intellectual and artistic accomplishments, I can't see that their brain tissue degenerated in the process.[14]

Yet most of our high schools provide only two or three periods a week of physical education, and none of them goes higher than a period a day. I know what a good deal of this physical education is like. In my high school days, we were required to resort to a damp, stinking gym two periods a week during our freshman and sophomore years. Then we lined up, 60 of us at a time, and stood there and shivered waiting our turn to do some death-defying trick on the apparatus. I well remember my first encounter with the parallel bars. They were so high and so wide apart that I could scarcely hoist myself up.

Then I had to wobble back and forth while my 60 classmates looked on and jeered, do a fancy flip-flop in mid-air, shear off my genitalia on the way down, and land on the back of my neck. It was all highly amusing to the class, but it scared the liver out of me. When I got home that evening, I considered the alternatives of suicide, running away, or learning how to do the parallel bars well enough so that at least I would not be laughed at again. I finally elected the last, but there was no possibility of getting access to the bars in the gym for private practice, so I had to make some. I had just one plank at home that I had been saving for another purpose, but I now dedicated it to self-preservation. I also had a rip saw that my grandfather had given me when it broke in two. With that instrument I sawed that heavy two inch plank from end to end. Eight mortal feet I sawed and made two planks out of it. It took me four hours of sawing and blistered my hands. Then I propped one end of the planks up on our back fence, and drove heavy stakes in the ground and braced them laterally, to hold up the other end. Then every afternoon as soon as I got home from school, I practiced gyrating on those goddamn boards until I learned the trick that we had been required to perform at our first encounter with parallel bars. It took me a month to learn it, practicing an hour a day. It was a race against time, because any day in gym we might be required to do that trick again. But we never were. The only other time during the year that the parallel bars were hauled out, the gym teacher did a totally different trick that was so obviously beyond my powers that I did a bit of fancy foot-work in the line and skipped my place. I think that the stinker was only showing off on the bars and sadistically enjoying his shivering pupils' discomfiture as they fell off. Naturally we got only one turn at the apparatus during our half-hour in the gym, with five minutes to dress. The rest of the time we stood and shivered. And that guy was the most popular athletic director in town because he had developed a State champion basketball team. May he rot in hell.

The next year I begged the family doctor to write me an excuse from gym. Mindful of that, when I began to teach I asked to have charge of the group of boys and girls who were excused from gym, and who had nothing to do during the gym period. I got all the dope I could on which of them definitely had bad hearts and which were probably just being cagey. Then I explained that we only had the job of figuring out together how to have the best possible time during the gym period at anything they wanted to do. To reassure them, we began by playing checkers, and then to limber up their imaginations a bit, we began changing the rules. We played four-handed checkers, which is a disconcerting business, and a sort of football checkers in which it is your job to get your one king over the opponent's goal line, and the top checker on the king may be passed from one checker to another according to a set of rules we devised to govern forward and lateral passes. Then we gradually moved outdoors as fast as we could invent appropriate games which did not require running. We invented lots of them. One is a modified golf in which we set up a wand and heaved our ball at it until we all hit it, counting throws as strokes; then we moved the wand to another place on the campus and heaved after it. The game which proved most amusing required each pupil to bring an old broom from home. We stood about 10 feet apart on the school lawn, and were not allowed to move more than three feet, so there was no running. Then I tossed in a volleyball, and the kids tried to sock it through the ranks of the opposition with their brooms. Such a flailing of brooms you never saw. That lawn was well dusted before we got through with it.[15]

We had so much fun and got so much exercise, sunshine, and fresh air without endangering anybody's heart (either physically or psychically) that to this day I suspect that things could be done to the old gym period that would take some of the fear and strain out of it (I personally could do with a little less smell in it too). Granted that most children like it as it is—but I suspect that even with some of these, this professed liking and apparent bravado in the activities themselves is the result of cultural pressure. They're supposed to like it; it proves they can take it. I don't want to make sissies out of them, and am willing to leave in plenty of activity that would take all the manhood they have—but the sort of experiences I had with the parallel bars does not develop courage. It develops fear where none existed before. To this day I am seized with panic in the face of any physical feat which I am not dead sure I can do. And just getting hurt is not in the picture; getting laughed at is at the bottom of it. If we remove some of this fear and strain we may well lengthen the outdoor period. Children could not stand more than a period a day of the high-tension activities they have now, but I suspect it would do them no end of good to have a long period daily of milder activity outdoors.

Outdoors. I keep repeating that word because the man who invented gymnasia was certainly inspired by the Evil One. They stink. They cost fabulous sums. They permit only highly organized games under constant supervision. They tempt the instructor to show off on the parallel bars. They permit schools to be built on sites that are not adjacent to parks or open field. They naturally overemphasize basketball, which takes more expensive space per man than any other sport. They shut out the ultra-violet rays and the fresh air and the beauty of the springtime.

The smartest thing the Beaver Country Day School [in Brookline, Massachusetts] ever did was not to build a gymnasium, even though they had money enough to build the Grand Central Station. They had a play room for rainy days, but no gym. Better yet, they leveled off only enough of the school grounds for a combined football field, baseball diamond, running track, and a few tennis courts. The rest they left rough and rocky as God made it. Consequently the children can climb trees or sit under them, play cowboys and Indians or cops and robbers, and have something like a Boy Scout "nature" program. They do this all the year round. In the winter they have splendid snowball fights. Nobody stays in because it is cold. I expected the Beacon Hill crowd to be at least neurasthenic, undernourished and ladylike if not deformed and misshapen after all these years of inbreeding, incest, and nameless perversions. But I never saw a tougher, healthier gang of young women anywhere in the thirty schools.

You know what else they do? They keep all school rooms at a temperature below 65 degrees throughout the winter. Whenever I visit the place I put on my warmest underclothes and make up my mind that I am going to shiver until my buttons come loose. One day I found a room that had not been used yet that day, so it was somewhat above freezing. I breathed a sigh of relief and huddled over the radiator and was just beginning to thaw out when, damn it, the bell would ring and in poured a gang of wild Indians for a singing lessons. They stopped short on the threshold, said "Oh, it's hot!" and threw open the windows.

One day I was reading the poems of Shelley and thinking about the life that man led. He was not very well house-broken so he spent most of his time sailing his boat or helling around in the wilderness. I began to wonder what sort of education we ought to provide for poets—not people who write poetry or even read poetry to any great extent, but people who get the juices out of living in the way that Shelley did: who respond to their experiences aesthetically as well as rationally and practically.

What does it do to your thoughts about education to think of millions of kids primarily as poets and artists? For that, I profoundly believe, is just what the genus homo is: the interpretive animal, the one most keenly alive to the spectacle of the universe. Up to the age of 18 he lives up to this role, in spite of everything we do to prevent it. If we wanted to preserve this awareness, this wonder, this sensitivity throughout life, what would we do to educate him?

I am pretty sure about one thing: we would keep in as much contact with nature as we could. I am aware that kids in camp do not fit any conventional notion of responding aesthetically to the beauty of it all, and that it would be poisonous to bombard them with sunsets, but I am still confident that somehow it seeps in. It does seem reasonable that kids need woods and water and growing things about them in order to grow up like the heroes of old.

With this thought in mind, let us look back at the program of physical education. We started with a field as God made it, costing nothing, full of rocks and weeds and humps and hollows. We spend about a million dollars to level this field and cement it, and in the middle of it we build a stinking gym. Now we have the kids right where we want them. Instead of letting them run around in the field and educate themselves, which would not have cost us a cent, we give them two 50 minute periods a week in this expensive and blasphemous establishment. Subtracting time for dressing, they have left about two half hours a week in it. Every movement during this time has to be directed by well-paid coaches, and motivated by the direst competition. The kids go off like a spring, having the aforementioned six hours daily of tail-sitting to work off. Instead of soaking in the sunshine they have the product of [utility company] Consolidated Edison, and instead of inhaling the fragrant odors of the springtime—need we go into that again? I mentioned once before what this does to the body, but now I beg you to consider what it does to the soul. What is the poet doing in a gym? What is an eagle doing in a cage?

I swear I am not saying my piece just because "summer is icumen in, lhude sing cuccu!"[16] Nor am I just being sentimental. Among other things, these sentiments would lop millions a year off the school budget. I realize that most schools have already spoiled their outdoors, and it would cost more millions to replace the fields they started with, but I defy any school to prove that it could not at least transport its pupils to a patch of green earth if it saw the importance of doing so. I am not asking for a landscaped park, nor acres of woodland, but for any neglected field or patch of scrub timber that is handy. There is not a square yard of any such place that lacks beauty and interest. Nor am I thinking just of summer camps, although I hope all children will eventually spend all the summer months in camp.[17] But this is not enough. Throughout the rest of the year I would advocate a long double period daily to be spent outdoors—in all but the most impossible weather—with relatively little supervision. I would like to have some organized games during this time, but also science field trips, woodcrafts, camp-fires, Indian wigwams, tree-climbing, fishing wherever it is possible, swimming, boating, dam-building, surveying, gardening, snowball fights, photography, sketching, and just passing the time. God forbid that we should try to extract the last ounce of perspiration during this time. It would be a time for growing up, consolidating gains, and getting intimately acquainted with clouds, winds, rain, snow, and all manner of growing things. It could be done for less money than we now spend on any educative activity, and it might well be the most educative of all.

This is a way, I think, to teach poetry. To explain patiently in class that a sonnet has 14 lines after substituting two periods a week of gym for a child's birthright of outdoor play is like castrating a man and then explaining the physiology of reproduction. I should want children first to live their poetry, and then they might have some referents for the symbols which get caught in the meshes of a sonnet. Even if they did not, the direct experience of the stuff is all that matters. Which would you rather have: love, or a poem about love? Me too.

15. **Conferences and Counseling:** Most of the publications of the child development people make me yearn for the millennium when we have a well-trained counselor for every 20 kids, with nothing to do but counsel them, and in addition a well-adjusted teaching staff, all of whom have psychiatric insight. They insist that teachers will have to carry most of the load, and they try to explain how to do it, bearing in mind the fact that teachers have plenty to do already. But what they recommend still seems impossible to me. Among other things, they assume that the teacher will have many chances to sit down privately with each pupil and get to know him as an individual. They do not seem to realize that most teachers in public schools see at least 150 pupils a day, and keep most of them only for a semester, or a year at best. There is absolutely no time during the school day for individual conferences, and conferences after school are always associated with punishment. Most American children are being educated by teachers who know nothing whatsoever about them but their names, their IQ, and their age. Whenever these teachers find out accidentally that a boy—whom they took to be a lazy lout—is working from midnight to eight in the morning to support his widowed mother, or that a girl who seems unreasonably high-strung has an insane father living at home who is always threatening to kill her—they are always dumbfounded. There is no way of learning such facts as these in the normal course of events. The 20 worst pupils in

school get individual conferences. The rest just buzz around in a gigantic bee-hive for three or four years with nobody there who knows them as a person, who keeps track of how they are getting along, or who feels responsible for their all-round development.[18] I know that home-rooms were started to provide such a person, but they failed. They simply became another class with an extraordinary number of things to do in less time than other classes, or else they became a study period, interrupted by announcements. This picture is slightly overdrawn because teachers somehow get to know a few things about their pupils, but how they do it is a mystery—the system makes it theoretically impossible to know anything at all about pupils. Under these circumstances we might just shake our fists at the system and do the best we can with one or two pupils each year. But I think we can do more than this.

In the first place, we should face the fact that teachers are not going to know all 150 pupils well enough to do what the child development people would consider a good job. We should work to have this number cut down, but that will take a long time. Meanwhile we might concentrate on the goal of getting to know well the pupils one has to counsel. If the pupils in any school were parceled out evenly among the staff, each teacher would have about 30 pupils to counsel. Allowing for differences in counseling competence, let us assume that teachers will have 10 to 40 pupils to counsel. It is possible, though difficult, to get to know this many pupils well, whereas it is absolutely impossible to get to know 150 well.

How to divide the pupils among the teachers is always a moot point. Some favor giving boys to men teachers and girls to women teachers. Some argue for assigning counselors to one grade, and others for having a sampling of all grades in all counseling groups.

Such considerations as those seem highly theoretical to me. I base my policy on two notions: first, that pupils should have a voice in choosing their counselor, for a counselor must first of all be a friend, and one can't assign friends; second, that it is very difficult to follow and understand a pupil's development unless one has regular contact with him in a class or activity. For these reasons I allow pupils about a month at the beginning of the year to get acquainted with their teachers for that year, and then to indicate their first and second choices among these teachers as their counselor. By utilizing second choices one can distribute the load as evenly as it ought to be distributed. Schools which have tried this system report uniformly that it works well.[19] No teacher is left out, and none is loaded unreasonably. Other things being equal, pupils are urged to keep the same counselor as long as possible; but if they want to make a change, the procedure above allows it with no questions asked.

I think the movement now on foot to have core teachers do all counseling is a serious mistake. It gives them too heavy a counseling load to do a good job. It eliminates many fine teachers from other fields who ought to be counselors. It furthers the separation of "progressive" core teachers from "traditional" teachers which is already tearing apart so many faculties. And it gives pupils no choice of counselor; they have to take the core teacher.

Some principals have told me that my system of choosing counselors makes a pretty picture, but when we get down to realities, some teachers just have to be kept out of counseling. The point admits of no argument. Anybody but a fool with a theory to uphold would see that these people are impossible.

I sympathize with this feeling. I have heard so many educational theories in my time that did not square with classroom realities that I know how these people feel. But here they happen to be wrong. I can name plenty of schools that have tried the system I recommend, fearing just the outcome these critics anticipate, and nothing of the sort happened. The critics are the victims of too lofty and too fixed a notion of what a counselor should be. All we want here, as a beginning, is a human being who has some obligation to get acquainted with a small number of pupils. Even the old battle-axes warm up when, contrary to their fears, they find themselves with a group of pupils, all of whom have chosen them as counselor of their own free will. And I should hate to exclude the teachers who need it most from the sort of contact with children that is one of the very few experiences that can truly change them. Lectures won't do it; conventions won't do it; most courses in education roll off them like water off a duck's back; and they won't read the books aimed at their salvation. The most potent influence we can bring to bear upon them is close contact with a group of children, to be studied as persons. Even that will not work in all cases, but compared with other means of influencing teachers, its batting average is remarkably high.

The next step is to find a time within the school day when pupils and their counselors can get together to talk things over. I say it casually, but this is the point at which every counseling system breaks down. There is no such time in the school day. Most schools get along with some unsatisfactory makeshift. The core courses have pupils read their books once or twice a week while conferences go on at the teacher's desk. What one can talk about in this goldfish-bowl setting is not reported. Some schools have counselors snake pupils out of other classes during the counselor's free period. That makes the counselor mad because it takes away the period when he corrects papers and gets ready for other classes, or has a quiet smoke in the boiler room. It leaves him no free time whatsoever during the school day. It makes the pupils mad because other pupils always wonder what they have done wrong when they are called out of class, and it gives them work to make up. It infuriates the teachers whose classes they leave, because of the interruption and because they will have to explain the stuff over again to these pupils at some later date. In order to avoid putting the conference outside the school day, as they look at it, this system puts regular work outside the school day. So nobody likes it, and conferences steadily decline under this system unless teachers are held in line by rigid pressure.

The only system I know that really works is to schedule no classes during the long noon period. It is a beastly administrative problem to schedule classes during this time anyway, and very little work gets done because classes are always interrupted by bells ringing and pupils rushing through the corridors. Instead of classes, have the student council figure out a program of recreational activities that the pupils themselves can manage with very little supervision: movies, dancing, conversation, reading, singing, radio and phonograph, quiet games, rest for those who need it, and so on. Those can be supervised by responsible older pupils appointed by the School Council with authority to send disturbers to a detention room, supervised by a hard-boiled teacher. Only a few teachers need be on patrol duty, strolling through the corridors and looking in on the various activities to make sure the lid is kept on within reason. Teachers can be scheduled for patrol duty in proportion to the lightness of their counseling load. Under this system while teachers are not at lunch they have up to an hour a day clear for private conferences, which have the right of way over all other activities scheduled during this time. Pupils do not resent being asked to come in for a conference once a month or so during this time, for even on that day they still have half their recreational time free, and on all other days of the month they have a long period of very enjoyable activity which they never had before. And teachers do not resent it, because the time is set up for this specific purpose and conflicts with none of their other duties. This system is not theory but practice, tried and proven. Not many schools have tried it, because the idea is just beginning to catch hold, but wherever it has been tried with anything like proper preparation for it and proper regulation in the initial stages, it works.

The next step is to set up machinery whereby all pertinent data on important aspects of pupil development, gathered in any department in school, pass through the hands of the counselor of the pupil concerned. The tangible part of the machinery is a box in the school office into which teachers put tests, papers, questionnaires, anecdotes, excuses, complaints, summaries of reading records, and so on, whenever they are through with them for their own purposes. The office clerk sorts them and puts them into the mailboxes of the appropriate counselors, who read them, take whatever action is indicated, and file them in the pupil's folder. This may sound like a big job, but the usual haul is not more than about a dozen items in a week. The intangible but important part of the machinery is a committee on school objectives which makes agreements in writing with each department as to what evidence of growth toward the various school objectives they will collect, with due dates and follow up. Until those agreements are made and enforced, the stuff does not roll in.[20]

If the school wishes to keep the old custom of reporting to parents, the counselor is the one who does it. This does not mean that on certain due dates teachers write reports on all 150 pupils in their classes and send them to the counselor, who relays them to parents. On the contrary, whenever teachers get any evidence of growth in some important aspect of development, they send it to the counselor without waiting for report time. It is the job of the committee on objectives to make them do it. Hence the stuff is flowing in more or less continuously from every department in school, and a good deal of it is evidence rather than unsupported opinion. It is on the basis of this evidence plus his own observations that the counselor makes his report. No counselor ever reports on all the kids in his classes. He only reports on the 10 to 40 kids in his counseling group.

The best form of report I know is an interview with parents at least twice a year, and whenever parents request it between times. This is possible even in public schools with large classes if the parents see only the counselor, not every teacher who has any contact with their child. They may, however, request the counselor to arrange an interview with some other teacher if the child is having any difficulty on which the parents can throw some light and offer suggestions.

The second best form of report is a letter written by the counselor and answered by the parents. If letters are written, they should not all be mailed on the same date. This piles work on counselors and on the office, leads to hasty and superficial reports, creates an electric tension around school while reports are being written with a corresponding letdown afterward, and leads pupils and parents to compare reports. To avoid this, the counselor agrees to write two or three letters a week, depending on the number of pupils he has to counsel, and these are typed and mailed as soon as they are received. In the same way, if reports are made orally, the school schedules two or three conferences per week with parents throughout the year, rather than piling them up at any report period. There is no other form of report which is any good at all. Marks are a menace—for reasons discussed earlier—and all the ingenious checklists and rating scales I have seen are only marks in disguise. Some schools, however, make quite a point of having the pupil report on his own progress. Although this coincides with our progressive doctrines of having everything come from the pupil, I don't like it. Maybe it would do my child some good occasionally to think on her sins and resolve to lead a better life, but as a parent I wouldn't like her to horn in on my conference time to do it. I would like a chance during this conference to say what I thought of the school, or to tell my troubles with the child at home and ask for some advice, or to get the low-down on her status in school, and I could do none of those things freely if the child were there. I also have a hunch that it tends to create self-conscious little prigs to have these kids continually evaluating themselves. I admit that this is only a prejudice with no scientific support. The Denver public schools had a long try at a "cooperative record," kept by pupils and teachers together, and they tried to appraise its effects, but all the evidence they got was questionnaire stuff—expressions of opinion for and against. Although this sort of evidence is usually unanimously in favor of whatever you are investigating, the testimony in this case was so mixed that I counted it as a moral victory for the opposition. I take it that whenever the parents wanted to find out how their child was getting along, they asked the teacher, and the teacher told them. The cooperative record was only one more side-show of the progressive circus.

Please note that I have not said anything about what the conferences are to be about. On this point the guidance people have more trustworthy information. I have only indicated how a public school under present circumstances can get the necessary minimum of contact with individuals to have any of this child development stuff function at all. If we keep on having an average of about .02 private conferences per pupil per year, there is no point in talking about developmental tasks or studying the whole child. And we are not going to leap from this point to having dozens of conferences per year with all the pupils we teach. Let's set our cap for what is within the bounds of possibility, and aim at an average of about six private conferences per pupil per year. I should like to enforce and jack up this figure by making it one of the standard measures to be reported to State departments of education and accrediting agencies. I know this is just the sort of thing the child guidance people abhor—getting data on mere number of conferences without regard to their quality—but I insist that here is a figure which would mean a lot more and be a greater force for educational progress than any of the statistics we collect now. It might be possible for a school to prove that it had an average of a dozen private conferences per pupil per year and still not suffer any change of heart—but I doubt it. Such contacts with pupils in circumstances in which they have at least an even chance to spill the beans are dynamite to any conservative faculty. And while one could not be sure that the school with lots of private conferences was a good school, one could at least be confident that the school which reported an average of .001 private conferences per pupil per year had not yet absorbed the doctrines of D. Prescott and Company.

16. **Integration** One of the most useful battles in the history of secondary education was fought and won under the banner of "integration," but never was a battle fought in which the real issues were so obscured as in this one.

As far as I am able to make out, the movement toward integration rested on two bits of primary data and no more. At the time of its inception the profession had just become aware that a "split personality" was characteristic of a form of insanity, and the psychiatrists were making the converse of this, an integrated personality seemed important. By a split personality they meant something pretty definite: a man who imagines at times that he is Julius Caesar or Napoleon or someone like that. The concept of integration was an observable mental state in which the subject was in control. The second bit of primary data turned up when [psychologist Wolfgang] Kohler's chimpanzee [Sultan] reached out of his cage and hauled in a banana with a stick.[21] For some obscure reason this ingenious act upset atomistic psychology and started a vogue for the adjective "whole." We went whole hog for the whole view of the whole child. We began bashing water-tight compartments between subjects. Since the only two subjects most children took at the same time were English and social studies, we scheduled them in adjacent periods and ordered the English teacher to teach in one the literature related to the century studied in the other. This was integration.

Now there has never been the slightest evidence, so far as I know, that a split personality was ever caused by teaching English and social studies separately nor cured by teaching them together. And if Kohler's chimpanzee had realized, when he reached for that banana, that he was inadvertently putting English and social studies together, he would have starved first.

Yet the movement went merrily on and developed some sense in the process. It soon became apparent that it would not do to drive history and literature in harness because then pupils began by reading Plato and Aristotle, and only when they arrived at problems of democracy in the 12th grade could they read Huckleberry Finn. But by now they had an integrated course established and a horde of angry conservatives yelling about it, so they couldn't just haul down the flag and go back to teaching English and history as usual. "What in hell shall we do in our integrated course, now that we've got it?" became the most pressing issue in secondary education.

I shall not recite in detail the entertaining history of the movement, but it finally turned out that if one tackled any real problem of children or of our society, it naturally called upon the resources of several subjects to settle it. This was legitimate integration, so real problems were OK. Thus we got around crab-wise to a sensible solution. Real problems were sought not because they were the most natural and obvious matters that ought to be dealt with in schools, but because we had to have something which would integrate our old subjects without too much strain on the imagination, and real problems turned out to be the only thing that would do the trick.

The search for real problems, in a profession not accustomed to dealing with them, was not without occasional mishaps. One Denver father was startled one evening by a request from his son for two family problems to discuss in class the following day. He and several others like him got the principal on the phone at once and told him sulfurously that their family problems would not stand a public airing. In Los Angeles lively hordes of children invaded homes and began rearranging the furniture and fixtures. Children everywhere began ringing doorbells and asking the inmates about their age, education, number of decayed teeth, favorite breakfast cereal, and views on presidential candidates.

It is a mystery to me how the movement survived, but it did, and a basic course or core course for all pupils, supposed to deal with real problems without regard to subject boundaries, now seems likely to be the next big step in the reorganization of secondary education. I have already indicated that one series of units in this course is oriented toward the central question, "how do we propose to get the things we all need?" and these units make plenty of sense to me and to all who have seen them.

Now that the shouting has died down, I wonder if the real motive behind this scrunching together of subjects was not the congestion of the curriculum with diverse and unrelated subjects which the elective system left in its wake. I have already alluded to the sorry state of the pupil exposed to all the competing demands of powerful associations of subject specialists. We knew in our hearts that this was bad for pupils, but could see no way to leave any of these subjects out, so we tried to find ways of teaching several of them at the same time in connection with some broad problem or topic that would lend unity and coherence to the school day. Once we let these problems in, however, we paved the way toward the gradual abandonment of the old subjects. We still justify these problems in terms of the amount of subject-matter we can tuck under their wings, but even now these problems are demanding attention in their own right, and to hell with the grammar and mathematics we pin on them. This is as it should be. The old subjects are not and never were a good way to bring up a child, and if we can integrate them out of the picture, I am all for integration.

17. **The Etiology of Critical Thinking:** This interest dates back to that momentous investigation last year with Richards.[22] We asked a great many senior high school students what was on their minds (or words to that effect), and it turned out that they had nothing on their minds. Nothing of any importance.

We were all set back on our haunches by the outcome of this inquiry, even though the state of mind revealed by the replies was familiar to us all. We began to ask one another what awakens the mind to speculation, to questioning the assumptions it has taken for granted, to thinking for itself. To assist and clarify this inquiry, we thought of friends of ours who seemed to have the quality we were looking for, and tried to think what started it. For many of the older generation it was the theory of evolution that set them off. For our own crowd it was mostly Marxism or Freud. Some even dated what they called their intellectual awakening from an innocuous psychology course in college, when they figured out how the body could get around without a soul to steer it. Some had come to life through reading anthropology, and finding out that their own mores did not reflect any fixed canon of right and wrong.

When we looked over our list, we had another shock coming. Every one of the common sources of intellectual awakening we had listed was a serious threat to religion, patriotism, or morals. We had been all set to bring about a new renaissance, but when we saw the means at our disposal which had worked with people we knew, we realized what would happen if we assembled them all into a battery and tried them out in school. We would be blown clean out of the water, that's all. Probably a sound instinct on the part of the culture. It might not be able to stand that amount of clawing at its vitals. The colleges, protected by an astonishing tradition of intellectual freedom, had been doing some discreet clawing for a long time, and we were not too happy about the result, even when the poison worked. It produced altogether too many disorganized, irresponsible, unhappy, ineffective people.

So there you are. Usually at this point I pull some rabbit out of the hat that solves the problem and saves the day, but I don't know what to do about this one. Maybe we were just a sinful crowd, and what we thought had aroused our minds was instead the cause of our corruption. This is something for the child development people to ponder: does the mind of man really mature only by picking fruit in the Garden of Eden? Can you think of any way to do it which does not threaten the foundations of society and produce unhappy, unadjusted people?

18. **The Star Spangled Banner:** Educators keep saying that it is the school's job not only to adjust the individual to the culture but to keep the way open for a return engagement. But they are always a bit vague about what sorts of changes in the social order would clear the tracks for better human growth and development. I should like to venture a few examples.

For one thing, I hope the individual does a job on the American home. Much as I abhor tampering with a sacred institution, there must be something wrong with this one. Why does it produce so many narrow-minded, pot-bellied, nagging, complaining, tired and dissatisfied women? Why does the healthy young bride, trained in the most progressive manner, regularly go neurotic after the second child or so? Why does the circle of friends and the circle of interests regularly contract after age forty until the husband and wife have nothing left to do but growl at one another?

I don't know the answers here either, but let us explore one possible alternative to the present set-up, just to dispel the illusion that the American home is the only type of home that it is possible to have. Suppose I found one of the old mansions built by the industrial tycoons in the 1890s on the theory that any marriage yielding less than 12 children was a flirtation. Then suppose I thought of two other families with whom I desired a closer acquaintance, and each of these families thought of other families toward whom they had similar sentiments until we filled the mansion to the rafters. Then we might set to work with saws, hammers, and paintbrushes and arrange the rooms so that each family had fairly secluded living quarters but shared a common large kitchen, dining room, nursery, laundry, social rooms, and recreational facilities. We might then pool our resources and hire a decent cook, who might be assisted by the wives whose talents lay in that direction. All the other jobs around the house might be divided up in any way that we could work out. If some of the wives wanted to work outside the house, they might contribute money rather than personal service. Most of the work would be done for their own families, as it is at present, but there are a few points at which we could get together. For example, the women might take turns riding herd on the children during their play-time rather than tending their own continuously. I think we could all save a bit of money on this set-up and have a better life. On the whole we now see too little of other people. Here they would always be handy, although each family would still have its private quarters. If you wanted someone to play poker or tennis or golf, you could just step into the corridor and yell, and someone would probably turn up. You could have one glorious Steinway rather than a dozen miserable little uprights. You could take on such luxuries as a billiard table and a tennis court—the backyard of the old mansion would probably accommodate one. The garage should have space in it for a work bench and some power tools. All the little adjustments we would have to work out in order to live graciously with other people would be good for us.

This might not work—although I know cases in which it has—but it at least illustrates the possibility that we could do things to the American home and family if we studied it critically and made up our minds to do something about its gross and obvious shortcomings. The way our home economics courses simply assume that the status quo will remain as is infuriates me. Most of the promising girls in high school now want to do more than devote their brains and talents to housework which any maid can do better. Yet they insist on a private house absolutely separate from all other houses. Those two desires, it seems to me, are incompatible. A few lucky ones may get jobs outside the house and pay a maid, but most of them will not. The only solution to their problem which is immediately available, so far as I can see, is cooperative housing. Just a footnote: I have known several experiments in cooperative housing which involved only three families, and these almost never worked.[23] I have a hunch that the smallest unit which would show advantages would involve about a dozen families. And even then one would have to be prepared for a rocky first year for the sake of the greater glory beyond.

Another job for the individual to do when he begins interacting with the culture is to make some change in our manner of electing our public officials. At the present time, democracy amounts to little more than the privilege of electing a set of crooks and incompetents to mismanage our affairs on the basis of no valid information at all about them. On the long ballot today the only man I knew anything about was Paul Douglas [a Professor of Economics at the University of Chicago who narrowly lost the Democratic primary for the U.S.

Senate in 1942; in 1948, he won an Illinois Senate seat]. I read the papers, but all they said about the candidates was utterly untrustworthy. It was stupidity on my part to vote for anyone but Douglas. I might as well have drawn the names out of a hat. I do not feel like a Nazi agent in expressing these sentiments because I find that Thomas Jefferson agreed with me. He said that the voting system would work as long as we continued to live in small agricultural communities where everyone knew everyone else, but it would break down the moment we huddled together in great cities. I have no alternative to suggest, but I wish someone like Ralph Tyler could be set to work devising Civil Service specifications for the selection of 99.9 percent of our government. To keep such a government responsive to public interests, I think we should have a series of radio programs devoted to the discussion of not more than one public issue a month, with safeguards to see that every shade of opinion was fairly represented. This would then be followed by a sampling of opinion on the various alternatives presented. I once made this proposal in *The Social Frontier*.[24] The response was surprising: hundreds of people wrote me enthusiastically about it, and whether it was coincidence or not, several radio programs of this sort appeared shortly after. None of them, however, was popular or influential enough to do the job I had in mind.[25]

All this may seem off the track, but here is the connection: there is a big push in the schools to organize their work around the idea of democracy, and I fear it may emphasize the wrong things. If we only instill reverence for certain outworn forms of democracy such as voting, it will have several bad effects. First, the native common sense of children will reassert itself when they come to vote. Then the whole notion of democracy may seem like an exploded myth. Second, it may distract attention from the important business of looking around for the changes that ought to be made in our social set-up, and finding ways to put them into effect.

What are some of these other changes? Well, take the fact that one out of 20 of us spends some time in a mental hospital, and more ought to. Perhaps there is nothing surprising in this; we all expect to spend some time in other sorts of hospitals, and think nothing of it. But I have faith that the incidence of serious mental breakdown could be markedly reduced if we set about it. One marriage out of four, I am told, ends in divorce. We have got as far as putting in a few aseptic courses in the physiology of reproduction in some schools, but these don't come within gunshot of the problems involved. I would not favor courses on marriage, but we need to do a lot more thinking throughout the curriculum on what it takes to make a successful marriage. Among other things, I would like to know a lot more about what it takes to develop a great capacity for loving. The measures we have taken have been in the opposite direction: we assume that children will love not wisely but too well. My hunch is that for every girl who "goes wrong" there are twenty who are too scared and frigid to sustain affection. Who has reliable figures on frigidity? A very good psychiatrist I knew last year claimed that 40% of New England women never had an orgasm. I think we might take our chances on a little fornication if we could do anything to improve this situation. Another great problem clamoring for attention is the fact that normally we have millions unemployed, and millions more who have work which leaves no sense of achievement. What this does to youth is well told in the recent report of the American Youth Commission.[26] A fourth great problem is that of war, especially this war, especially the ambivalent attitude of young people toward it. We trained them to abhor war and to regard it as a colossal blunder; now we have changed our tune, and wonder why they do not respond.

There are plenty more problems, but these are sufficient for the only point I have to make here. One part of our work in child development is to bring up young people in such a way that they will change things around, so that even better development will be possible in the generation to follow. We are usually a bit vague in our reports about the social conditions which interfere with normal development, and especially vague about measures which schools might take which would lead pupils, without sheer indoctrination, to remedy these conditions. I have given several examples of such conditions, and pursued one of them (the American family) far enough to indicate at least one promising course of action the schools might take. The other examples might well be analyzed in the same way, and even better examples might be found. I think we owe it to young people to point out some of the major problems they will have to solve collectively, and to give them all the tips we can about how to solve them.

ENDNOTES

1. "What is Wrong with Education" April 13, 1942 (Ben Wood Papers, Educational Testing Service Archives).
2. "Simplifying a Crowded Schedule" in *The School Review*, March 1945, v53, n3, 162-169.
3. Diederich to Morris Finder, July 14, 1994 (Finder Papers, Box 1, University of Chicago Archives).

4. Daniel Prescott, *Emotions and the Educative Process* (Washington DC: American Council on Education, 1938).
5. W.B. Townsend to Dean Mann, November 9, 1939 (General Education Board Papers, Box 280, Folder 2925, Rockefeller Archive Center).
6. Ellen Condliffe Lagemann, *Private Power for the Public Good: A History of the Carnegie Foundation for the Advancement of Teaching* (Middleton, CT: Wesleyan University Press, 1983), Ch. 3.
7. The Committee of Ten wrote an influential report in 1893 on the high school curriculum. Ten prominent educators outlined four secondary school programs; each one prepared students for college. The rigorous academic fare was designed to benefit all students, not just the small fraction who attended college. By the time of the Eight Year Study, far more high school graduates were entering college, but entrance requirements were often criticized as too narrow and inflexible. For the text of the Committee's report and a thorough discussion of its origins and effects, see Theodore R. Sizer, *Secondary Schools at the Turn of the Century* (New Haven: Yale University Press, 1964).
8. Smith was the first Headmaster of the Beaver Country Day School in Boston (1921-1943), a founder of the major testing service for independent schools (the Educational Records Bureau), and a coauthor, with Ralph Tyler, of *Recording and Appraising Student Progress*, one of the books generated by the Eight Year Study. For a profile of Smith, see Kridel and Bullough, *Stories of the Eight-Year Study*, 17-24.
9. Hugh Hawkins, *Between Harvard and America: The Educational Leadership of Charles W. Eliot* (New York: Oxford University Press, 1971), Ch. 3.
10. And it did. For the proliferation of courses until the 1980s, see David L. Angus and Jeffrey E. Mirel, *The Failed Promise of the American High School* (New York: Teachers College Press, 1999), Chs. 3-5.
11. Angus and Mirel reported a lower figure for foreign language enrollment (6.9%) on the basis of the massive 1933-34 federal survey, but they did not separate full year from shorter courses, so Diederich's claim about "time" is consistent with their numbers.
12. One of Diederich's assignments was to measure the effects of new programs in the arts. His research assistant for one year was art historian and psychoanalyst Bruno Bettelheim, an émigré from Austria whose first job in America was with the Eight Year Study. He and Diederich hung reproductions of famous paintings in the schools, asked students to write about what they liked and disliked, and then analyzed their reactions. They also printed a large sheet full of small reproductions and asked students to pick pairs that resembled one another. Diederich put his carpentry skills to good use by making portable collapsible stands for the paintings. Diederich to Siegmund Levarie, March 23, 1990 (Diederich Family Papers, Princeton NJ).
13. Some schools in the 1930s used bits and pieces of what Diederich had in mind, but none came close to the scope and duration of what he proposed. See Diane Ravitch, *Left Back* (New York: Simon and Schuster, 2000), 263-271.
14. Diederich's favorite educational philosopher, Comenius, had called for less time in school and more opportunity for play (he also yearned to simplify

Latin, perhaps another reason why Diederich admired him). Daniel Murphy, *Comenius: A Critical Reassessment of his Life and Work* (Dublin: Irish Academic Press, 1995), 18, 113, 210.
15. In graduate school, Diederich invented ring-toss games with the five year old daughter of his dissertation adviser, which prompted the eminent psychologist Edward Thorndike to say, "Paul, if you don't make it as a Latin teacher, you have a great future in kindergarten" Diederich to June and Duff Carr, October 17, 1988 (Diederich Family Papers).
16. "Summer is coming in/Loudly sing, cuckoo" From 13th century Middle English verse (Wessex dialect).
17. Historians have neglected the history of summer camps. For a good start at filling this gap, see Abigail A. Van Slyck, *A Manufactured Wilderness: Summer Camps and the Shaping of American Youth, 1890-1960* (Minneapolis: University of Minnesota Press, 2006) and Leslie Paris, *Children's Nature: The Rise of the American Summer Camp* (New York: New York University Press, 2008).
18. For more on the theme of anonymity in the American high school, see Arthur G. Powell, Eleanor Farrar, and David K. Cohen, *The Shopping Mall High School* (Boston: Houghton and Mifflin, 1985), Chs. 4-5.
19. The OSU campus school let students choose their counselors. Rudolph Daniel Lindquist, "The University School at Ohio State University: An Evaluation of Its Program of Education for Children and Youth" (unpublished dissertation, University of California—Berkeley, 1937), Ch. 12.
20. For the voluminous records gathered by the OSU teachers, see Jessie L. Rhulman, "An Approach to Revision of the Program and Procedures of Centralia High School through the Organization and Interpretation of School Records" (unpublished dissertation, Teachers College—Columbia, 1939).
21. Wolfgang Kohler, *The Mentality of Apes* (New York: Harcourt, Brace, and World, 1925).
22. Diederich was a research associate at the Language Research Institute in the 1940/41 academic year. His work there is discussed in Chapter 5 of this book.
23. He might have been thinking of the communal housing undertaken by several teachers at the OSU campus school, described in William Van Til, *My Way of Looking At It* (Terre Haute, IN: Lake Lurie Press, 1983), 88.
24. "A Proposal for a Monthly Radio Referendum" in *The Social Frontier*, June 1938, v5, n6, 304.
25. Diederich envisioned one million postcard ballots sent each month to a representative sample of registered voters, with a Washington DC bureau to tabulate the replies and share the results with Congress."A Proposal for a Monthly Radio Referendum" May 6, 1938 in "Diederich, Paul B." folder, UAV 350.284, Box 160, Harvard University Archives.
26. Howard Bell, *Youth Tell Their Story* (Washington, D.C.: American Council on Education., 1938), a study of 16-24 year olds in Maryland.

CHAPTER 2

RUNNING AWAY[1]

(1942)

Six weeks at a workshop? They usually last a day or two, but that was not the case during the Eight Year Study. In the summer of 1937, 126 teachers voluntarily spent six weeks on the Sarah Lawrence college campus. The group increased to 500 in 1938, and another surge in 1939 required ten different campuses to hold everyone.

The unprecedented length of those workshops let teachers create and revise curriculum. The slow pace of change in the Study's schools would supposedly accelerate if teams of teachers could focus on what they taught. The participants would have the time to concentrate on the hardest challenges they had identified, challenges that required more than a quick fix in a day or two of coaching by Diederich and his four colleagues on the Study's curriculum staff.[2]

How the teachers worked mattered as much as what they created. They experienced for themselves what progressive educators espoused: student centered learning. The teachers' needs shaped the workshops. For six weeks they were the pupils. The workshop staff modeled progressive pedagogy by serving as advisors rather than lecturers. For all participants it was a time to practice what they preached.[3]

One result was a greater likelihood that the teachers, in the fall and beyond, would use the changes they had devised. They had a keener appreciation of what it meant to start with the students' interests. They had sat on the other side of the desk--or, better yet, found ways to learn without desks.[4]

Renewal, invigoration, stimulation: those words describe another important benefit of the workshops. How teachers felt about themselves, their colleagues, and their profession changed. The esprit de corps stemmed not just from the pleasure of an all-expense-paid trip during the Great Depression. The design of the workshop consciously fostered camaraderie. Teachers rarely worked alone—they lived with and learned from other teachers. And they didn't always work—as in a truly progressive school, the arts were an important part of each day. Painting, sculpting, drawing, singing, dancing, and acting enlivened the summer.

Diederich wrote a favorable report on the 1939 workshops. He praised them effusively, but he privately acknowledged how hard it was to run them. For instance, the first two weeks were full of confusion whenever the staff refused to make decisions for fear of seeming undemocratic. For Diederich, a skeletal organization would have let teachers get to work quickly, with individual conferences in the first two days followed by grouping teachers according to the work they planned to do, not by their discipline (that approach had been tried and it failed).[5]

He also saw that the conversations at the workshops could drift aimlessly. He had heard "much random, uncoordinated, unfocused discussion" when teachers compared their educational philosophies. Within the Eight Year Study schools Diederich knew that teachers and administrators alike found ways to sidestep tough issues and avoid decisions. He admired the workshops and so did his former Ohio State colleague Robert Havighurst, who by the late 1930s lead the foundation that donated several hundred thousand dollars to fund them.[6] But Diederich conceded that educators in conference with one another made face-saving rationalizations for not doing anything about the matters at hand.

Running Away

Most educational discussions become, sooner or later, a desperate attempt to escape from the problem. This is often done clumsily, causing unnecessary embarrassment and leaving the group without the comfortable feeling of having disposed of the problem. Educational leaders have long since worked out adequate techniques for dodging the issue. The following list is tentative, partial, incomplete, a mere beginning, etc., but it should give group leaders a command of alternative modes of retreat and enable them to withdraw their forces gracefully, leaving the problem baffled and helpless.

1. Find a scapegoat. Teachers can blame administrators, administrators can blame teachers, both can blame parents, and everyone can blame the social order.
2. Profess not to have *the* answer. That lets you out of having *any* answer.

3. Say that we must not move too rapidly. That avoids the necessity of getting started.
4. For every proposal set up an opposite and conclude that "the middle ground" (no motion whatever) is the wisest course of action.
5. Point out that an attempt to reach a conclusion is a futile "quest for certainty." Doubt and indecision prompt growth.
6. When in a tight place, say something that the group cannot understand.
7. Look slightly embarrassed when the problem is brought up. Hint that it is in bad taste or too elementary for mature consideration, or that any discussion of it is likely to be misinterpreted by outsiders.
8. Say that the problem cannot be separated from other problems. Therefore no problem can be solved until all other problems have been solved.
9. Carry the problem into other fields. Show that it exists everywhere; therefore it is of no concern.
10. Point out that those who see the problem do so by virtue of personality traits. They see the problem because they are unhappy, not vice-versa.
11. Ask what is meant by the question. When it is sufficiently clarified, there will be no time left for an answer.
12. Discover that there are all sorts of dangers in any specific formulations of conclusions: of exceeding authority or seeming to, asserting more than is definitely known, of misinterpretation by outsiders—and, of course, the danger of revealing that no one has a conclusion to offer.
13. Look for some philosophical basis for approaching the problem, then a basis for that, then a basis for that, and so on back into Noah's Ark.
14. Retreat from the problem into endless discussion of ways to study it.
15. Put off recommendations until every related problem has been definitely settled by scientific research.
16. Retreat into general objectives on which everyone can agree. From this higher ground you will either see that the problem has solved itself, or you will forget it.
17. Find a face-saving verbal formula like "In a Pickwickian sense."
18. Rationalize the status quo; there is much to be said for it.
19. The reverse of "begging the question." Begin with a problem like, "What should be the content of our core course?" Conclude that maybe we ought to have a core course.
20. Explain and clarify over and over again what you have already said.
21. As soon as any proposal is made, say that you have been doing it for ten years. Hence there can't possibly be any merit in it.

22. Appoint a committee to weigh the pros and cons (these must <u>always</u> be weighed). It will reach tentative conclusions that can subsequently be used as bases for further discussions of an exploratory nature preliminary to arriving at initial postulates on which methods of approach to the pros and cons may be predicated.
23. Wait until some expert can be consulted. He will refer the question to other experts.
24. Say, "That is not on the agenda. We will take it up later." This can be repeated *ad infinitum.*
25. Notice that your time is up. If committee members look surprised, list your engagements for the next two days.
26. Conclude that we have all clarified our thinking on the problem, even though no one has thought of any way to solve it.
27. Point out that some of the greatest minds have struggled with this problem, implying that it does us credit to have even thought of it.
28. Retreat into analogies and discuss them rather than the problem.
29. Say forcefully, "Do we really want this laid out cold for us?" Obviously we don't.
30. Be thankful for the problem. It has stimulated our best thinking and has therefore contributed to our growth. It should get a medal.

[The National Education Association later reprinted this list in the form of a placemat]

ENDNOTES

1. "How To Run Away from an Educational Problem" in *Progressive Education,* v19, n3, March 1942, 167-168.
2. "Meeting of the Curriculum Staff" March 2, 1937 (General Education Board Papers, Box 281, Folder 2932, Rockefeller Archive Center).
3. For a glowing account of the workshops, see Craig Kridel and Robert V. Bullough, Jr., *Stories of the Eight-Year Study: Reexamining Secondary Education in America* (Albany: SUNY Press, 2007), Ch. 8.
4. Kenneth L. Heaton, William G. Camp, and Paul B. Diederich, *Professional Education for Experienced Teachers: The Program of the Summer Workshop* (Chicago: University of Chicago Press, 1940), Ch. 4. In that chapter Diederich reported that nearly all workshoppers whose classrooms he visited (over 20% of the 1939 corps) were using what they had created in the summer.
5. "What is Wrong with Workshops" April 10, 1940 (General Education Board Papers, Box 285, Folder 2977).
6. "Appraisal: Progressive Education Association Programs" (General Education Board Papers, Box 284, Folder 2971).

CHAPTER 3

FREE READING

(1942)[1]

In July, 1942, Diederich began work at the University of Chicago as an "Examiner" in English and an Assistant Professor in that department. He made an immediate contribution to the war by devoting half of his time to work on tests for the armed forces, especially the "GED" (general educational development) test which let several million veterans receive credits or skip courses when they returned to high school or college. The other half of his time was devoted to teaching—every Examiner taught—and he supervised the instructors of remedial English.[2] Diederich also oversaw the six hour comprehensive examinations in English, the product of weekly meetings with his colleagues in the English department. Many of these meetings he held in his apartment because "preparing an exam is thirsty business that should never be attempted except at an evening party at the home of the examiner after suitable refreshments have been provided" (See Figure 2, which Diederich claimed was an exaggeration that nevertheless caught the spirit of the sessions).[3] The work of a typical evening would yield items like "Apply Hume's criteria in "Of Miracles" to DeFoe's "The Apparition of Mrs. Veal" as well as short answer and objective questions.

The following paper tells us about the road not taken, a career path Diederich entertained in the spring of 1942, and it also reveals an earnest temperament that fit the ethos of the University of Chicago. It was the American campus most devoted to the life of the mind. Where else would a Dean quip that "going to the country is all very well for a few minutes, but there are no libraries."[4] As President Robert

---

Paul Diederich and the Progressive American High School, pp. 43–61
Copyright © 2014 by Information Age Publishing
All rights of reproduction in any form reserved.

A wildly exaggerated view of the final stage of a meeting to plan an examination ca. 1945 at the home of the examiner.

Hutchins said, "What is it that makes the University of Chicago a great educational institution? It is the intense, strenuous, and constant intellectual activity of the place."[5] Faculty memoirs from the Hutchins years make the same point; the President wasn't exaggerating. Historian William McNeill recalled that "fundamental questions were asked point blank, and no one could get away with a perfunctory answer."[6] Diederich's disposition matched the climate of the place better than it had and would in any other job he held—elsewhere he was more of a rebel among the moderates.[7]

The paper below is a passionate defense of lifelong reading. The best way to develop that habit is to "read all around" the topics discussed in class. Teachers should talk less, and when they do speak, it should be "elbow teaching," offering advice or asking questions that help the student who is reading find the answer or solve a problem. The best way to learn Latin, modern languages, and English is to read as much as possible rather than listen to lectures.

What should be read also excited Diederich. Good teachers needed a large supply of optional materials, not simply a decent textbook. They might never reach the size of Diederich's vast collection of Latin stories, but every teacher should be able to offer choices to students, including some books unrelated to the curriculum. Merely reading assignments in school was not what Diederich had in mind; a study hall could take care of that. Instead he wanted to foster a love of books similar to what helped him transcend the provincialism of the Kansas towns where he lived until he was 14.

Free Reading (1942)

Of all my experiences in the Eight Year Study, I have identified myself with two new developments which I should like more than anything else to carry further.

The first is a series of units oriented toward the central question, "How do we propose to get the things we all need?" The most common units in this series are probably those on housing, transportation, communications, recreation, conservation, taxation, public utilities, public health, and community planning. They are taught in social studies, science, mathematics, English, home economics, and vocational courses, but most of all in the new "core courses" which seem likely to become the next big step in the reorganization of secondary education. When these units attain their full possibilities, and connect with similar units which are now taught in elementary schools, they will enable pupils, over twelve years, to study a sample of the things we all need, from food, clothing and shelter up to freedom, justice, security, beauty, and a philosophy or religion. People will study how we get these things now, why we do not get enough of them, and how their generation could do a better job.

I worked last year to set up an experimental study to develop such units with the same group of pupils as they grew up through grades seven to twelve, to study the effects of these units upon them, and to publish the materials which they found most helpful. I sold the idea to Will French, head of the department of secondary education at Teachers College, Columbia, director of the Lincoln—Horace Mann schools, and chairman of the Committee on Implementation of the National Association of Secondary School Principals. He volunteered to get money to support the project in the name of NASSP, to match it from the research fund of the Lincoln School, and to provide the opportunity to develop those units at the Lincoln School. [Eight months of negotiations with the Sloan Foundation ended, unsuccessfully, in late January, 1942] so my thoughts have turned to the possibilities of doing something about the second new development which attracted my allegiance during the Eight Year Study: the development of an experimental free reading program.

The full significance of the proposal which I am about to make can be understood only with reference to several background items.

Experience in Teaching Latin

I taught Latin at the Ohio State University School exclusively by what might be called library methods. I told my pupils that there would be no regular class meetings. They were to regard my classroom as one department of the school library and drop in whenever they had a free period and felt like reading Latin. After some initial experimentation to find out whether I meant it, they came on the average better than six periods a week. They came in groups of friends, selected materials to be read from a long table at the front of the room, sat down around a table and read them together. When they encountered any difficulty which they could not resolve by their combined efforts, they raised a hand, and I came over to help. It was the only Latin class I had seen in which the pupils asked the questions and the teacher answered (or helped them find the answer), but it seemed more sensible inasmuch as the teacher knew how to read Latin and the pupils did not.

As soon as a group finished a story or a chapter in a book, they came to my desk and announced, "We're finished!" I would say, "Well, let's see," and one of them would hand me a copy of the text. I would ask each member of the group a question or two about the meaning or significance of the story they had read, and if all did not do as well as I expected, I told them that they had not really read it, and should go back and do a better job. Thus, while in the average class every man's hand is against every other's, in this one the reading of a text was a *group* responsibility. Everyone had to understand the story at the end, even though he might lean on the superior talent of other members of the group in coming to understand it. Conversely, the bright pupils could not simply read it themselves and let the less bright flounder; they had to help their friends to a clear and complete understanding.

Whenever a group did unusually well with a story which they thought particularly good, I asked them to write out a translation in their very best English, and either read it to the class or publish it in our little mimeographed newspaper. Since each group read different stories, these translations were usually well received. I asked for these translations only about once a month, and then we spent several days in polishing them. At other times translation was discouraged, since studies had revealed that only about seven percent of the usual oral classroom translation could be rated as "acceptable English." We spent about half of each period in this sort of reading in groups; the other half in various exercises and in the discussion of personal, social, literary, and artistic problems in the light of the experience of antiquity.

There was no formal instruction in grammar, because I had discovered as part of my research for the Ph.D. that one could tell the function in a sentence of 92 per cent of all the Latin words one would ever read by mastering 18 common endings as the Latin equivalent of English word order. We learned these endings incidentally in the course of reading.

No one was encouraged or even allowed to read any new Latin at home except for a few very bright pupils who could be trusted to do it properly. Home work consisted entirely of voluntary collateral reading in English. These pupils read, entirely in class time and with never any hint of compulsion to read at all, four times as much Latin as is recommended by the Report of the Classical Investigation (which is commonly regarded as excessive) and did very well on every test of power in reading Latin. Since each group read at its own best rate, the fastest pupil read *fourteen times* as much Latin as the slowest. This was good for both of them, for the fast pupil was challenged (he read practically four years' work in one) and the slow pupil thoroughly understood everything he had read, and never had to repeat a single syllable of it. He could start the following year just where he left off in the first, and continue at his own slow pace (although in his case we finally decided that it was so difficult for him that it would not justify the time spent). I found that I was able to handle as many as 35 pupils at a time with this method, even though they were a mixture of first, second, and third year Latin students. The only exception was that I finally decided it would be slightly more efficient to have the first year students meet together regularly as a group until Christmas; after that they were able to read well enough to proceed by my library method.

I have discussed this in detail because in a way it is the most important and the least generally known. Its significance is this: I did successfully for three years what anyone would regard as the most impossible part of my proposal. After a great deal of argument they are usually convinced that it might work in English; they have some doubts about its application to the study of modern languages; and they would never dream of trying it in Latin. Well, I did it in Latin for three years, and I have evidence that it works better than any conventional program in Latin ever dreamed of working. No regular Latin teacher really expects pupils to be able to read Latin with any fluency at the end. Mine could. Nor do they expect pupils to use Latin sources to illuminate important social problems, such as the development of fascism, but mine did, regularly, as a matter of course. In other words, I tried out my proposal in the hardest possible case—the one case in which the most dyed-in-the-wool advocate of a free reading program would admit that it would not work. But it did work. I am now in a position to say that if I could do it in Latin, I could do it in English.[8]

The Modern Languages

With this experience behind me, I looked with some amusement upon the teaching of modern languages, especially in small schools. In those schools the scheduling of language classes is a major administrative problem. The Registrar of Francis Parker [a private school in Chicago] told me that in making the schedule for the year, she had to start from the fact that a certain sophomore girl had to take beginning Latin. Such academic necessities not only play hob with the rest of the schedule, but equally play hob with the schedule of language classes. I found Alfred Adler, for example, a very gifted language teacher at Parker, teaching *eight* different language classes a day. Each year's class had to be split into two or three sections to fit the periods they had free. Some of these sections had only four pupils, but Alfred poured out his soul to them as energetically as to a class of 40—and was a nervous wreck at the end of the day. All the other language teachers were in the same boat.

I worked on these people a long time and finally convinced them that the major job in learning any foreign language is to read about a thousand pages of it, and standing in front of pupils talking about life, death, and grammar is a most inefficient way to get the job done. They finally set aside a large room in the basement as a foreign language reading room. Students of all languages were to report there two or three periods a week, rather than to their language classes, and read. Teachers were there to help at specified periods, and at other periods there were responsible older students who wanted some teaching experience. Although this was a limited and cautious application of my library method, pupils learned more and scheduling problems practically disappeared. I preached the same doctrines elsewhere, and all over the thirty schools now it is almost standard practice to have free reading periods in language classes at least two days a week (Not all my doing, of course). In the Dalton School [in New York City] the language classes now meet as a group only once a week—and Dalton students are conspicuously good linguists, as revealed not only by their school records but by our college follow-up study.[9]

Note that in many foreign language reading rooms, as at Parker, several different languages were being read by various groups of pupils at the same time. When this arrangement is desirable or necessary, the school does not have to provide a separate teacher for each language. Most language teachers are equally at home in two or three languages; at least they know enough to help beginners with their initial difficulties in reading. Apprentice teachers and senior students can also help out during periods when no teacher is available, if good teaching is going on concurrently in the regular language classes. When the library method carries the whole load, however, even a good teacher has to learn gradually and painfully how to make it work. The art of "elbow teaching" is not easy. The constant temptation, especially when one is pressed for time, is to tell pupils the answers to their questions. One then has to tell them the same answers at least twenty times. Gradually one learns how to give them just enough of a push at exactly the right point to enable them to find the answer for themselves. Then it sticks. One also learns that much of the apparent bustling activity of the regular language classes is really teacher-dominated, and how much more carefully one has to prepare and guide the work to maintain genuine interest in the activity itself rather than in the personality of the teacher. This is no mere rhetorical point. I could not have done it in Latin if I had not spent a large part of my leisure time for four years looking for materials that would really interest pupils. I found a large part of them in medieval Latin and in Latin textbooks written in England. When I began to teach by the library method, I had a card file of *sixteen hundred* short selections cross-indexed by subject matter and level of difficulty. Even then I was constantly annoyed and frustrated by the dearth of materials in Latin that are suitable for adolescents. It is a terribly mature literature—hardly a page in it was written for children. The modern textbooks, on the other hand, are too juvenile. I was driven at last to write and adapt most of my materials.

The Present Situation in English

Douglas Waples [a Professor at the University of Chicago] probably knows more than anyone else about the reading habits of the American people, and he claims to have evidence for the fact that the average American adult reads less than one book a year; that the greatest amount of reading in any community is done by junior high school pupils; that the greatest amount of reading among adults is done by women clerks and stenographers, and consists chiefly of sentimental romances.[10] It is almost impossible to get a reliable index of literacy for a community through its book reading, since so little of this is done; one has to resort to magazine reading. So far as using books to direct and sustain our lives is concerned, we are still functionally illiterate.

Present prospects are that reading will be further crowded out by radio listening. Studies in this field indicate that adolescents are at least within earshot of a radio for an average of two hours daily. When we put this together with other distractions such as movie attendance, riding in automobiles, sports, comic strips, picture magazines, freer social intercourse, and the increasing demands of required homework, it is hard to see how we can expect to maintain even our present low level of the use of books.[11]

The data on *ability to read* are no less discouraging. Tyler and Dale found that national syndicated newspaper columns had better be at a sixth grade level of reading ability if they were to appeal to a mass audience.[12] Most high school textbooks are well beyond the reading level of most pupils, to say nothing of the classics of world literature. Even with groups in which we should expect competence in reading, the results of every penetrating inquiry are uniformly disappointing. In the University of Chicago scholarship examinations, we included one short poem by Wallace Stevens that was certainly not above average difficulty in modern poetry, and below it we listed fifteen simple, unambiguous, short statements of ideas that either were or were not expressed by the poem. We asked these very bright students, the cream of our high schools, to indicate whether these ideas were in the poem or not, and on the average only 15% of the group checked each statement correctly. On a still higher level, I.A. Richards has written two books, *Practical Criticism* [1929] and *Interpretation in Teaching* [1938], loaded with evidence that even Cambridge undergraduates, the products of the most expensive system of literary education in the world, are quite often unable to get even the simple sense of typical passages of literary prose and verse.

This is the net result of teaching English might and main for at least a hundred years in almost universally required classes throughout the span of formal education. I think the English teachers should declare themselves professionally bankrupt, and sell their stacks of *Silas Marner* and *Ivanhoe* at public auction. They have failed to inculcate the habit of reading books in any way which can hope to direct and sustain life, and they have failed to develop even the ability to read beyond the level required in the conduct of business. How can such a population maintain and improve the democratic way of life when every test indicates that they would be unable to read even the Declaration of Independence and form any clear idea of what it meant? How can they hold fast to the basic ideas of democracy in the difficult years ahead, when clever would-be tyrants will attach all their beloved clichés to practices and institutions which are in fact the opposite of democracy? This picture may seem overdrawn, but who would have the courage to assert that our people are in general as clear about the principles of democracy as Soviet citizens are about the principles of socialism? I think we have been too complacent about this situation, and that it is much more serious than we think.

One immediate and pressing issue in the teaching of English should be noted. In the years just past English teachers who were abreast of curriculum trends have moved a long way from the required reading of the same classics by all pupils at the same rate, with recitations on them in class. At first they moved, and are still moving, in the direction of an "experience curriculum" as expounded by the National Council of Teachers of English.[13] While this is a healthy trend, the trouble with it (in the practice of the average teacher) was that it stirred up a large number of separate activities in short units, such as how to use the telephone, how to use the dictionary, etc., with no organic and compelling connections among them. Life in English classes became just one damn thing after another rather than a series of connected activities leading to a few major goals that truly mattered.

English teachers, it seems to me, are just now beginning to find big unifying themes around which they can organize a large number of specific activities. Some of the units which have become popular in English classes are "Understanding Ourselves" (largely human relations materials), "The American Dream" (democratic ideals expressed in literature), "Regional Groups," "Religions," "Recreation," "The American Language" and so on. Such units provide the best current answer to several concrete teaching problems. First, they unify the work around big ideas that matter. Second, they enable pupils to read a wide variety of materials at their own rate and still have something in common to talk about in class. Third, they relate reading to life's problems, which provides motivation and also a better basis for understanding. For these and other reasons I expect curriculum revision in English in the years ahead to center around the search for more and better unifying themes, advancing beyond the first crude stage of announcing a single theme for a whole semester or year and for an entire city system. Such themes have to be broad and vague enough to justify almost anything that a thousand different teachers want to do, so they become practically meaningless. But that is not what I mean. I have in mind the production of possibly fifty "source units" on important themes from which teachers can select and combine freely. I have been working with a committee on the revision of the English curriculum in the Chicago public schools, and this is just about the stage they have reached. While I support this trend, I recognize that it leaves out something which I regard, and most English teachers regard, as very important. That is the free reading development of the individual pupil: the relatively spontaneous selection of all sorts of books, unconnected with anything going on in class, which may—with good luck or wise guidance—meet a great variety of needs and interests as they arise. At some point in his development a boy ought to read *Treasure Island*, for example, regardless of whether it fits into a unit in class. These units will, of course, suggest and motivate a great deal of his free reading, but the course of his own private imaginings will not always fit those patterns. At times he will want to say, "To hell with home and family relations," and go in for a good bout of piracy. We don't yet know enough about the effects on personality of the adventures of a solitary soul among masterpieces, but I know from personal experience, growing up in a little Kansas town, that I first met in books the kind of people whose friendship I have come to value in the flesh. Without those people in books, I would have been terribly lonely.[14] I also got from them an idea of what a rich and full life would be like, and I still fail to see how I could have got it from any amount of participation in the life of that God-forsaken community. I can also testify that my reading did not divorce me from reality; it connected me to a higher level of reality. We must not leave this sort of experience out of the lives of the next generation. People like Jefferson grew up largely as a result of being given the run of a good library. The remarkable intellectual life of certain circles in England and America during the 18th century seems directly traceable to just the sort of free reading which threatens to be left out or neglected in the evolving English curriculum.

The Oakland University High School Free Reading Room

Another experience which opened my eyes to the possibilities of a free reading program was a visit to the University High School in Oakland [California]. I wanted to see the English teachers, so I look in the school schedule for English. To my surprise it was not listed. I asked, "What, no English?" The clerk explained that there was plenty of English, but at that time it was not taught in regular English classes. Most of the English teachers worked with core groups and other classes in which there were big jobs of reading, writing, and speaking to do. They suggested and initiated those activities, planned them with pupils, conducted them, praised what they had done well, and corrected what they had done badly. Among other things they suggested books to read, helped them in reading, and stimulated dramatic presentations of big ideas. Other teachers had drama groups as a regular elective during school time, with credit and status accorded on equal terms with any other educative activity. Other teachers had writing clubs, usually centering on a school publication. A few teachers offered college-level electives in English for a few advanced students.

The heart of the English program, however, was the free reading elective, which also had credit and status equal to any other elective. Two of the largest and most attractive English classrooms, near the school library, had been equipped as free reading rooms. The iron desks had been thrown out and replaced by about a hundred rainbow-colored canvas deck chairs that were comfortable, durable, and cheap. The boys had made attractive modern bookcases in the shop, and in them were placed all the books suited to free reading, leaving the small school library only for reference reading on school assignments. Pupils were allowed to elect free reading, with the consent of their counselor, for any number of periods per week they had available, from one to ten. They came to these rooms and just read—with absorbed attention. I can testify that at any time during my visit, one could have heard a pin drop in either of those rooms. Such absorbed activity was not characteristic of the other classes I visited.

Throughout each period the teacher in charge was continuously in conference with individuals and small groups in a small glass-partitioned office at one end of the room. Pupils might have a short conference at any time, and were required to have one at least every six weeks. The teacher discussed what they had been reading, how they liked it, what they had got out of it, and their plans for future reading. Difficult passages could be taken to the teacher for help at any time, and the teacher was also ready to suggest books to read on the basis of what the pupil had read and liked thus far. This sort of assistance was extended to "reading clubs" of pupils with similar reading abilities and interests who met once every two weeks or so to talk over what they had been reading, and to suggest directions for future reading.

While the curve of free reading went steadily down in almost every senior high school in the Eight Year Study, it maintained its level and even went up in these free reading groups. These teachers did not have data on the development of reading abilities in these groups which could be separated from the instruction in reading offered elsewhere in the program, but there is every reason to suppose that the effect was wholesome. I became convinced that here was an answer to the problem of free reading which worked in practice, while all the chest-beating of English teachers about the values of appreciating a great work together in a classroom just does not stand up. It may work occasionally with a gifted teacher, but on the average most English teachers have spoiled and will continue to spoil every book read under their tutelage, especially by bright and sensitive pupils, and perhaps equally by the dullards who have failure to fear.

I am also convinced that something like this program will have to be adopted increasingly by American secondary schools. We can no longer rely on free reading being done at home. There are too many competing distractions: radio, movies, social activities, the automobile, sports, comic strips, picture magazines, and increasing demands of home work. As I understand it, the school falls heir to the important jobs of youth-training which are no longer being done by the home or community agencies. Pupils no longer read books of their own choice at home to any considerable extent during adolescence. This activity is important, both to their own development and to the general welfare. Therefore the school must provide a time and a place in which free reading will get done—under conditions approximating those in which free reading is done by intelligent adults. Only thus will the habit of free reading continue into adult life.

Possible Effects on Other Subjects

I should like to indicate a few more possibilities in the free reading program which, so far as I know, no one has explored and connected with the other possibilities mentioned above.

I believe the program could enrich and extend interests in practically every field of study in school, especially for the bright and bookish students. To take my own experience as an example, I was thoroughly bored by most of the juvenile history textbooks I studied in high school. I was getting a great kick out of Plutarch outside of school, and learned more ancient history from him than out of the text, but I never realized until later that I would also have been able to understand and enjoy Herodotus and Thucydides in translation, as well as the more interesting histories written for adults, such as Tenney Frank's history of Rome and Alfred Zimmerman's account of the Greek city state. Both of those would have given me an insight into the economic bases of the events we studied. I never took biology, but I seem to have learned more about it out of Wells' *Science of Life* than most of my classmates, and now there are equally fascinating texts about the components of biology, such as Buchsbaum's *Animals without Backbones* and Romer's *Man and the Vertebrates*. Economics always seemed to me a matter of dry and sterile abstractions, but I might have thought better of it if I had read some of the reports of our National Resources Planning Board. I never even thought of the problems of agriculture, but I wonder whether I would not have been thrilled to the bone by some of the marvelous yearbooks of the Department of Agriculture.

These examples illustrate the point that a lot of bright kids would find new interest in all their subjects if they only had time free and books handy during the school day to *read all around these subjects* as they were being taught in class. They can learn the text with a fraction of their available energy, and get bored, but they would be challenged by being confronted with the materials through which adults renew and maintain their interest in these fields. The free reading program may, therefore, be one of the answers to the problem of the superior student.

For such students, moreover, this reading in subject fields may not only enrich courses but replace them occasionally. I once had a student who came to the point at which he wanted to get the main outlines of the history of the world clear in his mind. I lent him Wells' *Outline of History*, and he came back in a week knowing more history than we usually taught in a year. Every teacher can cite similar instances—the need of the hour and the right book happened to connect, and the result was a more vital experience than the average elective.

I have also felt that however much one enjoys reading, there will be times when one has to get away from books. This would not be a problem if pupils were allowed to come to the free reading room at their discretion, but in order to protect this time from competing demands, we may have to schedule their attendance. For this reason as well as the worth of the activity on its own merits, I think the well-equipped library should have about a dozen sound-proofed compartments for phonograph and radio listening, and several hundred albums of records. If the volume of sound or the privacy of the booths were a problem, an alternative would be to equip the room with ear-phones, as the poetry room is equipped at Harvard. In this room any number of people can listen to poets reading their own work without disturbing the fellow in the next chair. The library would presumably also supply quantities of good reproductions of pictures to look at. A room for viewing films sounds a bit utopian at present, but it will probably be standard practice in the future.

Possibilities of a Book Exchange

One of the habits which we must cultivate if reading is to continue in adulthood is that of buying books and taking pride in one's own collection.

This may be an ignoble exploitation of acquisitive impulses in the service of literary values, but a collection of books is certainly one of the most innocent forms those impulses may take, and it is a fact that most adult readers usually buy books and take pride in their libraries, while non-readers do not. In this case, as in so much of our behavior, I suspect that cause-and-effect relations are reciprocal: building a library contributes to the love of reading as well as vice-versa.

Since adolescents do not have much money, their book-buying must be done second-hand and at the lowest possible prices, eliminating the overhead and profit of a commercial establishment. This could be done if pupils would bring to school the books for which they had no further use, fill out a card for each book giving author, title, their own name, and the lowest price they would accept, and leave the book on a Book Exchange table in the free reading room. The school might supplement from other sources the books brought in by pupils so the Exchange would offer an interesting selection from the very beginning. I hope that this table would not be too tidy. If one cannot rummage in a heap of five cent books for buried treasure, and blow the dust off the top of it, it loses a good deal of its glamour. If there were a ladder on which one could sit and read, and a trap-door through which one could fall into the basement, that would help, but we must not hope to achieve the millennium in one bound. At the very least, however, the books must not be dusted. The savor of book dust and the love of literature go together.

Possible Ultimate Effects on the Schedule

I am not alone in feeling that it is not good for children to have as many different things to do in the course of a school day as they have now. They go from one activity to a very different one when a bell rings every 45 minutes or so all day long. Outside of school children are also torn apart by a multitude of competing stimuli. There is almost no time any more for a child to sit under a tree and think the long, slow thoughts of children. In a study of the philosophic problems and concerns of adolescents last year, I was seriously disturbed by the relative absence of speculation on what life was all about, what living was for, what constituted a successful life, what things were most worthwhile in life, what was the basis of right and wrong, and so on. These senior high school pupils reported almost no problems which I could classify as philosophical by any stretch of the imagination. I talked over my findings with the very sensitive teachers who had participated in the investigation, and they said they were not surprised. They asked me to consider the kind of life these children led as compared with that of our parents. The difference in tempo is roughly that between rural life and life in New York City. They said that their pupils literally had no time to think; consequently they were hyperactive, over-stimulated, unintegrated, blasé, and superficial. We must not add to the confusion by so crowding the school day with unrelated activities that young people have no time to think, nor even to assimilate the facts we teach them.

We annually deplore this situation and set out to do something about it in our school schedules. But then someone always rises to object that the schedule is an administrative matter, and should wait until educational issues have been settled. While those issues ought to include the rhythm and unity of the school day, in practice they come down to settling the competing demands of the various subjects. Simplifying the school day means leaving something out, and no one is willing to be left out. Consequently the old mill-race begins again. I fear this question will not be handled properly until someone recognizes that the school schedule is itself an educational problem, and a very fundamental one. I think we would do better to lay out first the kind of school day that would be good for children and then fit the various subjects into it, rather than vice versa.

This conviction deepened when I visited the George School [in Newtown, a suburb of Philadelphia], which has only three long periods a day: two in the morning, separated by a recess, and one in the afternoon. They achieved this set-up very simply. Formerly they had a six period day; then they decided to have each class meet for a double period every other day. Thus English, which formerly met the first period each day, would meet the first double-period Monday, Wednesday, Friday, Tuesday, and Thursday in a two week cycle. Social Studies, which formerly met the second period each day, would meet the first double-period Tuesday, Thursday, Monday, Wednesday, and Friday. While this solution to the problem may have been naïve, it was ideal for testing the effect on children of the single factor of a few long versus many short periods, since everything else remained the same. In the testimony of everyone connected with the school, the effect was wholesome. I myself had never encountered such a restful, unhurried, serious atmosphere in any other of our thirty schools [in the Eight Year Study]. This atmosphere did not pervade the other Quaker schools in our study, so I could not ascribe it to the Quaker tradition, and it was not characteristic of other schools in a rural setting, so I truly believe the schedule made the difference. I think they could have done still better by altering their curriculum as well, but even this much change was obviously good for the children.

I have also noticed this in my wanderings: teachers who find it congenial to work together love to have a block of time allotted to use, throughout the year, in any way they please. Some days they can use all of it for a field trip; some days their students can meet together to see a film; other days the time can be divided in any way the work is going on. If I were a principal, therefore, I would like to persuade the faculty to lay out the school day in three ample periods (with perhaps a fourth for lunch, recreational activities, and counseling) and assign each period to a group of teachers who could do what they liked within it.

I would like ultimately to assign one of these long periods to the core course and the free reading program; a second to a large "shop" in which one could practice all of the arts, including music, dramatics, home economics, typing, etc., and also perform scientific experiments; and the third to outdoor play, in which I would like to include something like a Boy Scout nature program, gardening, and science field trips. There would be no classes during the long lunch period, but a variety of recreational activities, rest for those who needed it, and counseling. What little instruction in foreign language remained might be included in the core and free reading period, and a thin strand of instruction in mathematics might be woven into the arts-science period. A possible first step would be to group the core and free reading together in one long period, academic electives in another, and the arts and physical education in a third. Any such simplification of the curriculum would have special value for small schools.[15]

Summary of Educational Possibilities

Putting all these considerations together, we get the following picture of the educational possibilities of the free reading program. It might share a long period with the core course throughout the span of secondary education, giving special flexibility to the core schedule, providing an opportunity for individual and small-group conferences, and continuing the usual collaboration of English and social studies without the usual artificial correlation of subject matter. The usual instruction in the arts of reading, writing, and speaking would be provided in connection with the core program, but the rest of the time allotted to English would be spent in free reading. The principal aim of this activity would be to reinstate reading for pleasure and growth among the activities of youth, and to carry this interest forward into adult life. The crucial test of the success of the program would be that the curve of interest in books would not decline during adolescence. We are not kidding ourselves that it would rise in any spectacular fashion. Under modern conditions the competing distractions are too powerful, but at least these pupils would not reach the threshold of adulthood as non-readers, as most pupils do at the present time.

Instruction in a foreign language might be offered in regular classes two or three periods a week. The rest of the time usually devoted to this subject might be added to the free reading program. During this time the pupils would read appropriate literature in the foreign language under supervision. Several languages on all levels of difficulty might be read by various groups of pupils in the same room at the same time, supervised by the same teacher. This arrangement would not only reduce the exorbitant cost of foreign language instruction and provide the utmost flexibility for individual rates of progress, but would improve present standards of attainment. It is high time that with all our instruction in foreign languages, some pupils actually learned to read them, and at least a few acquired the habit of reading them.

The director of free reading would endeavor to enrich and extend interests in other subjects by suggesting appropriate books, especially to superior pupils. Occasionally these suggestions would result in as great an enlargement of the pupils' cultural background as the average elective provides, and would do it in a week's time.

When pupils tired of reading, they might have the alternative of listening to selected radio programs or phonograph records, looking at good reproductions of pictures, or possibly even seeing educational films. Thus a substantial contribution might be made to the objectives of art and music appreciation, and the resources of radio and motion pictures might be utilized more completely than is possible in regular classes.

Pupils might also cultivate the habit of buying books and add something of the glamour of an old book-store to the library by maintaining a Book Exchange. This might well become the most popular section of the library, and indicate to what extent a school without an adequate library might hope to grow one by this method.

How the Reading Would Be Directed

I trust it is evident by now that there is more to this free reading program than shunting a group of pupils into the library during their free periods and just letting them read. True, they would just read most of the time, but first they would plan a reading program, and revise plans as they went along; next, they would learn to ask for help whenever they came to a passage which baffled them; and as soon as they had finished a book, they would come in for a conference, which would be the heart of the program. While no two conferences would be alike, in general they would release approval or condemnation of the book, find out how well the pupil could read crucial paragraphs, see where it seemed obscure or untrue to him and why, determine whether he was aware of some of its basic assumptions, and so on. It seems silly to enumerate those possibilities, however, for no actual conference follows such a pattern. The pupil usually comes in with something on his mind. One finally gets at what it is, and this leads to a discussion which very often brings out some relationship of what he has been reading, or what he might read next, to his problem. The pupil has certain vigorous objections to these books which suggest difficulties in reading them or in accepting them emotionally. One turns to the text to enable the pupil to back up or illustrate his objections, and then one sees more clearly what bothers him. Perhaps one can resolve the difficulty then and there; perhaps one has to let it lie fallow for a while, and bring it

Paul Diederich and the Progressive American High School 59

up in some other connection later. This may seem vague, but three years of "elbow teaching" in my Latin class left me completely unable to state any generalizations about what goes on in a reading conference. Anything and everything may happen, from a query about what to feed a dog to a confession of suicidal intentions. I can only reiterate what I said before: the chief thing to learn is not to tell the pupil the answers to his problems, but to apply the light touch at just the point which enables him to find the answer for himself.

There are certain more formal means of stimulating and directing the reading: book clubs meeting every two weeks or so, exhibits, working with other classes, reading records and summaries which reveal neglected or overemphasized areas, occasional tests and questionnaires, a classification of types of books with gentle pressure to read a variety of types, persuading a group of pupils to read on a given topic and to pool their findings, and so on. When one is not occupied with conferences, one goes among the pupils who are reading and chats with those who look as though they would not resent the interruption. Or one haunts the Book Exchange section and holds forth in the manner of an old bibliophile. The important elements in such activities are a contagious enthusiasm for books and a manner with pupils which suggests the charming host rather than the custodian of books. In conference, it is the fine art of being a person with whom any topic under heaven may be discussed with complete candor.

[The rest of the paper is a 13 step proposal for the introduction of free reading in the University High School at the University of Chicago in October, 1942]

ENDNOTES

1. "An Experimental Free Reading Program" [1942] in Box 29, Richard McKeon Papers, University of Chicago Archives.
2. Diederich was proud of several instructional strategies he used in his sections. He always found something to praise in the students' first few papers, and only then did he begin to offer one (and only one) suggestion for future papers. Furthermore, his students loved the exercise where he took lines from their papers and offered three alternative phrasings; the class then debated whether the options were better or worse than the original. "Teaching Critical Readings with Instructional Tests" Speech, National Council of Teachers of English, November 28, 1952 in "Diederich MSS/5" (ETS Archives).
3. Diederich to Morris Finder, April 9, 1995 (Finder Papers, Box 1, University of Chicago Archives). Another member of the Department of English later

recalled "lots of parties" alongside "fierce arguments" in those years. David Daiches, *A Third World* (Edinburgh: Sussex University Press, 1971), 46.
4. Quoted in George W. Plochman, *Richard McKeon: A Study* (Chicago: University of Chicago Press, 1990), 7.
5. William M. Murphy and D.J.R. Bruckner, eds., *The Idea of the University of Chicago: Selections from the Papers of the First Eight Chief Executives of the University of Chicago from 1891 to 1975* (Chicago: University of Chicago Press, 1976), 40.
6. William H. McNeill, *Hutchins' University: A Memoir of the University of Chicago* (Chicago: University of Chicago Press, 1991), 90. For a good sketch of faculty reactions to Hutchins, see Mary Ann Dzuback, *Robert Hutchins: Portrait of an Educator* (Chicago: University of Chicago Press, 1991), Chs. 8-9.
7. Chicago was also a good fit for his family. His wife Trudie, a biologist whom he married in 1937, worked with psychologist Leon Thurstone on a massive study of fraternal and identical twins to test his theories of intelligence. Diederich's son and daughter enrolled in the University of Chicago lab school. Chicago also revived Diederich's adolescent musical talents —Thursday evenings were devoted to his string quartet, and he also played his violin in Chicago's "collegium musicum," the nation's first society for student-faculty recitals. Interview of Siegmund Levarie, New York City, September 28, 2008.
8. By this time Diederich had no interest in promoting Latin in the high school curriculum. He called it an "intellectual luxury" suitable for only a few exceptional students, with most Latin teachers unequipped to teach it as literature and history. The reforms proposed in his dissertation "got no attention whatsoever," he recalled in 1994. Diederich to Levarie, October 2, 1994 (Diederich Family Papers).
9. Dean Chamberlain et. al., *Did They Succeed in College? The Follow-Up Study of the Graduates of the Thirty Schools* (New York: Harper & Brothers, 1942).
10. Waples' research is described in Carl F. Kaestle, *Literacy in the United States* (New Haven: Yale University Press, 1991), 182.
11. *The Training of Secondary School Teachers, Especially with Reference to English* (Cambridge: Harvard University Press, 1942), 36.
12. Edgar Dale and Ralph Tyler, "A Study of the Factors Influencing the Difficulty of Reading Materials for Adults of Limited Reading Ability" in *The Library Quarterly*, July 1934, v4, n3, 384-412.
13. National Council of Teachers of English, *An Experience Curriculum* (New York: D. Appleton and Century, 1935).
14. The way Diederich learned to read also banished loneliness. "I can recall sitting on my Uncle Bernie's lap, listing to the daily bedtime stories in the *Kansas City Star*. He would follow the words he read with his index finger just below them, and I watched intently. By the age of five I discovered that I could read the stories myself before he got home from work, but I never told him I could do it. I loved those daily sessions in his lap too much. I used to stand at the front door with a copy of the *Star* turned to the right page, dancing up and down with impatience, and pressing it upon him as he entered. First he had to remove the packing-house smells by leaving his working clothes in the attic and taking a shower before mingling with the rest of the family. The

smell was that of the stockyards and the slaughter houses. I never objected to it, but my elders could not stand it. I can [now] see these images with perfect clarity and also remember how it felt to sit in my uncle's lap while he read. I pity children who do not have such fond associations with the hard job of learning to read. To me every minute of it was a joy." Diederich to Levarie, February 1, 1995 (Diederich Family Papers).
15. The four period schedule is described in detail in Paul B. Diederich, "Simplifying a Crowded Schedule" in *The School Review*, March 1945, v53, n3, 162-169.

PART II

THE SPIRIT AND SUBSTANCE OF A PROGRESSIVE HIGH SCHOOL

At a conference with one session on school reform in the 1930s, historian Arthur Powell called the outlook of the progressives "midwestern." He was impressed by how sincerely they promoted the importance of social cohesion. Words like *democratic school community* were heartfelt priorities rather than clichés or slogans. Powell contrasted their allegiance to collective benefits with the "coastal" emphasis on the self, where personal gain in the form of upward mobility usually overshadowed the civic purposes of public schools.[1]

With the coastal values spreading everywhere in recent decades, it is easy to forget how many educators in the early to mid 20th century thought of schooling in terms of the greater good. A critical part of that mission was shaping the values and beliefs of the young. Cultivating particular attitudes and dispositions was not reserved for the family or the church. Diederich was confident that schools should foster what he called "the essential elements of a good life" and they included both personal and social benefits (thus the name of his favorite proposal, a 12 year core course in How We Get the Things We Need, was not How I Get The Things I Need). The scope of what he wanted schools to achieve is breathtaking. The first three papers in the following pages present the grand vision he believed must be accomplished.

The other papers reveal how Diederich would transform education to attain his ambitious goals. He thought the traditional high school was cumbersome; the last thing he envisioned was piling on more requirements or adding new programs. Part of the uniqueness of his vision is the combination of sweeping goals with a leaner structure in which daily life for students would be less burdensome and individual attention would be a priority. Both philosopher and inventor, he had, like his hero Benjamin Franklin, "an intellectual curiosity that challenged him to make sense out of things that others took for granted."[2]

By the 1950s and 1960s, Diederich said less and less about the "good life" schools should promote. During his 27 years at ETS, he stopped writing manifestoes calling on schools to cultivate virtue. Much of his time there was devoted to painstaking studies of student achievement in English. When he did publish on ethics, the subject was how to measure ethical development, not the ethics schools should foster.[3] When his thoughts turned to the ideal configuration of secondary education, the utopias he imagined used time in less wasteful ways. The good life there would be an efficient life. Diederich proposed various innovations that could be attractive regardless of the world views held by teachers, parents, and administrators. The inventor side of his mind eclipsed the ethical and social philosophy side, even if his prose style still carried an evangelical assurance that urgent topics should be addressed immediately. He also retained his old faith that difficult problems would yield to his solutions

It is a testament to his optimism that he believed that his goals could be achieved in public schools. Diederich habitually underestimated the widespread satisfaction with American education, where there was enough variety and choice within and among schools to please most students. If he were alive now, he might create a charter school where like-minded parents would embrace a four period day, free reading, and long discussions about what we all want and need. Most students today do not seek what Diederich had in mind, but it is not hard to imagine that quite a few would soon come around.

ENDNOTES

1. October 25, 2009, History of Education Society annual conference, Philadelphia, PA.
2. Edmund S. Morgan, ed., *Not Your Usual Founding Father: Selected Readings from Benjamin Franklin* (New Haven: Yale University Press, 2006), xiii.
3. Paul Diederich, "Methods of Studying Ethical Development" in *Religious Education*, 1955, v50, n3, 162-166.

CHAPTER 4

WHAT KIND OF SOCIETY DO WE WANT?

(1936)[1]

In his entry for the decennial report on the Harvard Class of 1928, Diederich listed his interests as chamber music and left-wing politics.[2] This article fleshes out what he meant by left-wing. Diederich's paper features economic justice and also sketches other traits of what he claims students want. There is no evidence that the schools he visited were nearly as wed to these doctrines as he suggests (which is why this essay is not in the first section of this anthology). But at the time, this short article reflected his conviction—a belief widely shared within the profession—that schools should articulate and promote a vision of social organization rather than reflect whatever the local community believed. As the book summarizing the Eight Year Study put it, high schools should "lead our young people to understand, to appreciate, and to live the kind of life for which we as a people have been striving throughout our history."[3] Diederich took seriously the task of expounding the overarching economic, social, and political ends of education, and he did so when more and more Americans began to favor less controversial, more tangible goals like the accumulation of credentials for individual competitive advantage.

Paul Diederich and the Progressive American High School, pp. 65–70
Copyright © 2014 by Information Age Publishing
All rights of reproduction in any form reserved.

What Kind of Society Do We Want? (1936)

An editorial in the April 1936 issue of *Progressive Education* offered a definition of a progressive as one who was dissatisfied with things as they are, who had a philosophy of what should be, and who was doing something about it.

During the past two years (1935-1936) the writer has assisted thirty progressive schools in developing a program of evaluation. The following outline is his personal impression of their philosophy of what should be, and what they are doing about it. It is in no sense an official statement; it would not be accepted in its entirety by any of the thirty schools. Neither does it pretend to be complete; many important elements of the new society which these teachers are helping to build are left unmentioned. It plots enough points, however, to show the direction of their thinking and its application in what they teach. It is a series of illustrations of a social philosophy at work in the classroom.

Our pupils do not have to accept the land of bondage and adjust to its demands; they can set out for the promised land. Even a small group of resolute and capable individuals who have formulated their goals clearly can influence the direction in which society will move. In this faith the teachers of the thirty schools have assisted their pupils in formulating something like the following set of propositions. They should be nailed to the doors of all our cathedrals of learning.

1. *We want a society in which everyone has abundant and good food, clothing, shelter, and means of transportation and communication.*

Our pupils therefore accept the provision of these essential goods and services as the collective responsibility of a well-organized society. As members of society they share that responsibility, even though their fields of specialization lie elsewhere. They are sensitive to the fact that our present provision for these basic needs is shockingly inadequate. They realize that we have the resources, technology, and workers to provide them for all; that the difficulty lies in our social organization. They welcome every honest and intelligent effort to solve this problem. They endeavor to analyze proposed solutions objectively, without being unduly influenced by the selfish interests of their group or class. They are ready to take an active part in securing the adoption of any measures which promise to lead to a solution of this problem. They are skilled in the techniques of social action by which such changes may be brought about.

2. *We want a society in which everyone has adequate, scientific health service and medical care, healthful working conditions, opportunities for healthful recreation, and healthful homes and communities.*

Our pupils therefore understand the scientific basis for good health and have acquired sound health habits and attitudes. They give interested support to the medical profession in its conquest of disease. They are keenly sensitive to the gap between our present knowledge and its application to the major sources of poor health in our society. They are interested in the possibilities of socialized medicine and are ready to support any measures which promise to extend adequate medical care to all.

3. *We want a society in which everyone has socially useful work suited to his capacities and interests.*

Our pupils therefore realize that the advent of the machine necessitates a readjustment of the economic order so that all workers may work part time, rather than part of the workers working full time and supporting the rest in idleness. They realize that the profit system makes such a readjustment difficult, and they are able to conceive, without emotional disturbance, a world in which the profit motive would be inoperative. They realize the significance in this connection of the labor movement and of the cooperatives. They have laid the foundation for a wise choice of a career, and they regard their vocation as a field of service to society rather than as an opportunity to enrich themselves at the expense of others. They feel the need for a national employment service, for adult vocational education, and for a continuing program of public works.

4. *We want a society in which everyone has leisure, and fruitful, expanding interests to occupy it.*

Our pupils therefore understand the fundamental importance in civilization of all the arts as leading to a more abundant life. They habitually practice at least one of the arts and enjoy several of them, both in and out of school. They have acquired habits of outdoor play and recreation which are likely to continue into adult life. They have learned to read widely and to enjoy various types of scholarly and scientific investigations. They have learned to make, keep, and entertain friends, and to enjoy both company and solitude. They look forward to continued education throughout life. They have learned to keep their work in proper relationship to other values.

5. *We want a society in which everyone has a share in the direction of his destiny.*

Our pupils therefore have learned to make their own decisions and to accept responsibility for them. They are committed to the principle that leadership for a particular purpose must be delegated by those who are led: that no one is authorized by virtue of superior wisdom or power to rule over another. They believe that freedom of choice is an indispensable condition of growth, and that growth on higher and higher levels is one of the supreme values of life, never to be discarded for the sake of greater efficiency in securing lesser values. They believe that those who own the means of production in our society should not have the power to dictate, to their own advantage, the conditions and rewards of labor to those who must use these tools and their products.

6. *We want a society in which there is no exploitation of human beings.*

Our pupils therefore have learned to respect the personality and rights of others. They will not use a fellow-student to further their own academic or social ambitions at his expense. They regard cruelty and selfishness, even in their more refined forms, in the same light as the torture of animals. They are aware of the extent of human exploitation in our present society and are determined never to tolerate it in the conduct of their own affairs. They have rejected the individualistic, competitive ideal of success and despise it when they see it portrayed in books, magazines, and films. Their attitude toward others in all relationships is marked by consideration for their interests and welfare.

7. *We want a society in which justice is done to all.*

Our pupils therefore have developed their own institutions and methods for the settlement of disputes and the adjustment of grievances. They feel no shame in submitting a just complaint to the arbitration of their fellows, and they respect and abide by their decisions. They are sensitive to all unfairness and are prompt to challenge it, even in a teacher. They realize that justice is not at present secured to large numbers of citizens, especially in industrial relationships. They feel that this is a problem for the whole community, not one to be settled between the contending parties by brute force.

8. *We want a society in which there is no war.*

Our pupils therefore have never learned in school to regard any war as justifiable, profitable, romantic, heroic, patriotic, or necessary. They believe that those who took part in the last war were deluded victims of circumstance who wasted their lives to no purpose. They have seen pictures and read books revealing the degradation, horror, and stupidity of war. They will not take part in the next war, and they will not go to jail on that account if they can help it. They feel that war is a problem to be solved, not an inevitable consequence of unchanging human nature.

9. *We want a society in which there is an equitable division of labor and its rewards among nations.*

Our pupils have therefore studied the natural and human resources of other countries, their conditions of labor and standards of living. They have investigated the problem of imperialism and the exploitation of undeveloped markets. They realize the consequences of economic nationalism; they deprecate the imposition of tariffs and understand the forces which cause them to be imposed. They are eager to support any promising measures leading to economic cooperation among nations.

10. *We want a society which is integrated with respect to its major common goals, and with respect to the behavior which is absolutely essential to the cooperative formulation and pursuit of those goals.*

Our pupils therefore have come through investigation and discussion to accept and live by such goals as are listed here. They have learned to accept the decision of the majority as a method of arriving at decisions on issues involving the interests and active cooperation of social groups, while they respect the opinion of the minority and give them every opportunity to express it. They realize the importance of this procedure as the central controlling principle of our society, while they understand and respect the methods of other countries in arriving at decisions on social issues. They will abide by this method until some other method is accepted by the majority to replace it, and they will defend it, even by revolution if necessary against the forces which would thwart or destroy it. They have also acquired such essential common patterns of behavior as honesty, tolerance, the scientific habit of mind, cleanliness, courtesy, responsibility, etc.

11. *We want a society in which all deviations from customary patterns of behavior which do not seriously threaten the cooperative formulation and pursuit of our major common goals are tolerated and welcomed.*

Our pupils therefore have associated with teachers and other persons of widely different personalities, points of view, manners and habits. They have traveled and read widely, and have learned to respect varying human customs. They have seriously studied the cultures of foreign and primitive peoples with an eye to the possible adoption of such alien customs and institutions as might enrich our own. They have learned to accept differences in dress, opinions, interests, the arts, race, religion, philosophy, and habits of living as natural and desirable. In all matters which are not absolutely essential to the effective cooperation of our society in the formulation and pursuit of its major common goals, they have learned to go their own way with confidence and without self-consciousness, and to accord others the same privilege. They will resist to the death any unnecessary standardization.

12. *We want a society in which the spirit and method of the best scientific inquiry is habitually applied to every problem situation.*

Our pupils therefore have been made aware at appropriate points in their development of a wide sampling of the important problems and conflicts of our society, and have studied them in the questioning, critical spirit characteristic of scientific inquiry. Their consideration of each problem has been extended to other problems to which it is logically related so as to provide for a continuous reconstruction of experience [a favorite phrase of John Dewey]. No problem has been withheld from such discussion, exploration, and resolution as is within their power. They practice scientific method not only as a pattern of thinking, but as a way of life. They endeavor always to adjust their behavior to the objective facts in a situation rather than to what they wish those facts to be.

ENDNOTES

1. "What Kind of Society Do We Want?" in *Progressive Education*, v13, n7, November 1936, 534-537.
2. *Harvard College—Class of 1928—Decennial Report* (Cambridge, 1938), 62.
3. Wilford M. Aikin, *The Story of the Eight Year Study* (New York: Harper & Brothers, 1942), 18.

CHAPTER 5

PHILOSOPHY FOR TEENAGERS
(1940)[1]

Ivor Richards left Cambridge University for Cambridge, Massachusetts in 1939 when he became a lecturer at Harvard. With the help of a five year grant from the General Education Board (the same foundation that underwrote the Eight Year Study), Richards and several assistants worked on simple ways to learn and use English. They were especially eager to promote Basic English—the 850 words that "let a man say almost everything—to say it well enough for his general day-to-day purposes in all the range of his interests however wide—in business, trade, industry, science, medical work—in all the arts of living and in all the exchanges of knowledge, belief, opinion, views and news..." (from a description of Basic written in Basic).[2]

Richards and fellow literary critic C.K. Ogden created Basic in the late 1920s and early 1930s, so by the early 1940s Richards was a promoter more than a scholar of Basic. He made the approach easily accessible in a range of formats—short books, primers with pictures, records, films, and even cartoons. Non native speakers were his main audience; that is, Basic was an introduction to, not a streamlining of, the English language. Learning Basic would be the first, not last, step to mastering English. Yet he also demonstrated Basic's merit by using it (and a few additional words) to translate and shorten by half Plato's Republic. Questions like "Shall you have any answer to make to that objection, my clever friend?" became "What's your answer to that?"[3] The book made headlines when the federal government gave two million copies to armed forces overseas in World War II.

Paul Diederich and the Progressive American High School, pp. 71–76

Diederich occasionally helped Richards with that translation, but he had been hired in September, 1940 to work on the high school English curriculum (Tyler thought it would be a valuable interlude for Diederich—"one of Paul's difficulties is his lack of depth of experience upon which to base generalizations regarding the curriculum," as the previous chapter suggested).[4] In his 1938 book <u>Interpretation in Teaching</u>, Richards lamented the lack of attention to how teachers responded to their students' incomplete and erroneous analyses of what they read. He thought that journals should have separate sections where teachers could report those mistakes and then relate how they helped students "come to see for themselves that what they regard as adequate reading and writing is not adequate."[5] Dentists tell one another how they fix rotting teeth, Richards observed, but the teacher is "oddly unwilling to confess in equal detail how he criticizes a bad essay."[6]

Diederich's work began as a casebook of exercises for teaching literature but very soon became more ambitious. Several teachers told him that the selections should all focus on adolescents' concerns. His survey of several hundred teenagers found that dating, parents, and jobs were the chief concerns, but Diederich nevertheless posed larger questions, the difficult questions he thought adolescents should be asking: "What is success in life? What is happiness? What sort of person do I want to be? What makes conduct right or wrong? What is truth? What are the chief virtues that others have found in living, and how can one obtain them (love, friendship, work, poetry, science, philosophy, etc.)? How should society be organized to attain these values?"[7] Most of the readings he preferred would have been suitable for a college course in philosophy, a subject almost never taught in high schools, where at best one might find, Diederich said, guidance books with "a little puerile moralizing on such topics as "Should one neck and pet?""[8]

We might think of Diederich's project as a marriage of two very different perspectives on schooling. That is, many educators in the 1930s and 1940s wanted to provide a useful and interesting curriculum for the non-college bound majority in high school. The time-honored academic courses supposedly lacked relevance in an era of economic calamities and international wars. A more engaging curriculum had to de-emphasize difficult books that were allegedly too difficult for the hordes of students with modest capacity and no appetite for hard work. In contrast, advocates of a "great books" approach to knowledge (including Chicago's President Hutchins) strenuously defended the enduring value of landmark works in many fields. Diederich thought he could combine both points of view. He believed that carefully chosen classics on serious topics of importance to thoughtful adults would also captivate teenagers and sharpen their minds.

Philosophy for Teenagers (1940)

This plan takes the form of preparing a book (to be issued first in looseleaf mimeographed sections, unit by unit, for trial by interested teachers) designed to assist adolescents in thinking through their philosophical problems, which would necessarily involve a serious effort at interpretation. The book would contain excerpts from all types of writing related to the philosophical problems of adolescents, each accompanied by exercises in interpretation and by suggestions for other classroom activities and further reading. In six weeks, we hope to complete the first unit of this book: "What kind of society do we want?"

Units and materials tentatively selected for the book:

1. Autobiographies of adolescence

    —H.G. Wells, *Experiment in Autobiography*
    —Lincoln Steffens, *Autobiography*
    —Goethe, *Dichtung und Warheit*

2. The nature and value of philosophy

    —Bertrand Russell, *The Problems of Philosophy,* Chapter 15
    —John Dewey, *Democracy and Education,* pp. 378-386

3. What is good? What is life for? What makes conduct right or wrong?

    —Plato, *Phaedo* (the long speeches of Socrates)
    —Plato, *Republic* (Book 6)—Aristotle, *Ethics* (the doctrine of the mean)—Walter Pater, *Renaissance* (Conclusion)
    —Fitzgerald, *Rubaiyat of Omar Khayyam*
    —Marcus Aurelius, *Meditations* (on Duty)
    —Thoreau, *Walden* (Where I Lived and What I Lived For)
    —*Sermon on the Mount*
    —*Fire Sermon of Buddha*
    —Matthew Arnold, *Culture and Anarchy* (Chapter 1)
    —Ruskin, *Fors Clavigera* (Letter 5)

4. The concept of scientific method

    —Bertrand Russell, *The Scientific Method* (Chapter 1)
    —Sinclair Lewis, *Arrowsmith* ("In a college laboratory")
    —Francis Bacon (to be selected)
    —Dante, *Latin Works* (excerpt to illustrate the pre-scientific way of reasoning)

5. The concept of evolution

   —Lucretius, *De rerum natura* (Book V, lines 769—end)
   —Darwin, *The Origin of Species* (Chapter on the struggle for
         existence)

6. A modern view of the mind

   —James Harvey Robinson, *Mind in the Making* (Chapter 2?)
   —Wanted: concept of the mature personality as seen by psychiatrists

7. Anthropology: the concept of a culture

   —Ruth Benedict, *Patterns of Culture* (Chapter 1)
   —Margaret Mead, *Coming of Age in Samoa* (Last Chapter)
   —Stuart Chase, *Mexico* (Last Chapter)

8. What kind of society do we want?

   —Robert and Helen Lynd, *Middletown* (Chapter on government)
   —John Dewey's speech, *Democracy and Educational Administration*
   —Boyd H. Bode, *The Democratic Way of Life* (Chapter 1)
   —John Stuart Mill, *On Liberty* (Chapters 1 and 4)
   —John Stuart Mill, *On Representative Government* (Chapter 1)
   —Thomas Jefferson, parts of the *Declaration of Independence* and
         selected letters
   —Michael Oakeshott, *Social and Political Doctrines of Contemporary
         Europe* (selections on democracy, socialism, fascism, and
         national socialism).

This list is quite tentative and incomplete. We hope to include much more fiction, biography, poetry, and drama. Some of the titles listed above may prove unworkable, but they give an idea of what we have in mind.

Problems: The form that a serious effort of interpretation of a great utterance should take remains to be worked out. Our exercises should coincide as nearly as possible with the way in which a good reader approaches an important utterance. At present we have only the following vague approach in mind: first, having pupils read the passage straight through to get a general idea of its contents, to be tested by marking a series of simple statements as being "in" or "not in" the passage. At this point the pupil should also formulate some questions and criticisms. Then we recommend a second and very close reading, to be tested by multiple choice questions on almost every sentence that was likely to cause any difficulty whatsoever. For example, the first sentence in the first selection from Mill begins, "The struggle between Liberty and Authority..." The natural questions to ask are, "What sort of struggle is probably referred to?" followed by five answers, each of which the pupil is to mark *plus* if he agrees, *minus* if he disagrees, and *zero* if he considers the answer doubtful or meaningless. Then, "Who is struggling?" and so on. The challenge here is to find the ambiguities that cause trouble and reward their clarification—and not to irritate the pupils to the point of revolt. After this intensive examination the way is open for more general questions on just what the author tried to prove, how he supported his proof, and where, if at all, the proof breaks down. There is also a place for comparisons of this passage with others, and probably many other types of questions. We shall also include suggestions for further reading and suggestions for classroom activities. Our second problem is the possible uses of Basic English in interpretation. My experiences with it thus far have not been too rewarding, and I have become a bit skeptical. Basic gets along because its words are terrifically ambiguous and can be applied most anywhere. I find I can do better with normal English. Perhaps the biggest problem is to find out just what techniques of interpretation are relevant and helpful, and then to introduce them in an orderly and systematic fashion so that they will become habits. About all we have to go on is the idea that words mean many things, and can be made to mean almost anything else by metaphor. It will take much more than that to interpret our passages, and we don't quite know yet what other techniques exist, or how to apply and arrange them.

In a book review published in January, 1941, Diederich described the challenge of shifting the teaching of English from <u>what</u> words mean to <u>how</u> they mean.[9] He did so through the example of a class in cooking:

It is as though a cooking-class were baking a cake and were not succeeding very well. One instructor advocated adding more eggs; another, more flour—both upon the respective authority of their respective cookbooks. Into this debate wandered an expert in the chemistry of foods and said:

> Look here! You people have been baking cakes by rule of thumb and by cookbook recipes long enough, and you are never sure that the cake will turn out well. Perhaps you are wrong in assuming that anyone knows perfectly how to bake a cake, and that all you have to do is to find his formula and follow it. Suppose we study for a while not *what* to do but *why* you do whatever you do in baking a cake. Let us study what these ingredients are, and how they react upon one another when we beat them and bake them together. This line of attack will be harder than learning to follow a formula, and many of you will make even worse mistakes than at present until you have thoroughly assimilated the basic principles, and are able to use them like an

artist. There is no guarantee that even at the end you will be able to do better than some are able to do now by native wit. But the cook-book approach has clearly failed, and if you want to improve your average performance as a group, some more fundamental approach seems to be necessary. Let us, then, study *how* these elements make a cake, and not merely *what* elements are supposed to make a cake.

ENDNOTES

1. "Interpretation Project" in General Education Board Papers, Box 570, Folder 6083, Rockefeller Archives Center.
2. I.A. Richards and Christine Gibson, *Learning Basic English* (New York: W.W. Norton, 1945), 7.
3. John Paul Russo, *I.A. Richards: His Life and Work* (Baltimore: Johns Hopkins University Press, 1989), 480.
4. Ralph Tyler to Robert Havighurst, March 26, 1940 (General Education Board Papers, Box 570, Folder 6083).
5. I.A. Richards, *Interpretation in Teaching* (New York: Harcourt, Brace and Company, 1938), 76.
6. Ibid., 74.
7. Paul Diederich to Flora Rhind, October 10, 1940 (General Education Board Papers, Box 570, Folder 6083).
8. Ibid.
9. Paul Diederich, "The Meaning of "The Meaning of Meaning" in *The English Journal*, v30, n1, 31-36.

CHAPTER 6

THE VIRTUES SCHOOLS SHOULD CULTIVATE

(1945)[1]

In 1967, Diederich attended a conference on evaluation. After the speakers finished, he stood up and declared, "Everything Ralph Tyler taught me has stood the test of time except for one thing." He then sat down. "And what is that, Paul?" someone asked. "I no longer write objectives!"[2] In the 1940s, he was still writing objectives (defined as the changes in students brought about by schooling) but he had become more and more interested in ethical values—the ultimate good students could obtain as a result of schooling. For instance, in a 1942 letter to Richard McKeon, professor of Greek and philosophy at the University of Chicago, he claimed that education "is a direct study of how to live well, and how to influence others to live well."[3] Teaching should therefore be "an open-ended inquiry into the problem of how to achieve happiness… this is a problem for which there is no answer in the back of the book, but one man's guess is not as good as another's."[4]

"Any part of math may turn out to be useful in connection with any ultimate value," and so too for other subjects, Diederich argued. What he sketches in this article would not in itself dictate a particular curriculum, although his "how we get the things we need" core course would have been "a direct study of how to live well." Diederich had no doubt that teachers should encourage and promote dozens of attitudes and habits rather than confine themselves to academic knowledge and intellectual skills.

The Virtues Schools Should Cultivate (1945)

For the past ten years I have been working with committees of teachers as a consultant on curriculum revision and evaluation. This work necessitates constant consideration, formulation, classification, and criticism of objectives. After trying every other basis for objectives which has ever been proposed, I have concluded that the most defensible basis is an ethical theory—a comprehensive, systematic, carefully examined set of beliefs about what are the essential elements of a good life and what kinds of behavior are most likely to attain them. The term "a good life" is here considered to mean a rich and full experience of human living, both the heights and the depths, excluding only experiences which make one something less than a man and incapable of further growth. A good life will include pain, toil, conflict, sacrifice, and even tragedy.

In this definition, democracy is not equated with the good life. Democracy is one form of social organization which men have evolved in order to achieve the good life together, since no man can achieve it alone. A sound theory of the good life is necessary before one can fully understand democracy or prepare the young for intelligent participation in it.

I hold that the following are essential elements of a good life:

1. *Health.* Mental and physical health, including the goods and services which are necessary to maintain and to protect life. Anything beyond necessity must be justified by its contribution to other values.
2. *Satisfying relations with others.* Relations marked by interest, mutual respect, affection, courtesy, tolerance, honesty, responsibility, freedom, justice, co-operation, fair competition, and the like. These relations should hold between both persons and groups.
3. *A sense of achievement.* A feeling of having accomplished something of importance or of having lived up to one's picture of one's self, both from day to day and in the course of a lifetime. If possible, the achievement should have in it some element which represents a man's own ideas and feelings (that is, should be "creative" achievement) and it should merge him in an undertaking which he feels to be greater than himself.
4. *Aesthetic experience.* A sensitive response to beauty in many forms, from contact with nature through all the arts, to delight in ideas. Fun, laughter, and excitement which involve a heightening of the senses, when they are not emotional accompaniments of activity directed toward other values but are sought as ends in themselves, may be classified under this heading

5. *Meaning in life.* A philosophy, religion, or integrated view of life which orders experience and provides orientation and security.

These five headings include in one way or another everything that is recognized as good for man. To attain them in reasonable measure constitutes happiness, or the good life. Serious deprivation of any one of them makes the good life to that extent impossible. Their balanced attainment enables a man to reach his highest development, and that development enables him to reach these goals ever more completely. Progress toward these goals, in fact, is what is meant by "development." Good conduct is that which increases the likelihood of attaining these values, both individually and collectively. Bad conduct is that which reduces the likelihood of attaining them.

These values are justified by the following criteria:

1. They are valuable as ends in themselves, apart from anything else which they may help one to achieve. This criterion rules out a goal like wealth, which is valuable only because it enables one to get other things that are valued for their own sake.
2. They are consistent with a tenable view of the nature of man. While it would take a separate paper to defend this proposition, the main headings of the argument may be indicated by saying that man is a physical organism, a social being, an active creature, an artist, and a rational animal.
3. They are consistent with a tenable view of the physical and social environment. Again the argument can only be adumbrated. The environment, for example, decrees that man shall either work or perish. He shares the planet with millions of fellow-beings with whom he must come to terms. The environment furnishes endless spectacles of beauty and sets innumerable problems for man as philosopher or scientist.
4. They are consistent with one another. Each of these values is dependent on, and contributes to, all the others. None of them requires the sacrifice of any other, although the intemperate pursuit of one value, such as a sense of achievement, might lead to the loss of another, such as health
5. They are attainable. From the standpoint of educational statesmanship, this criterion rules out such a goal as immortal fame, which could be attained only by a handful of men of genius.
6. They are innocent. The attainment of these values does not necessarily deprive anyone else of these or any other defensible values, although the ruthless pursuit of some of them, such as a sense of achievement, might involve the exploitation of other people; and

when two men fall in love with the same woman in our society, one of them is bound to be disappointed. When conflicts of interest arise, they must be settled in terms of merit and need, rather than in terms of power, rank, or privilege.
7. They are necessary. Serious deprivation of any of these values causes misery, disintegration, and degeneration. For example, the man who is starving, diseased, or neurotic is obviously not at his best. The need for aesthetic experience is not so obvious, but one sees it in the lives of people in a drab, ugly environment.
8. They are exhaustive—until someone proves the contrary. Every defensible value which I have discovered in the course of a protracted study of the good life may be classified under one or another of these five headings.
9. They expand indefinitely. If all values in any list could be attained completely by the age of thirty, thereafter there would be nothing to live for. These values can be attained on higher and higher levels, not only during the lifetime of an individual, but at any stage of progress of mankind.
10. They suggest courses of action. They are stated at a level of specificity which suggests activity directed toward these goals, without specifying it in such detail that it will not fit a wide range of circumstances.
11. They are universal. All men, everywhere, always, have either attained these values or suffered acutely for lack of them. We see no reason to suppose that these values are indigenous to any particular society.

The Nation's Failure to Attain Essential Values

As a nation, we have not yet attained these values in reasonable measure by any man's criterion. In more normal times a third of our people were said to be ill-housed, ill-clothed, and ill-fed. A great many lack medical care. Our public health services are still negligible as compared with what we already know how to do. One in twenty of us spends some time in a mental hospital. Most of us are probably neurotic to some extent and are driven by internal pressures to make life a burden to ourselves and our associates.

In the realm of satisfying relations with others, one out of every four or five marriages ends in divorce, and two or three others are probably held together by inertia and tradition. The birth rate declines as rapidly as people learn how to make it do so. The relations of parents and children, as every teacher knows, are far from satisfactory. The circle of friends of the average American family is unduly narrow and grows narrower after the age of forty, abetted by our nomadic habit of moving almost annually. The status of women is still inferior, while that of old age is pitiable. There are well-defined classes in our society, based not on personal worth but on race, religion, and economic status, with little friendly contact between classes. Our economic system assumes that the man who has capital has the right to control, in his own interest, the lives and fortunes of all the rest of us. Our public affairs, especially in cities, are usually mismanaged by a set of crooks and incompetents who are in politics for what they can get out of it. And now we are at war—the supreme disaster in human relationships, the gravest problem of our species, man's greatest tragedy and failure.[5]

At the moment our sense of achievement has abundant scope, but in more normal times millions are unemployed and millions more are employed in drudgery which leaves no sense of achievement. This condition would cut the heart out of the good life in any culture but especially in America where life is centered in a job. We may count on the fact that, with the disruption of the world economy by war and with the exhaustion of our national credit, the pupils now in our classes will live through a period of economic chaos which will make the most recent depression look like Thanksgiving Day in the Salvation Army.

In the realm of aesthetic experience, it is fair to say that, in spite of a few notable achievements, we are still cultural barbarians. The average American adult reads less than one book a year. Our cities, by and large, are blots on the landscape. Our American suburban architecture is more appropriate for doll houses than for the habitations of grown men and women. The modern miracle of radio provides subhuman entertainment about 95% of the time and could not secure an audience for anything better. We still have flowers and sunsets and pretty girls, but, in spite of these resources, it is safe to say that our people rarely feel the impact of beauty.

With regard to the meaning that we find in life, the gravest problem of our time is rooted in the fact that the majority of our people are no longer members of any church, and probably the majority of church members lack the depth of conviction which, in the past, made religion the center of orientation in life. We have lost the old faith without finding a new one. We keep on being "good" out of habit, because we were taught by our forebears who had a reason for being "good." We no longer accept that reason. Unless we find a new one, it can be only a question of time before the habit breaks down. Civilization cannot coast along indefinitely on moral inertia.

Many have tried to substitute a political faith for the old faith in religion. While one need not approve of this solution, it must be admitted that today one has to turn to zealots of the new political creeds to understand what Christianity did for people during its apostolic era. Our students who have acquired a passionate belief in the teachings of Karl Marx become quite objectionable in many ways (as did the early Christians, no doubt) but they have undeniably something to live for—something which gives them a whole new orientation in life, disciplines them, and channels their energy. We are told on good authority that Fascist youth in Germany and Italy have felt the same invigorating stir of a new idea, the same sense of devotion to a cause greater than themselves. The recent attempts of our schools to rebuild a passionate faith in democracy were undoubtedly suggested in part by the tonic effects on young people of Communist and Fascist doctrines.

The chief objection to the political solution is that it is incomplete. It leaves out many values which should be included in a faith by which men can live in the 20th century. Science, for example, is something in which our young people devoutly believe and which has no real connection with any political creed. Neither has aesthetic experience, whether derived from nature or from literature and the arts. Neither has love—in any more personal sense than love of our fellow-men.

Those who wish to use democracy as a central faith for our time should realize quite clearly what they are doing and what must be the measure of their success. Such a faith must do for people what Christianity did during its apostolic era and what Marxism does for some of our students today. It must provide orientation, security, discipline, and a central purpose in life. If democracy can do this, well and good. If not, it remains the chief task of the creative imagination of our time to build a new faith that men can live by.

What Shall We Teach?

If we face these problems in attaining the essential elements of a good life, what shall we teach our children? I venture to suggest that we should work toward such objectives as the following:

I. Health

  A. Attitudes

    1. Security: self-confidence, self-acceptance, poise, independence; flexibility (ability to adjust, to retain security amid change and disorder); cheerfulness, serenity, humor, courage; freedom from disintegrating fears, worries, obsessions, etc.
    2. Affection: ability to give and to receive affection freely; gradual emancipation from parental control without loss of affection; general good will toward men (traits listed under Objective II); freedom from disintegrating hatred, jealousy, suspicion, etc.

B. Knowledge: relevant portions of physiology, psychology, genetics, hygiene

C. Habits: diet, play, rest, cleanliness, control of infection, medical care, safety

II. Satisfying relations with others

  A. Personal

  1. Interest in people
  2. Personal attractiveness
  3. A pleasant speaking voice
  4. Conversational power
  5. Ability to make, keep, and entertain friends
  6. Ability to dance, sing, and play popular games
  7. Consideration for others: ability to sense reactions of others; courtesy and reasonable observance of conventions; willingness to help others.
  8. Tolerance of faults as well as differences
  9. Self-control, especially control of egotism, selfishness, desire for recognition, etc.
  10. Ability to assume leadership when necessary without being assertive or tyrannical.
  11. Ability to work and play amicably with others.
  12. Interest in the possibilities of cooperative housing.
  13. Resistance to the American practice of changing one's habitat at the slightest inducement.
  14. Cultivation of all the arts of living graciously and pleasantly at home.

NOTE: Other traits needed to get along well with people are listed in other sections of these objectives.

  B. Social

  1. Putting the general welfare above one's own.
  2. Respect for the rights of others, especially the right of self-determination.
  3. Repudiation of power (to control others by force) as a personal goal
  4. Deep suspicion of the ideas of national sovereignty, national interest, and national honor.

5. Willingness to devote time, effort, and money to public affairs.
6. Mastery of techniques of social action: ability to discover, evaluate and present relevant facts; some skill in using propaganda and detecting it; practical knowledge of methods by which social changes may be brought about, especially how to secure the passage of new laws.
7. Willingness to accept majority decisions.
8. Determination to protect the rights of minorities.
9. Determination to protect free speech.
10. Sensitivity to, knowledge about, willingness to promote, and ability to adjust to, needed social changes.
11. Acceptance of all deviations from customary behavior which do not seriously threaten the general welfare.
12. An acute awareness of interdependence: that a good life can be secured only by the organized efforts and controlled behavior of all men; a deep conviction that, in this joint endeavor, every man has his place, and every man should have his just share of the benefits secured.
13. Knowledge and acceptance of the American heritage—an unfinished experiment in democracy.
14. Realization that democracy may not be the best form of government or way of living and that fascism, communism, and anarchy are not the only alternatives. It is highly improbable that so early in the development of human society, men should already have evolved the best form of social organization. Loyalty to what we have should not interfere with a constant search for something better.

III. A sense of achievement

   a. The formation of an appropriate "ego ideal," a picture of one's self and one's role in life not too seriously at odds with one's capacities and temperament to be sustained.
   b. Acquaintance with the work of the world.
   c. Realization of problems to be solved in providing for our common needs; identification with some of these problems.
   d. A critical attitude toward the present economic system and willingness to co-operate in improving it, even at the cost of a temporary loss of security or of special privileges.
   e. Developing vocational interests and competence.
   f. Respect for common occupations, especially the role of a wife and mother.

g. Rejection of the individualistic-competitive ideal of "success."
h. Regarding one's occupation as a contribution to the general welfare rather than as an opportunity to make money at the expense of other people.
i. Good work habits, such as self-direction, industry, perseverance, responsibility, honesty, carefulness, thoroughness, mastery of time, initiative, good judgment, decisiveness, etc.
j. Determination to protect one's self and others against exploitation—especially through membership in unions.
k. Practical competence: ability to perform one's share of the common tasks which are necessary to maintain and to protect life: shopping, cooking, cleaning, caring for children, making things, banking, traveling, etc.

IV. Aesthetic experience

a. The habit of seeking contact with nature and of finding refreshment in it.
b. The habitual practice of at least one of the arts and the enjoyment of several: the ability to be moved emotionally and stirred intellectually by books which may be classified as literature; the ability to listen to a whole symphony with sustained attention to the music; the ability to sing a part in simple group singing and to play an instrument; interest in painting and sculpture and response to their artistic qualities rather than to photographic realism, story-telling, etc.; an appreciation of dramatic and pictorial values in the better movies; awareness of good architecture, good interior decorations, and good city planning; an appreciation of good design and color in objects of daily use (clothes, utensils, etc)
c. The habit and bringing order and beauty into one's immediate environment, whenever it is possible.
d. Habitual attention to aesthetic values in any problem in which such values are important.
e. Awareness of the dramatic, emotional, "human" significance of situations, issues, and problems as they arise in life.
f. Appreciation of the beauty of the human body, accepting but going beyond its sexual significance.
g. Attitudes preparatory to successful marriage.
h. The ability to find aesthetic delight in ideas.

i. The ability to face both high comedy and tragedy: seeing the world as incurably mad, and recognizing certain conflicts as essentially insoluble.

V. Meaning in life
   a. A scientific-humanistic world picture.
   b. A discipline of thinking, such as logic, scientific method, and creative expression.
   c. The development of a system of values and of ethics based on these values.
   d. Skill in reading, writing, speaking, and mathematics, beyond the kinds and degrees of skill required for the attainment of the preceding values

These patterns of behavior are not only objectives; they are virtues—and they are the only virtues which schools ought to cultivate. Good conduct consists in doing such things as these, and the good man is he who does them habitually and well. They are good because the more they are practiced by everyone, the better are everyone's chances of attaining a good life. Deviations from them hurt not only the individual but all members of his society. For this reason we have schools to make these patterns of behavior as nearly universal as possible. Unless most people practice them most of the time, none of us can attain the good life. Our moral obligation as teachers is to see to it that all the children of all our people learn to behave in these ways and to understand why it is imperative that they do so. Any subject which cannot make a genuine and significant contribution to the attainment of these objectives should be dropped from the curriculum.

ENDNOTES

1. "General Objectives of Education" in *The Elementary School Journal*, v49, n4, April 1945, 436-443.
2. Told to the author by Professor James Raths, son of Diederich's former colleague Louis Raths.
3. Diederich to Richard McKeon, May 21, 1942 in Box 29, Richard McKeon Papers, University of Chicago Archives. In comparison, a major report on the high school curriculum listed the appreciation of ethical values as one of five outcomes of education. See Educational Policies Commission, *Education for ALL American Youth* (Washington D.C.: National Education Association, 1944), 21.

4. "Reading and the Good Life" p12, Box 29, McKeon Papers. Diederich made similar points in one of his rare papers on the college curriculum: "What Should a College Program in the Humanities Do?" July 29, 1947 in Dean's Records, Box 15, University of Chicago Archives.
5. For a thoughtful discussion of why so many Americans shared Diederich's anxieties, see Ira Katznelson, *Fear Itself: The New Deal and the Origins of Our Time* (New York: W.W. Norton, 2013), Chs. 1-3.

CHAPTER 7

LATIN GRAMMAR WITHOUT TEARS

(1939)[1]

An angry mother asked Paul Diederich why her son did not know the genitive case. He had been in Latin class for three months and he should have learned it. Diederich asked her if she knew it. "You bet!" she said. "It's the second one from the top."[2]

The rote memorization of Latin exasperated Diederich. In his dissertation at Teachers College—Columbia, he proposed an easier way to learn Latin grammar. This chapter describes the shortcut and reveals how Diederich taught Latin during his three years at the University School, a "lab school" for 7th to 12th graders on the Ohio State University campus.

From its creation in 1932, the University School faculty wanted to be more than a convenient site for student teachers from the College of Education. Unlike the in-name-only lab schools, the University School adopted and evaluated new methods. The staff abolished grades, set aside one afternoon each week for special electives, required everyone to take art, encouraged interdisciplinary courses such as "The Nature of Proof," and in other ways justified its reputation as truly innovative.[3]

The first principal hired an extraordinary faculty. The founders of the school expected the teachers to resemble the instructors in a college or outstanding European secondary school. When the job market collapsed in the early 1930s, the base salaries—$3,000 for men, $2,600 for women—attracted talented applicants. "A *prize collection of prima donnas" was one result, with frequent meetings where "we argued ourselves hoarse," Diederich later recalled.[4]*

References to faculty arguments also appear in the diary of Robert Havighurst, head of the science department, but another theme occurs more often: the wide range of ability and motivation among the students. The pupils were not all as bright and focused as the gifted faculty. Remedial work was a topic the teachers often discussed, and in his own 8th grade math class, Havighurst divided the group to let the stragglers work on triangles and rectangles—with help they could "master the stuff very well" although he sometimes felt "they are incapable of understanding it." In his science labs, many pupils "crave routine" more than independence, which often bred "aimless" behavior.[5]

The students who took Latin also varied greatly. A future professor of theoretical physics completed a first year Latin textbook on his own during the summer before 9th grade, then read Genesis in Latin in order to compare it with the Hebrew and English versions. "He finished in a week and said, "That's really very simple Latin, isn't it?"[6] Another boy spent each period drawing grotesque faces in the margins of each reading. Only when the art teacher recognized his talent did he connect his skill with Latin, making portraits of the twelve Caesars. Diederich posted them in his room. "The boy blossomed under this attention, probably the first praise he had ever heard from a teacher. He left a permanent memorial of his talent in a huge mural over the main stairway in our school. Meanwhile he settled down and actually learned a bit of Latin."[7] In contrast, here is what Diederich wrote about a student with whom he did not succeed: "She is intensely combative. She is always in an attitude of defiance and opposition even to her closest friends. She undertakes a task as though it were nothing, then puts it off until the very last minute, and then does it in a way that does not nearly reflect her ability. I think she knew more Latin when she came here than she does now. I cannot persuade or compel her to do any work."[8]

To coax his students to become the sort of active learners the faculty prized, Diederich relied on persuasion more than compulsion. He let students work together in small groups and choose their reading from his collection of mimeographed literary excerpts—readings that adolescents liked more than the usual textbook fare. During two years at the Harvard Graduate School of Education, Diederich accumulated 300 selections, and he applied for a Harvard fellowship to spend a year in Paris to find more.[9] He withdrew his application when he enrolled in Teachers College—Columbia, where he expanded his collection of readings to 1,600.

When Diederich left the lab school in 1935, his approach also disappeared. According to a 1938 book written by the senior class, his successor reverted to grammar lessons. A year later, her successor assigned Virgil's Aeneid and downplayed the importance of grammar. The students protested and successfully demanded more time for grammar! And two years later, the school had yet another Latin teacher, and he chose Cicero along with readings in English on Roman culture.[10] But the lesson Diederich learned stayed with him. Throughout his life he was sure that new *methods could work with all kinds of students, notwithstanding the reluctance of some to be self-directed learners.*

Latin Grammar Without Tears (1939)

The writer's pupils were balked in their efforts to read Latin by the colossal apparatus of the traditional Latin grammar. We who have long since mastered this apparatus do not often realize just how colossal it is. To regain this awareness, graduate students in the classes of Professor Carr of Teachers College, Columbia University, make an annual count of the number of inflected forms to be memorized in high school Latin textbooks … [in 1932] the average number … was 1,572. The range was from 780 to 2,800. This did not include the inflected forms printed in the grammatical appendix; it was restricted to the forms printed in bold-face type in the body of the text with the directions expressed or implied, "Learn this by heart."

These forms, of course, are never mastered during the first year … pupils on the average throughout the country learn about half of the forms…. Even when the exceptional pupil attains a respectable mastery of these forms, they are organized in the worst possible way for reading. When a pupil encounters the ending a, for example, he has to think through five declensions of ten forms each before he can locate the possible interpretations of this ending. […] The traditional conjugations and declensions were never organized for reading purposes, but for speaking and writing Latin. The traditional definition of grammar is "*ars scribendi et dicendi*" [the art of writing and speaking]. Since pupils no longer have occasion to speak and write Latin, it is high time that we evolved a new Latin grammar: a system for the interpretation of word endings that may properly be called "*ars legendi*" [the art of reading]. Such a system would associate directly with the word endings commonly encountered in reading all possible interpretations of those endings. These interpretations would not include such meaningless concepts as "dative" and "ablative." The grammars commonly list more than ten uses of the dative and more than twenty uses of the ablative. Always in the plural and about half the time in the singular the dative and ablative endings are identical, so that the pupil cannot tell which is which. This means that when a pupil has finally located the dative and ablative among the possible interpretations of an ending like *is*, he must in theory think through more than thirty possible uses of these cases before he can tell the function of this word in the sentence. The only way to distinguish among several of these possible uses is first to discover by intuitive divination what the sentence means. With this in mind it is possible to diagnose the datives and ablatives. The meaning affords a clue to the grammar, rather than vice-versa. It is obvious that such a colossally inefficient instrument of interpretation is almost never used by beginners in learning to read Latin. They learn an acceptable smattering of the facts of Latin grammar on the side, as one of the mysterious visitations of Providence upon them for the sins of their elders, and pick up whatever skill in reading Latin they can through native wit.

As a step in the direction of organizing a system for the interpretation of the Latin word endings commonly encountered in reading, the writer selected a thousand running words from each of ten classical authors of prose and verse, and classified them according to their endings. The following classes of endings were found to occur in the following proportions:

> 18 "common" endings..................................66.5%
> Indeclinables (uninflected words)................23.4%
> 22 "rare" endings.. 6.8%
> 24 irregular pronoun forms......................... 2.6%
> All other endings.. 0.7%

The 18 common endings included all endings which occurred on one percent or more of the words studied. The 22 rare endings included all endings which occurred more than four times but on less than one percent of the 10,000 words studied. All other endings, none of which occurred more than four times among these 10,000 words, were rejected as of negligible importance in reading.

Try ... to put yourself in the place of a student ... who has been reading easy Latin for about three months without any systematic instruction in what the endings mean, and who has gradually become aware that Latin words assume a bewildering variety of forms to indicate their function in a sentence. He is now grappling with really difficult sentences which cannot be understood without knowing what the endings mean. He is left to flounder just long enough to gather the impression that the number of endings is infinite, and that they mean so many different things in different contexts that he will never be able to learn them. Then he is told that to master this intricate, bewildering system he has only to perform five definite, limited tasks:

1. To learn by heart 18 common endings and their interpretations, which will enable him to tell, within certain limits, the function in a sentence of 92.5% of all the words he will ever read in Latin. (These endings occur on 66.5% of the words, 23.4% have no endings, and 2.6% are irregular pronoun forms which he will learn as vocabulary).

2. To learn 8 rules governing variable endings which will tell him, in so far as any system of grammar is able to tell him, which interpretation of an ending which means several different things is most likely to apply in a given context.
3. To learn 22 rare endings and their interpretations, which will enable him to tell, within certain limits, the function in a sentence of 6.8% more of all the words he will ever read in Latin, or 99.3% in all. None of the few remaining endings will occur on the average more than once in 5,000 words.
4. To learn 14 "penultimate signs" which occur between stem and ending in 7.1% of all the words he will ever read in Latin, which will enable him to tell a few other important things about them.
5. To apply these 40 endings, 14 penultimate signs, and 8 rules in reading about a thousand pages of Latin, to find out by experience how they work. No system of grammar can give more than a clue to the meaning. It takes long practice to respond to these clues instantly, correctly, and almost unconsciously, and to recognize at a glance the patterns into which Latin words usually fall.

Students grasp at these findings as a drowning man grasps at a straw. Once again it begins to seem possible to learn how to read Latin. There are only 40 endings and 14 penultimate signs to learn, rather than the 1,572 inflected forms which have to be memorized in the average first-year textbook. Even this task is simplified by the fact that we never learn these 54 inflected forms outright. After the first three months of reading Latin without benefit of inflections we find that it restores the students' confidence to memorize the 18 common endings, which really carry about 90% of the burden of Latin grammar. It takes only an intensive drive of one week to get all pupils to the point at which they can give interpretations of any of these endings instantly, automatically, and without ever making a mistake. This is all the grammar we learn systematically for a long while to come. We paste the tables of rare endings and penultimate signs and their interpretations and the rules governing variable endings in our readers, and use them only for reference. When we finally come to the point of learning them systematically, most of us find that we know them already, and need only to nail them down for good and all with a little practice.

This system obviously applies only to reading, not to writing or speaking Latin. Since pupils almost never have occasion in later life to write or speak Latin, practice in these skills is usually justified in terms of its contribution to the ability to read Latin. No proof has ever been given that such practice contributes enough to the ability to read Latin to justify the learning of the traditional apparatus of Latin grammar which it entails. The usual argument, in fact, is devoted to proving that practice in writing and speaking Latin assists in the mastery of the traditional grammar. Of course it does, since this grammar was devised for the purposes of speaking and writing, but this is no proof that such practice assists reading.

Practice in speaking Latin is often defended on the ground that words and phrases learned through the eye and ear together make a stronger impression and are remembered better than words and phrases learned through the eye alone. No convincing evidence has been offered on this point, but the writer's faith in the oral method was shaken when he made up two artificial languages: one of nonsense syllables and one of random designs on paper which could not be pronounced, and which resembled nothing that could be pronounced. Both symbols and syllables were assigned meaning at random by drawing three-letter words out of a hat. All of the writer's pupils ... undertook to learn as many "words" of each language as they could in five minutes. While they studied the nonsense syllables, they were instructed to pronounce them softly, utilizing all the resources of throat and ear to memorize them. When they studied the symbols they were instructed not to pronounce even the meaning assigned to it but to associate one visual symbol with the other. So far as the writer could tell, these instructions were faithfully carried out. Each class was divided into two equivalent groups, one of which studied the symbols first, the other the syllables first. At the end of five minutes both groups were given a test consisting simply of the symbols or syllables in a different order than the one in which they had been studied, and were asked to write out the meanings which had been assigned to each. This was followed by another learning period in which the two groups exchanged their tasks, and by another test. Every group in the experiment learned the symbols better than the syllables by a wide and significant margin. This was contrary to the general expectation and aroused considerable discussion as to what it meant. It was agreed that the evidence was too flimsy to base a theory of learning upon it, but it put the burden of proof upon those who argue that speaking Latin is an invaluable aid in remembering words and phrases. The writer still uses Latin in routine classroom conversation for comic relief and for motivation, but he expects grammatical correctness in the response only by imitation or good luck. He never argues that this by-play is materially assisting the process of learning to read Latin....

An outline of the writer's method of teaching this system of interpretation may be helpful in showing how the results of this research may be utilized, since the system obviously calls for such a drastic readjustment of the usual content of a course in Latin that a teacher may well wonder how to teach it.

The principal activity in the writer's classes is the reading of new Latin, usually in small, congenial groups seated around a table. Each group chooses with the aid of the teacher a selection in mimeographed form from the files, or a small book from the shelves, that is related to their interests and adapted to their level of ability in reading. They elect a chairman for the day who reads through each sentence slowly in Latin. After each sentence the pupils in the group ask one another for help on any points which they have not understood. If no questions are asked, the chairman proceeds with the next sentence. The meaning of words is usually taken up first. Each pupil mentions the words he has not understood. As he mentions them, if any other pupil in the group happens to know the word, he tells the meaning, and, if possible, the dictionary forms of the word. If no pupil knows the word, it is underlined, and other unfamiliar words are mentioned until all the words in the sentence which no pupil in the group knows are underlined. The chairman then assigns one or more words to each pupil to look up in a dictionary. All look them up at the same time, thus dividing the labor of thumbing the dictionary by the number of pupils in the group. After each has reported the meaning and the dictionary form of the word, the chairman usually reads through the sentence again in Latin. In most cases the meaning will be clear, but if any pupil still has difficulty in putting the words together to make sense, he asks the group about the part that troubles him. Help is usually forthcoming on the basis of the content or of a rule that someone has remembered. If no member of the group can clear up the difficulty, they resort to a formal analysis of the endings in the part of the sentence that troubles them. This is understood to be the "next-to-the-last resort" and is done very infrequently. If the sentence will not yield to this formal analysis, they proceed to the last resort of all and call upon the teacher. He spends about half of each period going about from group to group, stimulating their endeavors and answering their questions. It is the only Latin classroom the writer has observed in which the pupils ask the questions and the teacher answers them, but it seemed a more normal procedure because the teacher knew how to read Latin and the pupils did not. Almost all of the teacher's instruction in grammar—as the art of putting words together to make sense—occurred during these brief conferences while pupils were confronted with a difficulty which they were unable to resolve by their own efforts, and which interfered with their getting on with a story in which they were interested.

Some of these difficulties, of course, required more elaborate explanation and more practice exercises to make the point clear than could economically be offered to one group at a time. In all such cases the teacher told the group to bring up the difficulty for "clinical study" and gave them the meaning provisionally. We reserved a part of almost every class period for such "clinical study" of especially difficult sentences. Each group brought up its unresolved difficulties one at a time. These were written on the blackboard, and the whole class, with the help of the teacher, endeavored to discover what the difficulty was and to resolve it for all time to come. When the point was especially important to remember, the teacher made up and dictated parallel sentences for the class to figure out as practice exercises. This "clinical study" afforded many opportunities for a comparative study of English and Latin ways of expressing the same idea.

As soon as a group finished a story or a chapter in a book, they applied for a test, which they took individually, either orally or in writing. It usually included some test of comprehension, preferably other than translation, questions on the interpretation of word endings and questions on the meaning of new words which occur frequently in reading. Any other elements might be included which were appropriate to the selection read. The writer at first tried to make objective tests on all of his stories, but this proved so time-consuming that the test became usually an informal discussion with the group around the teacher's desk. The ulterior motive of the test was to correct the tendency of the less energetic members of a group to take undue advantage of the activity of others in reading the story....

Some time was also given to reading aloud pupils' translations of stories which they had especially enjoyed. The pupils could see some point in reading their stories to one another if they had worked out a good translation, or in paraphrasing them if they had not, because no two groups had read exactly the same material; and the reading of each group could usually make a significant contribution to some problem of interest to the whole class.

The reading of stories aloud in separate small groups in the same classroom had the disadvantage of being rather noisy, but this proved more irritating to the teacher than to the pupils. As each group was concentrating on its own problem, it was usually not distracted by the discussion of other groups. It had the advantage of the interest aroused by working with a congenial group for a common purpose, not dominated by the teacher. All reading of new Latin during the first two years was done in class. "Home work" consisted chiefly of collateral reading in English.

The advantages of this system of interpretation over the traditional grammar are obvious. It is common knowledge that the traditional grammar is almost never learned by students in this country—except by a handful of professors after years of teaching and research. Senior high school teachers complain that their work is hampered because of poor preparation in the junior high school. College teachers complain that the basic forms are not mastered in the senior high school. Graduate schools complain that even the highly selected students who reach them after eight years of study do not know their grammar. Teachers of summer courses in education have reason to believe that even Latin teachers after years of experience do not know the traditional grammar. Of 65 Latin teachers, averaging better than four years of teaching experience, in the summer session of 1931 at Teachers College, Columbia University, only five out of the 65 were able to write the complete conjugation of *capio* without an error. The number of such grossly incorrect forms such as *capiebo* surpassed the most cynical expectations of the instructors.

The mastery of the elements of grammar has been the *sine qua non* of Latin teachers for a thousand years. They have exhausted their ingenuity and their patience in the attempt to drive the conjugations and declensions into the heads of recalcitrant youth. Is there anything in the present situation in education which would lead one to expect a marked improvement in the near future? On the contrary, the diminishing respect for formal drill in secondary education is likely to have precisely the opposite effect. We may count on a diminished rather than an increased mastery of Latin grammar as the years roll on. How, then, may the few pupils who really ought to keep alive the classical tradition in our civilization take their initial steps in learning to read Latin?

The system of interpretation of the 18 basic Latin endings presented in this study offers a way out. If the writer were content with traditional tests of interpretation—ability to give the possible interpretations of isolated words in objective tests—he could demonstrate conclusively that the 18 basic endings can be memorized to the point of absolute mastery, of never making a mistake, by practically every member of an average class in one week. This is not the real test, however. In the course of their first year of study Latin pupils should acquire a method of attacking difficult Latin sentences—of interpreting the function in a sentence of the words in the order in which they occur—that will function instantly, automatically and almost unconsciously. The writer is unable at present to prove that this occurred in his classes, since he has been unable to devise a convincing test of this subconscious analysis of Latin sentences. His case therefore must rest upon the likelihood that a system of interpretation, easily held in mind, that attaches directly to each ending all its possible interpretations in terms which do not require further definitions, is more effective in reading Latin than a system which was never devised for reading Latin, which scatters the possible interpretations of each ending among fifty or more forms in paradigms, which interprets the function in a sentence of these forms in such ambiguous terms as "dative" and "ablative" which may mean thirty different things, and which is never mastered even after years of study.

A second advantage of this system of interpretation is that it relegates the study of grammar during those all-important first two years to a properly subordinated place. The Classical Investigation revealed the fact that 69% of the pupils who begin the study of Latin drop out in the course of the first two years.[11] If they have 1,572 inflected forms to memorize during the first year and more in the second, it is obvious that they will learn little else—and equally obvious that they will never learn these forms. Any substantial progress toward such broad objectives as literary culture, language consciousness and a social outlook is out of the question. On the other hand, if they attempt to master only 18 basic endings in the course of the first year and 22 more in the second, they will be unconscious of the fact that they are studying Latin grammar. The writer's pupils, stimulated by their parents' concern that they have never heard of conjugations and declensions, continually clamor for the study of grammar. If progressive education consisted of giving pupils whatever they wanted, regardless of why they wanted it, the writer would long since have capitulated. As it is, he is at great pains to convince his pupils that they have actually studied Latin grammar in a more carefully thought out and effective fashion than any of their contemporaries. The time saved is devoted to extensive reading, to the study of etymologies and linguistic developments that really have something to do with English (which the repetition of *amo, amas, amat* decidedly has not!) and to the investigation and discussion of significant social problems in the light of the experience of antiquity. The pupils read entirely in class time on the average about four times as much as is recommended by the Classical Investigation as a desirable minimum, and during one trial period of three months the fastest pupil read fourteen times as much as the slowest.

After the second year a carefully selected class consists chiefly of those enthusiasts who wish to learn all there is to know about Latin. These pupils may be taught more and more of the traditional forms without harm, since their reading habits are already well established, and by the end of the four year course, if the instructor is interested in this outcome, they will be able to impress their college instructors with their knowledge of "grammar" and even with their ability to write Latin. Such knowledge, however, is appropriate only for specialists, and can only be acquired with satisfaction and success upon the basis of at least two years' direct experience with the language. The first two years of a high school course in Latin are no place for it.

ENDNOTES

1. From *The Frequency of Latin Words and their Endings* (Chicago: University of Chicago Press, 1939), 21-25, 33-35, 37-43.
2. Diederich to Morris Finder, August 24, 1995 (Box 1, Finder Papers, University of Chicago Archives).
3. Robert W. Butche, *Images of Excellence: The Ohio State University School* (New York: Peter Lang, 2000), Chs. 12-16; Rudolph Lindquist, "The University School at Ohio State University" (unpublished dissertation, University of California—Berkeley, 1937); Class of 1938, University High School, *Were We Guinea Pigs?* (New York: Henry Holt, 1938).

4. Diederich to Finder, August 12, 1995 (Finder Papers). Debate over the merits of abandoning traditional subject-specific courses in favor of problem-centered interdisciplinary courses sparked much of the acrimony, according to William Van Til's autobiography, *My Way of Looking At It* (Terre Haute, IN: Lake Lurie Press, 1983), 81.
5. Entries of December 21, 1932, May 7, 1933, and May 17, 1933 in "Diary—OSU University School—1932-34" (Box 41, Folder 4, Robert J. Havighurst Papers, University of Chicago Archives).
6. Diederich to Siegmund Levarie, June 12, 1995 (Diederich Family Papers).
7. Diederich to Finder, June 23, 1995 (Finder Papers).
8. Jessie L. Rhulman, "An Approach to Revision of the Program and Procedures of Centralia High School through the Organization and Interpretation of School Records" (unpublished dissertation, Teachers College—Columbia, 1939), 622. "Centralia" was the pseudonym for the University School at OSU.
9. "Application for a Sheldon Fellowship" UAV 350. 284. Box 160. Harvard University Archives.
10. *Were We Guinea Pigs?* 124-128, 132, 135-136.
11. Advisory Council of the American Classical League, *The Classical Investigation* (Princeton: Princeton University Press, 1924), 31.

CHAPTER 8

A MONSTROUS SCHEDULE OF CRAMPED INACTIVITY[1]

(1959)

One of the most important studies of 20th century American secondary education was The American High School Today *by James Bryant Conant, former President of Harvard University and ambassador to West Germany. Published in 1959, this short book praised "comprehensive" high schools where students of different abilities and ambitions could pursue a wide range of academic and vocational courses. An ideal school would challenge the talented and less talented without creating invidious distinctions. The future lawyers and laborers would like and respect each other regardless of their different goals. Conant did not invent that mission for the high school, but he was its most influential advocate in the 1950s and 1960s.*

In 1957 and 1958, Conant and several research associates visited 55 high schools in 18 states, and in 22 schools they scrutinized the course selections of seniors whose standardized test scores before 9th grade ranked them in the top 15%. Their programs were of special interest to Conant. He wanted to know how many of the most able pupils finished high school well prepared for college. In gathering the data he relied on the advice of ETS President Henry Chauncey, and later ETS helped publicize Conant's book.[2]

Conant concluded that the smartest students rarely worked hard enough. Foreign languages did not attract a majority of the brightest for 3 or 4 years. Math and science enrollments were slightly better, especially for boys. Friendships rarely brought the future lawyer and laborer together, and romances usually stayed within rather than crossed socioeconomic lines. The majority of the 22 schools left much undone, and because Conant only examined schools with good reputations, the state of affairs elsewhere was worse, he assumed, particularly in small rural high schools unable or unwilling to offer calculus, physics, Spanish IV, and other rigorous courses.

For Conant, a college preparatory course of study exerted too little push. So many students were there that the talented were constrained by less able and less motivated classmates. In the late 1950s the college prep courses included considerably more than the top 15%, as they had for a long time—there was no golden age when they held only the top 15%.[3] With college entrance requirements modest in most states, and easing fast with the expansion of community colleges and branch campuses of state universities, the desire to attend college was no guarantee of sustained exertion. The most able students needed more than college prep courses provided. Advanced Placement was too new and too small to do the job alone. Only 10,531 students took the AP examinations in 1960.[4]

More than his published work, Conant's notes and correspondence were full of examples of the detours around academic exertion. After a visit to Bloomington High School in Indiana, he wrote that many students there told him they wanted to work part-time to buy a car rather than study foreign language. "This is a factor I hadn't thought of before," Conant confessed.[5] He had thought about the lure of music. "I know all of the temptations under which high school students now suffer," he told the President of Bennington College. "They would gladly take music rather than a foreign language if they could find any excuse."[6] To John Gardner, the President of the Carnegie Corporation, he claimed that high schools let the academically talented cultivate non-academic talents because "it is easier and pleasanter" for the students. In his opinion, which is borne out by course enrollment data, "this temptation is far more a matter of concern than the life adjustment courses we hear so much about."[7]

But in public Conant did not despair. "Most of the schools which I found unsatisfactory in one or more respects could become satisfactory by relatively minor changes."[8] His book offered 21 specific recommendations, including a model program for the talented students: four years of English, mathematics, and foreign languages; three years of science and social studies, and at least 15 hours of homework each week.

At the time, Conant's proposals were well received. They extended efforts already underway to make high school education more rigorous. Although some educators worried about the cost of full time guidance staff, seven period days, smaller English classes, new foreign language classes, and other recommendations, Conant's suggestions were praised as timely and realistic.

Diederich was one of the rare dissenters. In this withering paper, he tore into Conant's endorsement of a tougher daily schedule and the exhaustion that it could produce.

A Monstrous Schedule of Cramped Inactivity (1959)

As we consider the recommendations of the Conant Report that are likely to have the most effect on school policies, "there is need," as the man who rises to speak so neatly puts it, "for a return to basic fundamentals." By this redundant expression I mean the fundamentals we sit on.

The fellow who is one standard deviation above the average in scholastic aptitude, according to this report, ought to sit on a hard chair for seven or eight classes a day listening to other people talk. Five of these periods are for English, a foreign language, mathematics, science, and social studies. One or two are for everything else the school teaches, including art, music, shop, business, home economics, an extra period for lab, gym, assembly, home room, and student activities such as student government, dramatics, debating, and the school paper. If there is another, it will presumably go for library or study hall. After school, the student has a little time for work, practicing an instrument, games, hobbies, talking with friends, and blowing off steam, but right after supper he must settle down to what Dr. Conant estimates as three hours of homework.

As we advocate a "get tough" policy with these superior students, we should realize that we are advocating a daily schedule for growing boys and girls, at the most social and fun loving period of their lives, that is a lot tougher than any adult puts in, except for a few harassed executives with ulcers. Whenever we teachers go to educational conventions, do we regularly attend seven or eight meetings per day, sitting on hard chairs in cramped quarters the whole time, and then return to our hotel rooms to put in three or four more hours boning up on what the speakers wanted us to know, so that we could prove that we understood it and remembered it in seven or eight almost identical sessions the next day? This is really too easy a comparison, since the speakers have a long time to prepare what they have to say, and try hard to make it interesting, while teachers have to make it up as they go along. If we ever tried this routine for three consecutive days, would we then prescribe that our dearly beloved sons and daughters should undergo an even tougher routine, not just for three days but every day of their lives, barring vacations and weekends, while they are fizzing with all the juices of adolescence? Would we further prescribe that even this inhuman schedule would never be enough to satisfy the demands of their teachers, so that they would regularly go back to their chairs the following day with feelings of inadequacy and guilt, and be publicly put to shame if their sins of omission were found out?

You may say, "Oh, that is just Diederich's exaggerated way of putting things. Surely going to high school is much nicer than this." No, it is not, and I know whereof I speak. I have been sitting in classes day after day … in sixteen excellent school systems … to find out what their above average teachers are teaching about English. At the end of each day visiting classes—even though I am treated like a VIP, not a guilty student—my fundament is sore, my legs are cramped, my eyes are tired, my brain is reeling, and I would rather do anything else on earth than study for three or four hours what these youngsters are expected to study. It is not that the teaching is bad; there is simply too much sitting down, listening to talk, talk, talk. Flesh and blood rebel at the monstrous, inhuman schedule of cramped inactivity listening to voices talking nonsense, endlessly repeating themselves, scolding, prompting, belaboring the obvious, and scampering over the obscure.

If we just once looked at our youngsters as healthy young animals and tried to figure out for the first time what would make them smart and strong, understanding, kind, resourceful, able to do useful work and bring up families, would we prescribe seven or eight periods of tail-sitting in class followed by three hours of tail-sitting in the evening? There is no instance in which we do it to our animals except in a kennel where space is cramped, and even there we provide a little runway for the dogs to get out and stretch their legs. Our children do not get the runway, except possibly two or three periods a week in gym, where they go off like a coiled spring, but they have all the other dismal features of a kennel, including the noise. When we put our very intelligent poodle into the car to take her to the kennel, she trembles all over; and when we get her out, she is so overcome with joy that she cries all the way home. Why our children do not behave like that poodle is more than I can understand.[9]

It is equally deadening to teachers who have to impose discipline on five successive large groups of youngsters whose instinctive drive is to stand up, move around, do things, and talk to people, while we make them sit still and listen. The teachers come out of it as scarred and tired as the pupils. The art of teaching is so delicate and difficult that I would be willing to bet that we shall wind up the next century of experimentation with the fully documented conclusion that no one can do it effectively for more than two hours a day—each class hour accompanied by at least two hours of preparation and checking students' work.

All of the present dreary, ineffectual round is based on the assumption, unsupported by a shred of evidence, contradicted by common sense, and contrary to the practice of almost all colleges for hundreds of years, that learning proceeds best when administered in doses of five periods a week plus homework for all academic subjects. Dr. Conant even repeats this fantastic prescription in his report, without saying one word to justify it. I can appreciate his reticence on this point, since it lacks any rational or experimental foundation.

When I was teaching in high school, I thought that my twenty five class hours per week were simply the way God made the world, and nothing could be done about it. But when I made the transition to college teaching, I never had more than twelve class hours per week and averaged about ten. When my load got up to twelve hours, my chairman would apologize and promise to make it up the next semester. I would look stern and say, "See that you do. How can I get my research done? How can I see all my students?" But privately I was saying to myself, "I never had it so good."

Some years later I helped introduce a new English program in the Detroit high schools that permitted just two class meetings per week, along with two periods of independent reading supervised by assistants and one period of programmed instruction, also supervised by assistants, while the teachers had this whole day free for conferences. While we were planning this program, the two teachers were wondering how they could ever cover five days' work in two. I said that a college teacher would regard this as much easier than what they had been doing—covering two days' work in five. When they were still skeptical, I said, "If you could afford the financial sacrifice, wouldn't you like to teach in college?" Yes, they would. "Don't you realize that all your college classes would meet either two or three times a week?" Yes, that's true. "How long would it take you to adjust?" After a moment of silence, someone said, "About thirty seconds."

I do not blame Dr. Conant for his recommendations. He was looking squarely at The American High School Today and recommending the best practices that he found. I only wish he had thought what would happen if he recommended a similar program for the institution with which he is most familiar: Harvard College. Riot and insurrection would break out among both students and faculty.

But what about The American High School Tomorrow? I am encouraged by the fact that, in the most advanced high schools I have recently visited, the modal expectation is that each subject will have one large-group meeting and two small-group meetings per week, plus access to a daily double period reserved for study. This allows time for five academic subjects, independent reading, two double periods per week for "labs and arts," and a daily double period for outdoor play. It permits almost all assigned work to be finished in school, and there is also plenty of time for individual conferences—the only element in college teaching that is superior to high school teaching.

I have figured out a schedule that includes everything that Dr. Conant wants us to teach to superior students in *two* periods per subject per week. It averages just two periods per day with homework, which will mean an average of two hours homework per night, even if each academic class requires an hour of homework. There is time in the daily schedule for art, music, shop, lab, library reading, and all those activities of a modern school that involve standing up, moving around, doing things, and talking to people. These are *not* "progressive education." They go on in the most conservative schools, and students obviously learn a great deal from them in the most natural way possible. They also serve to reduce the tail-sitting and listening to the span of time that the young organism can absorb. If you think that the two periods per subject per week would teach only two-fifths as much of the academic fare Dr. Conant wants, my best guess is that they will learn as much or more. Five of these heavy doses per day are too much for anyone to absorb, but an average of two, followed by truly adequate time for homework, are possible. My schedule resembles the college schedules that are and have been in daily use for hundreds of years all over the world. Why we think youngsters fourteen to eighteen years old can stand more of a classroom grind than college students is something for the historians of our culture to figure out.

The only thing that might be labeled "progressive" in my schedule is a double period once a week for something that I have called "core" for want of a better name. This is all that survives of the "core courses" that were so popular and, on the whole, so invigorating among the thirty schools of the Eight Year Study. The subject that I would recommend for this core is the careful study of how we get the things we need—from food, clothing, and shelter up to freedom, justice, scientific knowledge, beauty, and the satisfaction of our spiritual needs. It would be a systematic eight year study of how the *work* of our communities is organized and carried on: what the farmer does, the factory hand, the executive, the newspaper man, the judge, the mayor, the doctor, the scientist, the artist, and the minister. There is a great deal of education to be gained from a thoughtful study at first hand, reinforced by plenty of reading, of how our people go about their work. I have recommended only one double period per week for this important study, supplemented by a trip whenever a trip can be arranged, because we have not yet worked up enough teaching materials and techniques to make a more extended study profitable in this area. But I think we could handle one long period per week with profit even now, since so many leaders in the community would gladly come in to tell about their work, and would invite groups of students to come out and see it for themselves.

However that may be, the rest of the schedule is a good, solid, academic one with English, a foreign language, mathematics, science, and social studies every year, interspersed with enough ambulatory activities to relieve the tail-sitting, even for these superior students. We commonly regard them as cherubs in Italian renaissance paintings—all heads and wings, no bottoms. Let us return to fundamentals. They have a bottom, and it is sore.

ENDNOTES

1. "The Conant Report" [1959] in "Diederich—Miscellaneous Writings" (ETS Archives).
2. Robert L. Hampel, *The Last Little Citadel* (Boston: Houghton Mifflin, 1986), 62-65; Ellen Condliffe Lagemann, *The Politics of Knowledge* (Middletown, CT: Wesleyan University Press, 1989), 200.
3. David L. Angus and Jeffrey E. Mirel, *The Failed Promise of the American High School, 1890-1995* (New York: Teachers College Press, 1999), Chs. 2-4.
4. Arthur G. Powell, *Lessons from Privilege: The American Prep School Tradition* (Cambridge: Harvard University Press, 1996), 160; John A. Valentine, *The College Entrance Examination Board and the School Curriculum* (New York: College Entrance Examination Board, 1987), Ch. 6.
5. "Trip Report—Bloomington High School" October 16, 1957 (Conant Papers, Box 7, "Indiana" folder, Harvard University Archives).
6. James B. Conant to William C. Fels, March 17, 1959 (Conant Papers, Box 6, "Correspondence 1957-1964" folder, Harvard University Archives).
7. James B. Conant to John W. Gardner, July 23, 1959 (ibid.)
8. *The American High School Today*, 40.

CHAPTER 9

"PROGRESS TOWARD COMPLETE LIVING"

Guidance and Counseling in High School (1949)[1]

Arthur likes archery, collects guns, drinks cocoa occasionally, and learned about sex on the day his parents bred the family's cat. Praised by most teachers for his painstaking work, especially in the sciences, Arthur seems "reserved" in class, has few friends, and is encouraged by his overprotective mother to consider himself an invalid with a weak heart (the school nurse is unconvinced). Diederich initially doubts if Arthur should take Latin, but later praised his progress—"his translations were uniformly excellent and attained a high degree of ease and freedom in the course of the year."[2]

Test scores, counselors' interviews, student questionnaires, "incident reports" from teachers, quarterly academic progress reports, hour-by-hour diaries of a typical weekend, and other material engorged the files of students at the Ohio State lab school in the 1930s. Excerpts for six students filled 675 pages of one dissertation on the school's student record-keeping. Some parents just wanted a grade rather than narrative reports and conferences, but the faculty retained its commitment to thoroughness.[3] Other schools in the Eight Year Study were not as meticulous. Diederich had read many "anecdotal records" from teachers who blurred the significant with the trivial, reported unusual rather than typical events, and settled for brief and vague entries.[4]

Paul Diederich and the Progressive American High School, pp. 109–127
Copyright © 2014 by Information Age Publishing
All rights of reproduction in any form reserved.

Diederich wanted to organize the mass of information and devise better methods for its use. He admired the approach of Ralph Tyler—Don't just ask what work the student has done; ask what the work has done to the student. In this paper he sketched how to do that at ETS, which he joined in 1949 thanks to an offer 50% higher than his Chicago salary of $5,000. A few friends teased him for "selling out to the enemy," but Diederich felt that "the enemy [the College Board, ETS' major client] has capitulated and reformed. It no longer tells high school teachers what they may teach. They tell ETS what it may test. It will be part of my job at ETS to keep it that way."[5]

President Henry Chauncey was also interested, throughout the 1950s, in creating measures of personal growth. "Our tests cover only a fraction of the aims of education and lack continuity for those they do cover," he wrote in the 1952-53 annual report.[6] *He told the ETS trustees in 1953 that "the situation is ripe for a major effort" in personality research.*[7] *Critics of ETS later mocked Chauncey's enthusiasm for personality tests, which was part of his expansive vision of ETS as helping people understand themselves and make wise educational and occupational choices.*[8] *Those critics don't acknowledge that many psychologists outside ETS agreed that personality research was a suitable and promising topic to explore. Not one scholar who participated in a ten-year-review of ETS research in 1958 criticized the organization for chasing a will-o-wisp.*[9] *But by the early 1960s, after dozens of investigations (including studies of ministers, engineers, and businessmen), the need for more research was so clear that Chauncey became more cautious on its prospects.*

Yet in the 1950s and 1960s the fields of school counseling and school psychology flourished, and keeping informal notes on students' character traits became common practice. In many districts, employers and government agents had access to those notes when parents and students did not. Not until 1974 did federal legislation guarantee parents the right to inspect the official files and sharply limit their disclosure to outsiders. Even before that law, most teachers did not compile potentially hurtful information on students' social, emotional, and ethical development. An elementary school report card might require teachers to give blue or red checks for habits like 'works well with others' or 'follows directions', but high school teachers rarely had to appraise "progress toward complete living," which for Diederich should have been the scope of their evaluations. Close surveillance of behavior seemed inappropriate—and even ridiculous, as a National Lampoon parody of a high school yearbook made clear. In that 1974 issue of the humor magazine, the four page spoof of a student file included many familiar items like grades and IQ, but it also had 19 items for Personal Appearance (Unusual shoes? Tight pants? Loud colors?), 38 items for Personal Hygiene (from underwear to lunch bucket), and the hilarious 63 items for Aspects of the Home Environment—messy soap dish? musty closets? attic disorder? frayed upholstery? Diederich would have deplored the trivialization of school records, but he left the door open for that result by encouraging the collection (in a long "Profile Index") of a vast array of information apart from academic performance. He once said that he sought to collect observations, not ratings, but that thin line was hard to see and easy to cross.[10] *For instance, in 1968 Diederich wanted to revive Edward Thorndike's 297 indices of goodness of life in American cities. If someone read that there were two chiropractors in the Princeton New Jersey phone book and seven pages of listings in Kansas City—Diederich wanted to add the per capita number of chiropractors as another indicator—would that be an observation or a rating?*[11]

"Progress Toward Complete Living": Guidance and Counseling in High School (1949)

My purpose in joining ETS is to change the public secondary schools of this country from a system of marks in courses (with attendant promotions, failures, and credit toward graduation) to a Comprehensive Evaluation Program in which data on all important aspects of a pupil's development are collected systematically throughout the year, are summarized to reveal whether changes are needed in the school program, and then are turned over to the pupil's adviser, counselor, or home room teacher, who will record them and, if necessary, take or recommend action upon them.

I regard our public secondary schools as the one place above all others in which we have made good on the promise inherent in the democratic way of life. [Thomas] Briggs estimated rather conservatively in 1932 that we had already educated in free public secondary schools about 16 times as many pupils, in proportion to population, as any other nation in the history of the world. The difference may have narrowed since, but when I talk to schoolmasters from England or France, for example, and still more when I talk to school people from Brazil, Egypt, or Persia, it is clear beyond question that our program of public secondary education is an order of magnitude hitherto unknown. When I tell them that about 90% of our young people now enter the 7th grade and about 50% complete the 12th, they can hardly believe it. Nothing like this has ever been done in the world before. In almost every small community in the land, the high school is the finest building. It has replaced the cathedral as the symbol of what our people believe in and hope for. We have wasted about all our natural resources except the most important of all—brains. There we have at least made an honest effort to educate all the children of all our people at public expense above the elementary level. Our execution of this unprecedented effort may still be imperfect, but it is in good, loyal, devoted hands, and steadily improving.

It should now be obvious why I am not quite so interested in private secondary schools. They are not the great, unique contribution of our people to the progress of civilization. Furthermore, many private schools already know so much about their pupils from direct, personal contact that an elaborate data-gathering program of the sort I envision would not be necessary to keep in touch with the development of their pupils.

I am not much interested in colleges, because I believe that in most instances the quality of their thinking about educational policies and procedures is about 50 years behind that of our public secondary schools—although they may be more expert in particular tasks, such as the teaching of Hamlet. When I decided to come here, I was asked why I could not remain in my comfortable job at Chicago and there develop the sort of program I had in mind. The answer is that in the College of the University of Chicago it would be simply inconceivable. I discussed my pet idea with many people there, and while they regarded it with amused tolerance, as the sort of scheme an educator would dream up, they could see no possible use for it in the program of the College. Education, they say, is by definition restricted to the acquisition of knowledge and the training of intelligence. The particular aspects of the growth of the mind that they want tested are limited by the syllabi of the various College courses. Anything outside that Aristotelian edifice is no-man's land.[12] It is particularly that no-man's land I wish to explore.

Public secondary school people, on the other hand, are ripe and ready for the sort of program I have to offer. They are always interested when I explain it. They understand what it is all about. They know at first hand the kinds of problems in secondary education which it is designed to solve. They know that they need help and are willing to cooperate. Here and there I am sure to find fervent disciples who will regard this scheme as an answer to prayer.

Finally, I regard the adult educators as an exceedingly intelligent lot with a broad, flexible, and well-informed view of educational possibilities and procedures. Their only handicaps for my purposes are the limited time they have to get at their clientele and the rather narrow range of human attributes which they are prepared to investigate. The result is that they cannot give me testing time, and they do not want to test very many things. When an adult has paid $50 for a course of 12 lectures, he naturally does not want to give up two of them in order to try out some tests. He would be particularly annoyed if one of the testing periods dealt with his manners, morals, hobbies, philosophy, or use of scientific methods in his daily affairs.

I hope that something like my Profile Index will be developed for elementary schools—by someone else. I do not know enough about elementary schools to attempt it. Early in my career I decided that I was not good enough to teach in elementary schools; I was just about up to teaching in secondary schools; but I would be damned if I would lower myself to teach in a college. I receded from that lofty position when I accepted employment at the University of Chicago, but I never felt quite at home there. Now I am back where I belong—in secondary schools. The Lord's Vineyard.

The situation which my proposed program is designed to correct is this: a small pupil enters the door of an enormous high school, like the hole in a bee hive, and buzzes around inside for four years, usually without meeting anyone who knows him well as a person, who regularly receives reliable information on all important aspects of his development, and who feels responsible for supplementing the efforts of his parents to bring him up as a fine human being. There are people who feel responsible for doing whatever the social studies, or the sciences, or literature can do to make him a fine person, but usually no one puts the whole picture together and does something about it. True, there are home room teachers, advisers, and counselors, but their main job at present is to fill up a home room period with busy work, or to inform pupils of school regulations and see that they are fulfilled, or to give occasional advice on problems which the pupil brings up. If they receive any reports about the pupil from other sources, it is usually in the form of course grades or very infrequent standardized test scores. In some progressive schools they receive occasional written reports from other teachers for editing and transmission to parents. Those reports are usually masterpieces of vagueness and generality. "Mary has made a marked improvement in her adjustment to the group. She now participates more freely. She is more willing to take responsibility, and on several occasions she has completed her work on time. In the future, she should spend a little more time in preparation for class." After such reports have been edited by the home room teacher to remove any offensive statements, and then edited by the headmistress to screen any relics of the blunt truth that the home room teacher missed, their meaning is as close to nothing at all as the art of composition can achieve. The ten most troublesome pupils may receive reports which crack down rather sharply, and the ten best may receive reports which, out of sheer appreciation of merit, are detailed in their eulogy, but the great middle group tends to receive reports which could be interchanged among them without anyone noticing the difference.

In contrast to that vagueness, marks in courses seem clear and definite, and they spare teachers the anguish of composing a hundred or more letters about pupils every two or three months. Marks, however, have their drawbacks also, and while these shortcomings have been frequently pointed out, I intend to outline them briefly; otherwise the feeling will persist that there is nothing wrong with marks, that only sentimentalists and progressive educators object to them, that some form of marking is inevitable, and that all fancy variants on marking systems are only marks in disguise, and are readily translated by pupils and their parents into the marks they really represent.[The next 11 paragraphs are omitted—they repeat the attack on grades at the start of the 1942 "Eighteen Shortcomings" essay]

Marks should be replaced by a scheme which is focused upon the important dimensions of human growth and development. The time has come for a major revision in our methods of academic bookkeeping. Marks alone, supplemented by a few tests, are not enough.

The steps necessary to introduce my version of a comprehensive evaluation program into a high school would be roughly as follows:

1. Prepare for the proposal by discussing it first with administrative officers and influential teachers. They will probably say that it is a fine idea but will not work in practice, and anyway the time is not ripe. What is wanted, they will say, is a change of heart rather than a change of machinery. Ask them how one gets a change of heart except by giving teachers things to do that will gradually lead to a change of heart. The only other way is exhortation, and it seldom works. Ask them if the idea is not worth a trial, and whether they will object to your proposing it in a staff meeting.
2. Propose the plan in a staff meeting. Make sure that several teachers are ready to speak in its favor. Explain why evaluation should be done on a school wide basis rather than leaving it entirely to individual initiative: (a) Getting reliable evidence on even one objective is a herculean task for one teacher, and getting evidence single-handed on all objectives is impossible. Shouldn't we try a division of labor? (b) Leaving it all to individual initiative has never led anywhere to anything but piddling results. (c) A common concentration on school objectives, rather than confining attention to course objectives, will multiply the educational effect. (d) Real progress toward certain objectives is revealed only by the extent to which students apply what they have learned in classrooms other than those in which they have learned it. (e) Effective guidance depends on assembling the significant evidence on pupil development from every department in school. Usually it is hopelessly scattered, and no one has access to all of it.
3. If the counseling program or home-room program is not in good order, propose the necessary changes. Any setup in which each adviser has responsibility for keeping in touch with the all-round development of not more than 40 pupils will do, but if advisers have to look out for more than 50 pupils apiece, keeping the Profile Index may prove burdensome. I favor the system, used in many schools, in which pupils are given about one month at the beginning of each year to get acquainted with their teachers for that

year; then they indicate their first and second choices among these teachers as their counselors. It should be understood that these counselors are not to engage in psychotherapy but only to keep an eye on how pupils are coming along in all their courses and activities. There should be *one* person each year in a position to see the pupil whole.

4. Have a Committee on Evaluation appointed with one representative of each main sector of the program (e.g., one for all the foreign languages) and one administrative officer. The responsibilities of this committee are to see to it that evidence is gathered on as many of the major school objectives as possible, to schedule the collection of this evidence at various times throughout the year and among all departments, so that the load is distributed as evenly as possible, to summarize each type of evidence as it is gathered and to report any significant findings to the faculty, to see to it that the evidence then gets to the counselors, and to make certain that the counselors record the evidence on the Profile Index and file it in the folders of the pupils concerned.

5. Get this committee to accept some *prepared* list of school objectives. I have gone through the Tyler technique of asking each school to build its own objectives from scratch dozens of times, and, while it has value as professional stimulation, it always takes at least a year, and never results in a list of objectives which is markedly different from the lists of comparable schools.[13] Where lists differ, it is chiefly because one school did not happen to think of objectives which others included, and vice versa. When the additional objectives are pointed out, they are readily accepted. The major objectives which have emerged from the prolonged and intense curricular discussion of the last few decades are readily accepted by secondary school faculties; they only like a little leeway in the headings under which these objectives are to be arranged. I am willing to be tolerant on this point, but they also ought to be tolerant for the sake of collaborating with other schools and with ETS. I tell them that however one cuts the cake, it is still the same cake, and why not adopt *any* sensible classification? The precise form of statement is unimportant, for it is the *data* we classify under these headings that will determine their meanings. Let us save a year of futile wrangling, largely over the meaning of words, and get on with the job of collecting data. Most faculties are more than willing to agree. They have been asked so many times in the last two decades to "clarify their objectives" that now, if one proposes to do it again, they are likely to lie down on the floor and kick and scream.

6. Have the Evaluation Committee make a survey of the evidence relevant to school objectives which is already being gathered in all departments, with approximate dates on which it is gathered.[14] Make a big calendar with columns for months and rows for departments. Enter all available evidence on this chart and also on a Profile Index to see what areas of growth are now completely ignored. Consider adopting a *few* new sources of evidence each year so that these neglected areas will have at least token recognition. Consider where this evidence can most conveniently be gathered, and on what dates. Adopt definite legislation to make sure that it will be gathered. The Evaluation Committee is to make all necessary arrangements and check up to make sure the work is done properly. After each type of evidence has been gathered, the Evaluation Committee is to summarize it and report any significant findings to the faculty.

7. Set up a box in the central office labeled "Faculty Exchange" or any other ambiguous title. Evidence should be dropped in this box. Each piece of evidence should be marked with the number of the school objective to which it refers and with a letter indicating the pupil's status with respect to this objective. I have recommended the letters W (weak), N (normal), and S (Strong) to indicate standing in the lowest quarter, the middle half, and the top quarter, respectively. In some cases it may be possible to report the exact percentile rank on national norms. An office clerk will sort these pieces of evidence into the mailboxes of the counselors concerned, who will record it on the "Profile Index" and then file it in that pupil's folder. Thereafter he may take or recommend any action which is suggested by the evidence—from giving the pupil a pat on the back to calling him on the carpet.

8. Each counselor should probably write a brief summary and interpretation of the evidence in each folder at least once a year. He might add, with discretion, his own impressions gleaned from observation. The summary might be sent to parents and a carbon copy might be filled in the folder. At the beginning of the following year, the folder might be sent intact to the counselor for that year, but he should discard everything in it which is not of continuing interest, and keep only the Profile Index and the summary.

9. Some principals will be silly enough to want all this evidence filed in their own office, where they but no one else can get at it conveniently, while others will want everything on carbon copies so that duplicate records may be maintained. I am strongly opposed to those practices. The data on pupil development should all pass through the mind of someone who knows the pupil and feels

responsible for his all-round development. The simple busy-work of recording the evidence on the Profile Index was devised only for the purpose of insuring that the counselor will look at the evidence and understand what it means. No principal could possibly look over the volume of evidence that will come in. The burden must be shared by all teachers. Therefore, the evidence should be where they can get at it, not where the principal will never find time to get at it. If a principal wants the evidence on any pupil, he can send for the folder, and the counselor will give it to him—with a sharp injunction to return it immediately.

The preceding outline of steps in the establishment of a comprehensive evaluation program should give a fairly clear idea of the sort of program I envisage. We may now revert to the question, what good will it do? What is it designed to accomplish?

It is designed, first of all, to bring about a change of heart in teachers. Many devices have been adopted for this purpose and few of them work. There are conventions, summer schools, institutes, professional literature, faculty meetings, supervision, and exhortation. For the most part, they only keep the wheels moving in the same old grooves. The only devices that I have *seen* make drastic changes in practice and in attitudes are three: summer workshops (under certain conditions), a serious effort at evaluation, and counseling. I made a year's follow-up study of a representative sample of 200 participants in the [eight week] workshops sponsored by the Progressive Education Association in 1939, and I became convinced that a good workshop experience can make startling changes in teachers.[15] As one department head expressed it, "I do not take much stock in these 'miracle stories' that crop up in educational literature, but I have a genuine article right here in my own department. The old lady next door just attended one of your workshops last summer. Just visit one of her classes and take a look at what she is doing. You would never believe that last year she was the most conservative teacher in my department."

A city superintendent told me: "Every year we spend about $50,000 on supervision, and everything goes on as usual. Last year we spent $1,800 to help a group of our key teachers to attend one of your workshops. We practically got a new curriculum out of it. It was the best investment in supervision we ever made."

A serious effort at evaluation produces much the same sort of change in teachers: namely, a lively interest in the major goals of general education, and a determination to work directly toward them rather than trusting the usual subjects to work, when swallowed, like a pill. I worked on both the curriculum and evaluation staffs of the Eight Year Study, and I have no doubt as to which staff produced the decisive changes in attitudes and practices. The approach of the curriculum staff may be represented by the questions, "What are you teaching? How can you teach it better? Should you be teaching anything else, or in addition?" All that got us was a bumper crop of fusion courses. The approach of the evaluation staff may be represented by the questions: "What should be coming out of all this? Is it or isn't it? If not, what can we do about it?" This stirred up the curriculum as with a spoon. The curriculum staff never began to get to first base until the evaluation boys had been there to pitch the ball.[16]

Most members of the evaluation staff, however, and most of the thoughtful leaders in secondary schools we visited gradually became convinced that the most fruitful line of attack upon evaluation was through school objectives rather than course objectives, and through a concerted effort to gather evidence on school objectives in many departments and activities. Said one principal, "It is the program that educates, not the individual course." However paradoxical this position may appear, in our experience we got along better on that assumption than on any modification of that assumption. The evidence we gathered through this approach was more important, of more interest, and more upsetting to traditional routines than anything we got through helping particular teachers to evaluate the unique outcomes of their own teaching.

Finally, I have known counseling to work wonders with teachers, but only when the counselors regularly received information on how their advisees were getting along in all their courses and activities. When they received genuine scientific data on their status and growth in important aspects of development, the effect was even more striking. In this relationship the counselor has to consider the pupil as a human being rather than as a consumer of the particular wares that he, as a teacher, has to peddle. He becomes concerned with serious deficiencies in character, personality, attitudes, interests, social adjustment, and the like, and begins to question whether the school is doing the right things for its pupils. He begins doing some of these things for individual advisees in his capacity as counselor, and to make provision for them in his class work. Sometimes he realizes that even the sum total of all the things that can be done toward such objectives in traditional courses does not begin to equal the job that needs to be done—even after all the potential contributions of agencies other than the school have been taken into account. Then he begins to agitate for major changes in the school program. As a result, he may get a really intelligent core course, rather than a mere combination of traditional subjects, and a richer program of student activities. The whole faculty may gradually become more concerned with the main dimensions of human growth and development, and less concerned with how much the student knows about chemistry, Latin, or English literature. I have never observed an instance, however, in which this concern with pupil development led to an *un*concern about whether the pupil knew anything about anything (as the progressive schools are parodied in the popular press). Remember that progressive education has as yet affected very few secondary schools, and almost all of the incredibly ignorant students we get in college are the products of the traditional college preparatory program that was forced upon secondary schools by the colleges themselves.

A second good effect of the program I advocate is to make the process of evaluation more objective, more reliable, more cooperative, more continuous, and more comprehensive. I group these points together because they add up to improvement in the process of evaluation above the stage represented by marks in courses, supplemented by a few standardized tests of intelligence, reading, grammar, and foreign languages, when teachers are on one side of the fence and pupils are on the other. When reliable evidence is gathered in all courses and activities on aspects of growth that pupils as well as teachers regard as important, and the counselor merely pools the information and records it on a simple, meaningful chart, the counselor is not making any personal judgment; he is reporting evidence, with the intention of helping the pupil to capitalize on his strengths and to overcome his weaknesses. Usually that evidence is hopelessly scattered and never brought together into one picture. A system in which counselors automatically get this information from all over the school, record it, and file it will overcome this difficulty. There will not be recurrent hectic periods when pupils are taking tests in all subjects simultaneously, followed by slack periods of unexamined living; the evidence will be flowing in all the time. Finally, we should not put all human attributes on one linear scale of academic achievement, nor conceal important attributes behind marks which are supposed to represent academic achievement; we shall put the evidence under appropriate and meaningful headings. Evidence on punctuality, responsibility, social grace, and the like will not be reported as hidden components of grades in English, mathematics, etc. but as evidence on those particular traits and abilities. Then we shall find that everyone excels in some things and everyone has weak points. The picture will be closer to reality, more encouraging, and more stimulating.

A third good effect of the program that I advocate is that pupils will have a clearer idea of what education is for, and of where they stand with respect to important characteristics of human beings. The objectives in my list will probably have a more immediate appeal for pupils than the objectives commonly listed by teachers of the traditional subjects, for the main headings are values that we all cherish—things that are obviously necessary for happiness—and the objectives listed under these headings will be traits, abilities, and habits clearly related to the attainment of those values. I should not want to conceal from pupils any of the evidence on their progress toward those goals. No secret dossiers should anywhere be accumulated that are not open to inspection and challenge by the person concerned. I view with alarm the growth of our own Gestapo, the FBI, and its compendious files, and I should not want to assist in the establishment of anything like it in schools. With time and training I think we can reveal even intelligence test data to pupils with beneficial results. But if any evidence would be really damaging if revealed, it should either be communicated orally, or read and at once destroyed, or, if absolutely necessary, kept in a separate folder in a locked drawer. Everything else should be discussed freely by the pupil and his counselor in periodic conferences.

The ultimate effect of this sort of examination of progress toward complete living might even be to regenerate some sort of morality. I have set forth in my paper on "An Ethical Basis for Educational Objectives" my reasons for suspecting that we are in the midst of such a breakdown and confusion of values as the world has not seen since the decline of the Roman Empire.[17] I do not believe that our *conduct* is much worse than the conduct of previous generations, but we no longer have any clear idea of what is right, nor any convincing and compelling reason for acting in ways which our forefathers thought were right, for reasons which we reject. Unless we find a new definition of what is right and a new reason for acting in accordance with it, I fear that it is only a matter of time before conduct itself will lapse below the standard which is necessary to maintain that large-scale cooperation on which civilization depends. We cannot coast along indefinitely on moral inertia. While I am somewhat surprised to find myself in the role of prophet, my Profile Index will at least keep before the eyes of pupils five major values on which all schools of ethical thought can agree, and their attention will be called repeatedly to the kinds of behavior, attitudes, traits, and the like which conduce to the attainment of those values. In the absence of widespread agreement upon a system of morality with divine sanctions, such a rough-and-ready lay morality may serve at least an interim purpose.

In the past few decades, adults have been extremely unwilling to help children with the problem of what things in life are most worth having, and of how they may be attained, on grounds that "nobody knows the answer," "all values are relative," and "each one must make his own pattern." It seems to me about time that these fashionable clichés were confronted with a blunt "stuff and nonsense!" There is no problem on which adolescents need and want help so much, and almost any thoughtful and experienced adult is qualified to help, once he puts his mind to the problem and does not run away from it. He has been over the road and knows something about where it leads. The idea that each individual must have an absolutely unique pattern of values seems to me just as foolish and dangerous as the idea that each school must have a unique set of objectives. The similarities among men are more important than their differences. Unless there is a wide area of agreement on what the durable goods of life are, and millions of people are acting intelligently and cooperatively to reach those goals, there is no possibility of attaining anything like the good life. We have to pull together, not each in his own direction. There will be minor differences, to be sure, just as each man, having the physical characteristics which enable him to be classified as a man, still has certain features which enable him to be recognized as a person. But the way educators have talked in recent years, one would think that each man was at liberty, if he chose, to have two heads, six legs, and no thorax. I am fed up with this relativist and laissez-faire position. There are a large number of things that all of us want and need, such as the necessities of life, health, and protection; friendly relations with others, a free society, a sense of worth or achievement; aesthetic experience; and knowledge integrated in a philosophy which gives orientation, direction, and security. "But these things are so obvious and general!" Not obvious to pupils who are just beginning to struggle with the problem of what things in life are most worth striving for, and not so general but that we can derive at least six pages of fairly specific objectives from them, and begin to build tests and other instruments that will put teeth in them. The main headings *have* to be rather obvious, in order to secure widespread agreement, and rather general, so that a lot of particulars may be classified under them. But there will be nothing vague or woolly about the particulars.

A fourth and last good effect of this proposed change in academic bookkeeping will be, I hope, upon the policy and direction of ETS itself. Despite its notable achievements in the field of test theory and methods, there is some feeling among educators here and there that the organization is apt to be tied too closely to measuring the conventional outcomes of conventional courses—having to seek the least common denominator among them, and to become immersed in refinements of analysis when what we need is at least crude evidence of growth in great untouched sectors of human development.[18] I do not state this as my personal criticism, for I have just spent the better part of a week acquainting myself with what ETS and its member organizations have been doing in recent years, and I am amazed at the number of new trails they have blazed. Nonetheless, I have heard the opinion expressed by many educators who ought to know better, and can think of no better way of combating it than by launching a program that is considerably ahead of current educational practice than merely abreast of it.

In order to develop this program, I shall need dozens of new measures, many of them in areas of growth as yet scarcely touched by objective techniques. I can develop some of these measures myself, but I should like as many members of the organization as possible to devise some of these measures or to send me ideas on how to devise them. As bright and able testers, they must have dozens of wild and woolly ideas for new types of tests and other instruments which they have never developed or completed, because no contract calls for them. My contract <u>does</u> call for them. Here is a capacious bag in which everyone is invited to thrust any instrument of evaluation which is too hot for the usual contract to handle.

~ ~ ~ ~ ~ ~ ~ ~ ~ ~ ~

Now for the other side of the picture. What are the objections to the proposal? What possible harm may it do? What dangers and difficulties should be avoided?

The chief objection I hear is that the headings in my classification of school objectives have no discernible relationship to most of the courses now taught. For many of these objectives, it will be said, no particular teacher feels any responsibility, even though the faculty as a whole might feel a vague concern; and for many of the things that teachers now spend most of their time teaching, there is no place in my classification. Would it not be better to make the main headings the natural sciences, the social sciences, the humanities, and the like, and under these headings put official lists of the objectives which teachers in these areas are now striving to attain? Then at least something would be done about the evidence collected.

The "subject approach" to evaluation is simply not fruitful, holds no possibility of educational progress, and is not even interesting to high school faculties which have any life in them. It is dull, outmoded, sterile, divisive, narrow, unimaginative, and unprofitable. It is bound to neglect most of the important aspects of human development and to emphasize certain hallowed bits of knowledge, such as the position of French pronoun objects, out of all proportion to their importance. It prevents collaboration between teachers of different departments in getting evidence which would be of interest to all, and which should be sent to all, rather than locked up in the files of one department. It is not even necessary, for teachers can find out readily enough what students know about the subjects they teach. It is on the larger aspects of human development that they need help. The "subject approach" to evaluation, as to education, is a blind alley. I should know, for I have been forced up that alley dozens of times in the Eight Year Study and later, and I have never known it to lead anywhere.

On the other hand, it is untrue to say that teachers feel no personal responsibility for the kinds of objectives I have in my list. Teachers have come a long way from the days in which mastery of facts and principles of the subject taught was their sole concern. They now not only feel concern for broader educational objectives but often take quite definite steps to attain them. They realize, too, that a great variety of things are being done about those objectives in almost every department in school; therefore, the collection of evidence to ascertain progress should be a school-wide venture, with all the economy of effort that comes from a division of labor. If each department set out single-handed to collect evidence on all the broad objectives to which it was contributing, it would exhaust itself before getting to first base; it would duplicate similar efforts on the part of other departments; and it would wind up with a collection of fragmentary, incomplete evidence in its own files which ought to be supplemented by data from other files and become the property of the whole school.

Furthermore, even if teachers are indifferent to some of these broader objectives in their capacity as teachers, they are either already interested or can readily be made interested in them in their capacity as counselors. Even if they do nothing about the evidence in their own classrooms, they will have plenty to do about it as counselors; and if nothing comes of their efforts, they will soon be proposing changes in the school program in order to obtain the objectives on which the evidence has consistently been unfavorable. I see no possibility that a steady flow of unfavorable evidence on some of the broader objectives will long be ignored.

Finally, even if the school regards some of my objectives as primarily the responsibility of other agencies, it would still be desirable, if time allowed, to check up on how well those other agencies were doing their share. The school as evaluator for society can look beyond the boundaries of its responsibilities as teacher. If some important areas of development are sadly in need of attention, the school can either report to the agencies concerned or take over the functions itself. This will only make the process by which the curriculum grows more scientific and more systematic.

A second objection may be that we now know how to get reliable evidence on only one or two of the main aspects of growth included in my classification. Why include objectives for which we have no tests?

The answer is to stimulate the production of such tests, both in our own organization and in schools using the form; to get people, in the meantime, to look for any sort of informal evidence that will give some ideas of where pupils stand in those areas; and, if all else fails, to remind ourselves that we do not have a complete picture. I do not want at this point to eliminate any important objective because I have no test for it. If the objective remains in the list, someone may think of a way of testing it tomorrow.

A third objection I have heard is that my objectives, as stated, are too vague and general, so as to stand above controversy, but as soon as one gets down to particulars, people will disagree. That is all right with me. I have provided a series of empty boxes on five different shelves, labeled only distinctly enough for us to sort our data into them. If School A takes my objective, "knows how to buy wisely," and teaches one set of things about it, while School B teaches a different set, the tests of each school can still use this box. What goes into the box determines its meaning, not the label that I put on it. If, after we examine the contents, any label proves grossly inappropriate, we can readily change it. While I do not object to criticism of my labels in advance, I suspect that the best time to change them will be after we see what sort of evidence each one brings in.

A fourth objection which was expressed rather vigorously to me is that I am creating a mechanical monster to do a job which can only be done rightly by direct personal contact between a gifted teacher and small groups of pupils.[19] Perhaps my monster is necessary in mass education, it was admitted, but only because mass education is wrong. While education is wrong, my monster will be crude and ineffective, and if ever education becomes right, the monster will be unnecessary.

I object to that position, not only because I do not propose to spend my life waiting for the millennium, but also because I believe my "monster" would be useful even in an ideal school system. There are many things about pupil development that only a rather impersonal testing program can reveal accurately, no matter how small the group. The most striking instance of this I recall was the time the son of our last Dean entered the College for the University of Chicago along with about 1,200 other students. The first thing he had to do was take my tests in reading and writing, and before the following morning I had him placed in our remedial classes in both of these arts. His father was nationally famous, and justly so, as a teacher of reading and writing; he had only three sons—as small a group as one would find even in the ideal school—he knew them all quite well, and got along famously with them. Yet, in talking over the matter, he confessed that it was only during the preceding year that he came to realize that his youngest son was not reading or writing as well as he should, and he did not realize how badly until he saw the results of the tests. It gave me some pleasure to think that I knew it within the first 24 hours the boy was in college, and all our subsequent experience with the boy confirmed that diagnosis. And, in the same operation, I had similar data on 1200 other students. The moral of this little tale is that there are plenty of things about a boy that one cannot tell just by looking at him or by living with him. The machinery I propose to set up to find out those things need be no more "monstrous" than a clinical thermometer.

A fifth objection, related to the preceding, is that my scheme will bury teachers in paper work and leave them no time for their true function, which is, presumably, teaching. The scheme requires each counselor to put down *one number* in a certain position in the Index for each piece of evidence that he receives. I should expect that on most days he would receive none at all; occasionally, three or four pieces; rarely, a windfall of ten or a dozen. How long would it take to write down twelve numbers?

To my mind, this is the absolute minimum of paper work that any record system could require, for it is impossible to write less than one number as the sole record of a piece of evidence. If the counselor cannot take the time to write down this single number before filing the evidence, it will simply be dumped into the pupil's folder without any record at all, and—very likely—without the counselor's knowing what the evidence is or what it means. Then we shall simply have folders bulging with unsorted and unexamined evidence, like those which have been kept for over 30 years by the Laboratory School at the University of Chicago. I have tried to use those records, and it takes, on the average, at least two hours to look through one folder and make any sense at all of what it contains. If the evidence had been recorded on the Profile Index as it was filed, one could see at a glance the school objectives on which evidence had been gathered, the status revealed by this evidence, and the serial order of each piece of it in the folder. If one wanted to examine the evidence on any particular objective, such as growth in reading, one could locate it instantly. There are so many benefits to be gained by pausing just an instant to put down that single number that I do not believe any conscientious teacher would begrudge the time.

Furthermore, we have passed over the slippery assumption that the sole function of a teacher is to teach. So it is, to be sure, but we must never forget how important and how integral a part of teaching is proper diagnosis and evaluation. Let us remember the analogy of medicine: in the old days, doctors "wasted" little time on diagnosis but spent it all on treatment. Now a doctor will spend about nine-tenths of his time with a patient on diagnosis, often involving the most elaborate tests and measures; the rest goes for treatment—and how immeasurably more effective it is! Analogies must not be pressed too far, but I strongly suspect that educational efficiency would be increased to about the same degree if teachers would take all the time necessary for diagnosis and evaluation, regarding it as an essential part of their job, and then teach, but with a full knowledge of their patient's condition.

A sixth and final objection is that we shall be getting a great deal of evidence on pupil development into the hands of untrained counselors who will not know what it means or how to use it, and great harm may ensue. The only answer is that we shall have to be very careful and then run the risk. The initial experiments will all be supervised by me personally or by some other member of ETS. We shall explain patiently and repeatedly what each type of evidence means, how to interpret the scores, and how to use them most effectively. As we see what misunderstandings arise, we shall print all necessary instructions not only where teachers can see them but also where pupils can see them. Our fears in this connection arise largely from past misuse of intelligence test data and of scores on tests which were to serve as the basis for a year's grade in a subject. Those were the most dangerous figures one could possibly hand to an untrained counselor; almost all of the evidence I propose will be far more innocent and fool-proof. Finally, even if occasional harm is done, the beneficial changes in teachers' attitudes and practices will more than offset the damage. The responsibilities of counseling a limited number of pupils, when linked to an effective evaluation program, do so much for teachers that I should not want any teacher to be excluded from these benefits on the ground that he is not a thoroughly qualified teacher already.

ENDNOTES

1. "Toward a Comprehensive Evaluation System" in Green File, Series 5, R 15, ETS Archives.
2. Jessie L. Rhulman, "An Approach to Revision of the Program and Procedures of Centralia High School through the Organization and Interpretation of School Records" (Unpublished Dissertation, Teachers College—Columbia, 1939), 92-185, 116-117.
3. *Thirty Schools Tell Their Story* (New York: Harper & Brothers, 1943), 736; Margaret Willis, *Three Dozen Years: A Report on the University School, 1932-1968* (NP, 1968), 44.
4. Diederich, "After Tyler, What?" (Unpublished paper, January 25, 1965, ETS Archives), 28.
5. "Long Range Plans for ETS services to higher education" October 5, 1973 (Folder 650, William Turnbull Papers, ETS Archives).
6. *Annual Report to the Board of Trustees, 1952-53*, 27.
7. Henry Chauncey to the Board of Trustees, May 20, 1953 ("Research Board, 1950-56" folder, Box 17, Series 6 A/B, ETS Archives).
8. Nicholas Lemann, *The Big Test: The Secret History of the American Meritocracy* (New York: Farrar Straus Giroux, 1999), 86-93; David Owen, *None of the Above: Behind the Myth of Scholastic Aptitude* (Boston: Houghton Mifflin, 1985), 195-196; "Minutes of the Board of Trustees," May 3, 1954 and November 23, 1954 ("Research Board, 1950-56" folder, Box 17, Series 6 A/B, ETS Archives).
9. "Minutes of the Meeting of the Standing Committee on Research" November 10, 11, 19 and 20 ("Research Committee, 1958-1961" folder, Box 35, Series 6 A/B).
10. "Methods of Studying Ethical Development" in *Religious Education*, v50, n3, May/June 1955, 164.
11. "Indices of Goodness of Life" February 28, 1968 (Folder 54, Henry Chauncey Papers, ETS Archives).
12. Diederich probably had in mind the Dean, Richard McKeon, a philosopher known for, among other achievements, his work on Aristotle.
13. In 1935, the Eight Year Study schools listed their instructional objectives. The result was 12,000 note cards that Diederich summarized in a 20 page

single spaced list. Tyler then reduced that enumeration to eight clusters of objectives. From "After Tyler, What?" 13.
14. One study of 35 school districts found that an average of 50 pieces of information were collected, including eight items on personality traits. But teachers rarely used the data or saw their relevance to classroom instruction. Roger B. Maas, "Recent Trends: Schools Records, Child Accounting" in *Wisconsin Journal of Education*, April 1942, 377-78, 382.
15. Kenneth L. Heaton, William G. Camp, and Paul B. Diederich, *Professional Education for Experienced Teachers* (Chicago: University of Chicago Press, 1940), Ch. 4; Craig Kridel and Robert V. Bullough, Jr., *Stories of the Eight Year Study* (Albany: State University of New York Press, 2007), Ch. 8.
16. Ralph Tyler recalled that the schools in the Eight Year Study saw the evaluation staff as especially helpful. Morris Finder, *Educating America: How Ralph W. Tyler Taught America To Teach* (Westport, CT: Praeger, 2004), 100.
17. Paul B. Diederich, "An Ethical Basis for Educational Objectives" in *Ethics*, v58, n2, January 1948, 123-132.
18. Diederich in 1958 recalled with approval Ralph Tyler's slogan: "Better crude evidence of something important than the most refined evidence of something that doesn't matter" (Paul Diederich, "A Fund for Special Measurement Services for Educational Projects Supported by Research Grants" 3/26/1958, p. 15, in Folder 54, Henry Chauncey Papers, ETS Archives).
19. In September, 1952 Diederich drafted a "profile index" that had 97 items in six categories, but he hoped that any school that tried it could condense his six pages to one or two. "The Profile Index" ("Values" Folder, MSS/5 Diederich, ETS Archives).

CHAPTER 10

WAITING WITHOUT GIVING UP

(1969)[1]

Progressive education was a broad array of practices designed to make schooling more pleasant and more practical. As with other amorphous constructs like modernism and romanticism, the meaning of progressivism varied from person to person, place to place, and era to era. Diederich is an example of how one individual could embody several strands of progressive education. His faith in research, desire to reconstruct American society, and vision of teaching as coaching make it impossible to pigeonhole him as only an "administrative progressive," a "social reconstructionist," or a "pedagogical progressive," three categories often used by historians of education. In 1969, Diederich described five examples of progressive education where he had been the teacher, parent, or observer. For all five, he underscored the importance of patience and empathy in order to see the world from the child's point of view. Diederich also stressed that the activities could and should be structured by adults—as he put it, "students are the ones who play the game but not necessarily the ones who invent it." He rejected the notion that child-centered work required the young to create their own tasks and projects. "A progressive teacher tends to contrive situations in which his students willingly carry on activities that educate because they seem interesting." This essay began with a memorable vignette from 1943:

Waiting Without Giving Up (1969)

Since people who talk about progressive education have varied notions of what it is or was, I'll start this article with some instances of what I regard as progressive education.

First, let me tell you about a day [in the Spring of 1943] when my daughter and I were walking to her nursery school.

At we started out she said, "Daddy, we musn't step on the cracks in the sidewalk or a bear will come out and bite us." That seemed a sensible precaution, so we carefully avoided the cracks all the way to school.

Next day, she wanted to play the same game again, but, tempted to find out whether she was ready for a mild dose of science, I asked her, "How do you know that a bear will come out if we step on a crack?"

She replied scornfully, "Oh, everybody knows that!"

I wanted to say that the things "everybody knows" are most likely to be false. Since she would not understand, I said, "I just can't believe it, because I haven't seen any bears around here lately. They may have all gone north. Couldn't we step on a crack and find out?"

Since she seemed alarmed at that idea, I suggested, "You go and hide behind that tree where the bear can't see you and let me step on a crack. I'm big; I'm not afraid of bears. Besides, I can run faster than they can."

At first she thought this would be too dangerous but finally consented. When I could see her little face peeping out from behind the tree, I shouted, "Come out, bear!" and boldly stepped on a crack.

At once she pointed to a bush behind me and said, "See, Daddy, there's the bear!"

Some parental instinct prompted me to say, "Let's run!" Since her legs were rather short, I scooped her up and ran all the way to school. Once inside the gate, we turned around and shouted insults back at the bear.

I thought the imagination of childhood had defeated the methods of science, but this judgment turned out to be premature. Next morning she said to me, "Today, Daddy, you hide behind the tree and let me step on the crack."

Well! I could not tell without further evidence whether she had caught the spirit of "Let's try it and see" or whether this was another part of the game of make-believe. But at least she was not afraid to put herself in the position of danger, and her belief in the reality of the bear had perceptibly diminished.

I regard this as an instance of progressive education because I approached an objective through the natural concerns and activities of a very young child. I was willing to accept apparent defeat on the first trial in order to save face for her and to give her time to mull over the results of the experiment. Arguing would have done no good at this point, and I still think my impulse to pick her up and run was wise.

If this first trial had really failed, I would not have given up on the objective but would have waited for other opportunities to get my child to submit her hypotheses to experimental tests. A large part of progressive education consists of waiting—but waiting without giving up. In fact, my daughter needed many repetitions of this sort of lesson before she began to say, "Let's try it and see" on her own.

I was willing to accept rather inconclusive evidence that the bear lesson had attained the desired result for two reasons. First, any attempt to pin her down at this point might have involved an admission on her part that she had been wrong, and I did not want this first step toward science to be unpleasant. Second, I was quite confident that if any change in attitude had come about, it would reveal itself on numerous occasions as we went along.

Perhaps the overriding consideration is that this incident showed willingness to listen to a child and to take her ideas seriously. One of the wisest teachers of my acquaintance says, "A teacher does not have to understand children. He only has to be willing to."

Now let me go on to the more mature problems of the first grade. A few years ago I was asked to help develop measures of intellectual development and potential in disadvantaged first graders in New York City schools. The group intelligence tests previously used had given obviously false readings. As many as 70% of the children in some schools scored at the feeble-minded level, but the things these children could do showed that they were anything but feeble-minded.

I soon guessed several reasons for their low scores. They were afraid of tests; they were upset by time limits; they hated answering questions (especially those in official looking documents); they had the life-saving art of switching off their attention so that they never fully understood the directions. Above all, when they came to a question that they could not answer, they did not skip it and go on to the one that they *could* answer but sat there and sulked the rest of the period.

Early intelligence testers tried to avoid using tasks children learn in school, believing that some children are handicapped by poor instruction. They used unfamiliar tasks, such as making a string of beads exactly like a model string or finding a path through a maze. This procedure is all right for secure children, but insecure children freeze up when they are asked to do something they have never done or even seen. For this reason I decided to use tasks involving familiar words, numbers, and pictures and to disregard the effects of poor instruction, which, after all, constitute a real handicap to further learning. I attempted to avoid invidious comparisons by developing norms or standards of performance only within individual schools.

For one typical test I devised a sort of scale, a "balance beam." It was a stick two feet long with a screw-eye in the middle. This was hung from a hook at the top of a small stand so that the stick balanced. Each end of the stick had 10 pegs sticking up at one-inch intervals, numbered from 1 to 10 to show their distance from the fulcrum. A heavy bolt at each end of the stick could be screwed in or out to make it balance. Lead drapery weights could be placed on the pegs to show that a 3 and a 6, for example, would balance a 9; if the weights were even one position off, the stick definitely would not balance.

The children played with this scale in pairs. One boy might place a weight of 9 and ask his partner to balance it with two weights on the other side. The partner might put one weight on 4 and—after a few false moves—another on 5, and the beam would balance. If he made it within three moves, he won, which gave him the privilege of copying that solution on a piece of paper that was later dropped into his "mailbox" as a record of his successes. If he did not make it in three moves, the other player tried it.

I taught the children to copy their solutions in this fashion: "4 + 5 = 9," which they read as "Four and five balance nine." I taught them that the plus sign was just a handy way to write "and" and that the equal sign meant "balance."

At this point I ran into trouble with the people of the curriculum division, who said I must not use plus and equal signs before the second grade because research had shown that children of this age and ability could not understand them. I said I had seen disadvantaged first graders using these signs quite accurately and cut short the discussion by saying that I had no desire to interfere with the curriculum, but this was not curriculum; it was measurement, and I was authorized to do something about that.

Of course, that was not the whole truth. Which do you think it was: curriculum or measurement, teaching or testing? In my view, one mark of a good measure is that you can't tell which it is. To put the issue even more sharply, what would you say if someone wanted to throw out the balance beam on the ground that it took too much time away from teaching?

This device had several features that seem to me to show various facets of progressive education.

First, the children set the problem for themselves or for one another, and they were soon setting much harder problems than any I would have dared to give them. By the end of the year, one child even discovered that three weights on the third peg plus four weights on the fourth will balance five weights on the fifth—which leads straight into the Pythagorean theorem.

Second, as soon as the children found the way to balance a number, they began to look for other ways to do it. Hence they began to think in terms of more than one correct solution for some kinds of problems.

Third, everybody got everything right because they kept on until the beam balanced, and then the answer was automatically right. The numbers they copied and gradually remembered represented correct solutions that would not be contradicted in subsequent experience—unlike the sums they got by counting on their fingers.

The children varied widely in the number and difficulty of the problems they attempted to solve with the balance beam and the other "toys and games" I used in this testing program. This implies a fourth advantage to this kind of testing: In their free activity periods these children had a wide choice of "games," could play whenever they liked, and could stick to any game as long as they wished without the panicky feeling that comes when time is limited. They could get accustomed to the rules of each game gradually and not have to understand and remember a set of directions they had received at the beginning of the period.

In all the "games" we always found some way for the children to record the solutions they found, and in their eyes these constituted the record of their successes—never of their failures. They always deposited the slips recording their solutions in their "mailboxes" with a feeling of triumph, never realizing that I was an old meany who would look into the boxes from time to time, count their slips, and record them under various headings.

The number of points a child accumulated over a period of several months was, of course, far more reliable than the scores on a conventional test, and it indicated the bent of a child's interests and the depth of his understanding as well as the number of problems solved. These were scores—as solid as anything one could get out of a Binet [I.Q.] test—but scores on performance when the children were doing their best, not when they were frightened or confused or sullen or hostile. This is the sort of testing that I hope to see vastly extended in the schools of the future.

[A description of an ETS colleague's use of pegboards in 4th grade is omitted]

To illustrate how certain aspects of progressive education can be combined with even a strictly regimented program, let me discuss a remedial English course I taught at the University of Chicago. Most of my students were in grades 11 or 12. As remedial material, we used a series of objective tests for reading and writing that a colleague and I had prepared for the United States Armed Forces Institute.

Each of these tests was built around a single topic. Students took them home and came to class with their answers already marked. Although they could answer 50 multiple choice questions in the time ordinarily devoted to homework, time in class limited discussion to about 10 questions, so our first problem was to select the 10 that most needed discussion. Our procedure was to ask, "What did you do with Item 1?" and each student held up one, two, three, or four fingers to indicate which answer he had chosen. If nearly all students chose answer 3 and that was correct, we would say "Yes, 3" and go on unless someone wanted to argue about it. But if one faction wanted answer 2 and another wanted 4, we might say, "Mary, why did you choose 2?" "Jim, why did you choose 4?" "Does anyone else have a different reason?"

By this time, hands would be waving all over the room, and all we had to do was to recognize students who wanted to speak, and occasionally to ask a question in order to clarify what a student was trying to say. As soon as the arguments began to repeat themselves, we would say, "That's enough. We now have heard all the reasons we need to decide which answer is better. How many now want 2? How many want 4? The 4's have it. If you still want to argue, take up your point after class with someone who chose 4."

The reason I regard this class as an instance of progressive education is that it relied almost exclusively on students' arguments with one another as a means of improvement. We did this not as a matter of principle but because it worked. Whenever we lost patience and simply told a class which answer was correct and why, they promptly forgot it and never referred to it again. But if they argued with one another until they were convinced that one faction was right, they would refer to that case as a precedent in subsequent discussions.

It is well known from numerous observational studies that nearly all teachers talk at least 50% of the time they spend with a class; many of them talk as much as 80% or 90% of the time. Arguments by students with one another are relatively rare. But if our experience is any criterion, the student arguments on clearly defined issues are what really produce change, while most of what the teacher says goes in one ear and out the other.

[The Dalton School's provision of time for doing assignments in school is omitted]

All of my examples dealt with student behavior that was not exceptional in any way. It was only the treatment that I regarded as progressive. What are some of the salient features of this treatment?

First, all the examples showed an ability and willingness to enter imaginatively into the world of children, to see things from their point of view, and then to suggest things to do that they would regard as sensible and interesting and that always had an educational purpose—an objective. I hope that rather than being heavy-handed, the educational purpose was just a nudge in the direction of learning something that they would come to value.

Second, the teachers in the examples were not hesitant about setting a task, inventing a game, devising a procedure, or even designing a schedule that the students did not and probably could not originate. Some progressive teachers talk as though nothing in education can be progressive unless it "comes from the students." Getting students into the act is indeed important but not necessarily at the point of devising things to do. Students are the ones who play the game but not necessarily the ones who invent it.[2]

Third, the teachers' role was limited to setting the stage, providing the necessary material, equipment, or time, and then acting for the most part as observer or referee. In the activities that are most easily recognized as progressive, you will probably agree that the teacher is not very conspicuous. When the disadvantaged first graders were playing with my "toys and games," for example, the teacher was not even looking at them. He was on the other side of the room trying to teach something to a group of eight or ten pupils.

I disagree with the doctrine that nothing is progressive unless the children think of it and then carry it out all by themselves. I prefer less sweeping conclusions. One would be that it is an unworthy ambition for a teacher to try to prove to his class that he is the brightest boy in the 10th grade. Another would be that it is not so much what the teacher does but what the students do that educates them. A third would be that a progressive teacher tends to contrive situations in which his students willingly carry on activities that educate because they seem interesting.

Critics have often charged that with progressive methods students do not learn anything, or at least not as much of the usual school subjects as do students taught by traditional methods. I can think of three reasons for this charge, which, by the way, is refuted by an enormous body of evidence.

First, many weak teachers who were having trouble with discipline in traditional schools excused their shortcomings on the ground that they were practicing "progressive education." Second, a few progressive schools during the thirties became infected with an early and incomplete version of Freudian theory and applied it to the education of normal children in a way that no psychiatrist would condone. Third, when the shortcomings of the average public school graduate became the subject of national concern after the Russians put Sputnik in orbit, people blamed it all on "progressive education," forgetting that this movement had never reached more than about 1 percent of our high schools. Progressive education was only a convenient scapegoat.

The Sputnik-inspired demands for superior education did not toll the death knell for progressive education. When my little daughter stepped on a crack to see whether a bear would come out, she was performing a far more scientific experiment than many carried out in traditional high schools. As long as there are teachers who are willing to understand children, progressive education will continue.

ENDNOTES

1. "You May Not Agree but Progressive Education Should Continue" in *Today's Education*, v58, March 1969, 12-19.
2. Diederich's criticism of one of his Ohio State lab school colleagues illustrates this point. "In his first meeting with a seventh grade class, he asked these students to think of something they would like to know about the outer world and report it in the next class. Two little boys, aged 12, brought in a handful of dirt from the schoolyard and asked, "How can we find out what this stuff is made of?" The teacher was flabbergasted and could not think of a way to begin and later he told other science teachers that "it would take these students at least four years to begin to realize what their question meant, let alone find an answer." To Diederich, "he was taking the question farther along than the students wanted to know. They would have been satisfied with a lower-level answer like "use a microscope and a soil-testing kit." Diederich to Levarie, January 29, 1989 (Diederich Family Papers).

CHAPTER 11

WHEN SHOULD HIGH SCHOOL BEGIN AND END?

(1954)[1]

When should high school start and end? There is nothing inevitable about the traditional four year span of grades nine through 12. Throughout the 19th century, high school could be a smattering of additional work offered in the same building as the common (or elementary) school—or it could be any stretch of time in a preparatory department on a college campus—or in a few cities it resembled what is typical today. When it began and when it was over was not sharply defined until the early 20th century, and even then educators wondered if the cut points before and after high school should be repositioned. For instance, a "6-4-4" alternative sparked much interest. The middle four years would finish students' basic education; after 10th grade they could take, free of charge, vocational or collegiate work. Graduate school or professional training could begin around age 20, the point where most undergraduates start their major.[2]

The 6-4-4 option rarely caught on. Splitting secondary education (defined as grades 7 through 12) into junior and senior high school was more popular than fusing grades 7-10. Few high schools wanted to lose their upperclassmen. Exceptional students in grades 11 and 12 have been accommodated within high school through Advanced Placement courses rather than accelerated to college, although that is possible for gifted students who skip grades or live in a district where "early college" is an option. And what would the beloved high school sports teams have

Paul Diederich and the Progressive American High School, pp. 137–144

suffered without the older students? Furthermore, most parents think 18 is the right age for high school graduation—sixteen might be the time for a driver's license or a part-time job, but sixteen seems too soon for college, especially away from home. Anyone brave enough to do it runs the risk of what Diederich's mentor, Ralph Tyler, encountered when he entered college "in short pants." When the 15 year old Tyler asked a girl for a date, "she looked at me and said, "With a freak like you? What would the girls in the dormitory say?"[3]

When Should High School Begin and End? (1954)

I amused myself last weekend designing a small high school for grades 7-8-9-10, complete with floor plans and a schedule. This dream school dramatizes certain possibilities that grow out of imminent needs for more schools, more colleges, more teachers, some saving of time to make room for military service, and to offset the alarming trend toward an unreasonably long apprenticeship before qualifying for professional and technical occupations. Knowing your [Henry Chauncey's] interest in acceleration, I thought you might be interested in a way to get it that might conceivably come off, since it is so well adapted to relieving the strain on educational facilities and teachers during a period of almost explosive expansion.

For example, in Princeton, we have barely finished doubling the capacity of our elementary school when we are told that it is already crowded, and some rooms will have to be added within a year or two. The high school is bursting at the seams, and a huge bond issue to increase its capacity will have to be passed immediately. We don't know where we are going to get teachers for all these new rooms, although we are probably more favored in this respect than other sections of the country. By the time the pupils in these new classrooms are ready to enter college, the colleges will be full to the brim, and many who ought to go to college will probably be turned away.

Under my plan, we would add nothing to Princeton's three existing elementary schools or the high school, but the three elementary schools would all service grades 1-6, and the high school would become (within five years) Princeton Community College, serving grades 11-14. We would build two new high schools along the lines of the appended plan to serve grades 7-10, absorbing two grades from the elementary schools and two from the high school. I would insist that we call them high schools, not junior high schools. My plan could easily be expanded to accommodate up to 600 pupils, but beyond that size I would prefer to add a third school rather than to increase the size of each unit.

Each high school should be large enough to accommodate at least two sections in each grade: one for able pupils who would be ready to enter any four year college at age 16 after ten years of schooling; the other for pupils who would either drop out and go to work at age 16 or else enter Princeton Community College for technical education for from two to four years. The College would not be restricted to the less able students, however; there would be a liberal arts and pre-professional program for very able pupils who either preferred a college in their home town or could not afford to go elsewhere. Thus the present organization into academic, commercial, and technical curricula would, in effect, be continued, but at a level two years higher.

Since there would be twice as many pupils who could qualify for education only to community college at age 16 as there would be potential entrants to Harvard, Yale, Smith, Vassar, and the like, there probably ought to be three sections in each grade in the high school rather than the two indicated in my plan: one for accelerants and two for regulars, or even one regular and one slow.

The curriculum for accelerants in the new high schools is conservative by my standards, designed to meet every reasonable demand of existing first rate colleges by the end of grade 10. The time saved comes from the elimination of two periods of duplication of effort in schools and colleges. Much of the work traditionally assigned to grades 7 and 8 in eight grade elementary schools is either review of what has gone before or a foretaste of what is to come after. I saw the effect of this on my son, who was greatly interested in math through grade 6 but lost all interest in grade 7. He said, "It's all review. We aren't learning anything new." He perked up again in grade 8 when he had a foretaste of algebra, and voluntarily did all the problems in every chapter. I know only too well what will happen next year when he has to do essentially the same problems over again in high school on the ground that "they don't really teach algebra in elementary school." Maybe not, but he and a great many of his friends managed to learn it. He is also learning the same American History he will have to learn twice again: once in the junior year of high school and once in the college freshman year. He is learning the English grammar that will be taken up from the beginning, as though he had never heard of it before, next year in high school. He even has a smattering of Latin and French that will be completely disregarded and taught from scratch in high school. While dull and uninterested students may need such repetition, the able and interested chafe under it and lose rather than gain from it. We shall have none of it in our program for accelerants. We start the first day in grade 7 with algebra and go on either to geometry or, as I would prefer, to elementary statistics (or possibly two years algebra, one geometry, one statistics). In all other fields the program for accelerants would be a genuine high school program from the beginning of grade 7.

At the other end, high schools and colleges have both been working toward a well rounded program of general education along the same lines: the one to grades 11-12, the other to grades 13-14. This year my daughter has a course in American history that is a good deal tougher than the one she will probably be required to take in college. Next year will come the Modern European History that she will undoubtedly meet again, not only in history courses but in literature, art, and music. Among other old friends she will recognize the introductory courses in literature and science as what she had in high school.

We shall try to avoid as much as possible of this duplication by leaving out course content that will probably be covered in college. We shall have no surveys of literature from the Beowulf to Thomas Hardy or from Cotton Mather to Hemingway. Instead, all students will be required to read an hour a day in a well-stocked library, with occasional discussions of what they have been reading. We shall probably not teach physics or chemistry as such, since they are stiff courses for most students below age 16 and far too likely to be taught again. Instead, we shall probably have two years of biology and then two years of general science. I should like to get in the biology first because grade 7 is our last chance to take up reproduction before pupils become self-conscious about it, and it leads very materially into genetics, and from that into evolution. The last two years in general science could have vocational applications for students who will be leaving us shortly, and should leave all with an understanding of scientific method and of scientific operations in everyday life.

While I suppose it is impossible to keep a social studies teacher from teaching history that will be taught over again ad nauseum, I shall do my best to make the central theme in grades 7-10 "How We Get The Things We Need"—from food, clothing, and shelter up to freedom, justice, beauty, and scientific knowledge. It should afford a bird's eye view of how the work of our society is organized and carried on, and a first hand acquaintance with the major groups of occupations as a basis for a wise vocational choice. I may have to get an enlightened Industrial Arts or Business Education teacher to teach it, since social studies people regularly pervert units of this kind into history. That is, they teach a unit on transportation in almost every grade now, have the students draw pictures of everything from an ox cart to a space ship, and imagine that students then understand the problems of transportation. Understanding the history of a problem is not necessarily the same as understanding the problem.

In language, the accelerants would acquire a reading knowledge of one modern language and spike it with enough related work on modern English grammar, semantics, linguistics, and philology to develop the same kind of awareness of and interest in our linguistic environment that geology develops with respect to our terrestrial environment. In math, as I said before, accelerants would probably get algebra, geometry, and elementary statistics; non-accelerants would probably take general math and elementary statistics. I propose putting in statistics because it is valuable for everybody, is a good way of maintaining computational skill and arithmetic reasoning, is suitable for this age range, and is unlikely to be taught later except to a handful of graduate students.

The principle behind this allocation of subject matter is that the years of puberty and early adolescence—ages 12 to 16—are years of vigorous exploration in all directions, while later adolescence—ages 16 to 20—is more appropriate for the systematization of knowledge. While this is an over-simplification, one simply cannot imagine very many wiggly 8th graders settling down to a survey of English literature from Beowulf to Thomas Hardy. I have some doubt that such a survey is wise at any age below 70, but people in grades 11-14 manage to survive two successive doses of it, and some even enjoy it.

One bit of evidence for the exploratory tendencies of the younger group is that, in the massive surveys of what the American people read, the greatest amount of book-reading is done by junior high school pupils. Reading declines thereafter with each increment in age and education. That is why I would reserve an hour a day for library reading during this period of growth. I have also set aside an hour a day for such activities as assemblies, student government, orchestra, chorus, play rehearsals, and clubs. Students not involved in these on any given day could go to the room of their choice and do homework, with the teacher present to help, or continue library reading, or go out and play games. I put in this period because there are certain highly educative activities that must necessarily draw upon talent from all four grades, especially in a small school. It is almost impossible to schedule such activities within the school day unless one period is set aside and kept free from all regular class and laboratory engagements.

The afternoon would be kept free for library reading and for creative work in the shops, the labs, and the studio. Possibly we should add some practice rooms above the lockers at the rear of the gym for pupils who wished to devote their creative work period to music. While this work would have to be organized to some degree, so that all would have a chance to use the facilities they needed, the organization should be kept to a minimum. Except for certain reserved periods, therefore, pupils would simply sign out in their homeroom for the rooms in which they wanted to work and report there at the specified time. Periodic checks would be made to be sure they got there.

It may be argued that I have gone too far in restricting regular class meetings in academic subjects to two hours a day. My reasons are, first, that two hours a day of sitting on hard chairs listening to other people talk are about all that most people can stand, and certainly all that youngsters at the onset of puberty ought to stand. Second, if there is to be a college preparatory emphasis in this program, teachers will be full of zeal to cover as much of their subjects as possible. If four teachers full of zeal are left free to assign homework each day, there will be too much homework. There is no way to prevent it, no matter what theoretical restrictions one imposes. Two assignments per school night are enough. Third, if we are getting these youngsters ready for college in minimum time, we may as well get them accustomed to a college-type schedule.

A fourth reason for scheduling different types of activities at separate times of day is the saving of space. Each room serves several functions. From 9 to 11 it is a regular academic classroom. From 11 to 12 it is a study hall or a meeting room for one of the student activities. At noon it is a lunch room; students go down the hall to the cafeteria, pick up their trays, and return to their own home room, with its familiar chairs and tables, to eat. There is no need to provide separate space for this function, to be used only once a day. From 1 to 3, the social studies and language classrooms, lined with shelves full of books, are used for library reading. There will be space for every pupil to sit in his own comfortable chair at a table an hour a day. I know of no high school with one room set apart as a library that could make such an offer. At the same time the two science classrooms become laboratories, one probably for biological experiments, the other for general science experiments. The two math classrooms, fitted with hand tools and few power tools, can be used as shops. Incidentally, both the art room and the laboratories need ready access to a shop; and while the first two are usually on the top floor and the third is in the basement, here they are side by side. The auditorium, with steeply rising tiers of seats permanently in place, can be used for assemblies, play and music rehearsals and performances, movies, public meetings, dances, and athletic events—with plenty of room for spectators. It reverses the common practice of moving in temporary seats on the floor of a gymnasium to convert it into an auditorium, with a small stage at one end. That practice is unsatisfactory because all seats are on the same level, and the smaller children can't see. Besides, it provides no space for spectators when the gymnasium is used for athletic events. In my plan, the gymnasium becomes the stage rather than the auditorium; the tiered seats are always in place, and can be used to watch either stage performances or athletic events. Thus, a small school with only 10 rooms and a gym can boast a huge library, shops, labs, studio, cafeteria, and an auditorium.

A fifth and somewhat unexpected reason for this type of schedule is that this arrangement would enable us to draw upon the talent of former teachers among our housewives, who would not be attracted by the rigors of full-time teaching with four or five classes, plus activities, per day, but who might well be attracted by a part-time appointment for two or three hours a day. The academic teachers could report at nine, teach two classes, remain for a third hour to help pupils who dropped in to study, and go home at noon. Perhaps one day a week they would supervise some student activity during the third hour. Some of them might be persuaded to stay for lunch, simply to keep order, while some of the afternoon teachers might find it possible to begin their work by supervising lunch for those academic teachers who had to leave. In the afternoon a former librarian or English teacher could supervise the library reading, while others with appropriate backgrounds could supervise work in the shops, the labs, and the studio. Only the work in science would bear very much relationship to what had gone on in the morning, and the lab supervisors could easily keep in touch with it. Two music teachers, one for orchestra and the other for chorus, would come in only an hour a day, from eleven to twelve, and probably not more than four days a week, to keep one day open for assemblies. The dramatics coach would have a similar appointment. At three all pupils would go outdoors to play games, do woodcrafts, or work in the school garden, and a third shift of supervisors would take over—the kind of people who now serve on community playgrounds.

By so spreading the work load, no one would have more than three hours a day on duty, and only two of these would be at all rigorous. I should think that even a sensitive soul who would recoil in horror from full time teaching in a typical public school would find such an assignment pleasant. There would still be plenty of time for housekeeping. The only requirement would be that their children should be old enough to attend school. If they got sick and required care, it should not be difficult to get a substitute for as little time as three hours a day.

Of course, if a professional teacher wishes to remain throughout the day and even supervise some of the sports, he would be welcomed and given proportionate compensation. I should think that the full-time service would be an advantage only in science, so that the laboratory work could be integrated very closely with the course. In the other fields I doubt that it would make any difference.

Note also in the proposed schedule that it would be possible for the same teacher to teach his subject to all four grades, thereby making possible a continuity that is not likely to be achieved when we pass a group from one teacher to another. A science teacher, for example, would teach grade 9 MWF and grade 10 TuTh at nine a.m.; grade 7 MWF and grade 8 TuTh at ten a.m. I think the argument for continuity outweighs the danger of getting stuck with a poor teacher for four years. The poor teacher can be fired, but achieving continuity is not easy.

ENDNOTES

1. "A high school for grades 7 through 10" in Box 6, Folder 54, Henry Chauncey Papers, ETS Archives.
2. Robert Orrill, "Grades 11-14: The Heartland or Wasteland of American Education?" in Michael Johanek, ed., *A Faithful Mirror: Reflections on the College Board and Education in America* (New York: College Entrance Examination Board, 2001), 81-101.
3. Ralph W. Tyler, "Education: Curriculum Development and Evaluation" oral history conducted by Malca Chall, Bancroft Library, University of California, Berkeley, 1987, 8.

CHAPTER 12

A SEAMLESS EIGHT YEAR LIBERAL ARTS EDUCATION

(1958)[1]

Henry Holmes, the Dean of the Harvard Graduate School of Education when Diederich was there, described the shift from high school to college as "more or less convenient and justifiable socially and psychologically"—he was thinking about the emotional well-being of youth—"but quite inconvenient and unjustifiable, indeed quite accidental, from the standpoint of education."[2] Despite strenuous efforts in the early 20th century to define the appropriate work of a legitimate high school and a bona fide college, the end of secondary school and the start of higher education still overlapped . For instance, the difference between a strong 12th grade American history course and the college survey of the same subject was hard to see. For weak students, the review might be helpful; for strong students, there were less admirable benefits: "College survey courses in American history are being elected by average students from good independent and public schools who are looking for a "free ride" and even by abler students anxious to hold on to scholarships or to fatten their academic averages" (as the editor of this book did in his freshman year at Yale, taking an easy French course in an otherwise exhausting year).[3]

In the 1950s, the new Advanced Placement program promised to reduce duplication. Diligent high school students could take three hour examinations to demonstrate they had mastered college-level material. There were no certainties and many ifs: if the high school offered AP ... if the student took the AP exam after taking the

---

Paul Diederich and the Progressive American High School, pp. 145–154 course … if the student did well on the exam (usually part or all essay, graded 1 to 5) … if the college granted course credits or course exemptions at all (and if so, for what grade?). What was not in doubt was the content of the course—each AP test was tied to a published syllabus. Students and teachers knew the topics and skills that the AP exams would assess.[4]

AP notwithstanding, grades 11 through 14 were usually less coherent than the first two years of high school and the last two years of college. With basic skills in 9th and 10th grade and an academic major for college juniors and seniors, what lay between? With so many opportunities to take electives and so little consensus on liberal education, linear progression was less common than "shreds, patches, impulses, without thoroughness, logic or coherence," in the words of Abraham Flexner.[5] In some nations, college encompassed those four years. That has rarely been the case here, apart from a few experimental colleges and small programs for the very gifted. What we have instead is exposure to many fields, with little or no effort to tie them together. The burden is on the student to see if and how the various courses connect. The upshot is what one former College Board officer called a "wasteland" rather than the "heartland" college might have been.[6] In Diederich's vision of a seamless education, there is much less choice among courses—students could choose _within_ a course how far to extend themselves—in order to reduce the curricular sprawl that jeopardizes intellectual coherence. He would keep students together for eight years, as several European nations did, thus reducing the transitions that foster the sort of duplication he had seen in his children's education. Moreover, his school is for the gifted. With those three major changes—less choice, less segmentation, and more attention to the brightest—Diederich believed that a coherent liberal arts education by age 20 was possible.

A Seamless Eight Year Liberal Arts Education (1958)

The entire span of education between grades 7 and 14 needs overhauling in order to reduce duplication of effort and lost motion and thereby get closer to a liberal education in those eight years than we do at present. There is obvious duplication between grades 11-12 in good modern high schools and grades 13-14 in college. Grades 11-12 attempt to round off and polish the student's education in the humanities, social studies, and science, usually with the addition of courses in foreign languages and mathematics. Grades 13-14 attempt to "introduce" the student to those fields, as though he had never heard of them before.

The survey of American literature commonly offered in grade 11 and the survey of European literature in grade 12 are usually followed by a similar survey in either the freshmen or sophomore year in college. It differs chiefly in being reduced to one year in length, thereby requiring the books to be read at a faster clip. American history, modern European history, and Problems of Democracy in high school are followed immediately by a course in college that attempts to combine all three, ignoring the fact that all three have previously been taught at greater length and in greater detail than is possible in a one-year introductory course in college. Courses in biology, physics, and chemistry, or an integrated course in the physical sciences, are followed immediately by a one-year introductory course in these areas. Protests of students that they have already studied these subjects are usually brushed aside with the remark that the high schools do not *really* teach these subjects; take the college course and then you will know something about them.

Even when colleges give placement tests, purporting to pass students to a more advanced course if they already know the elementary course, it is notorious that the examinations are geared so closely to their own introductory courses that it is doubtful whether a student who had had courses with similar titles in any other institution could pass them. Pressey, in his monograph on acceleration, notes that exemption examinations are often harder and are marked more severely than the course from which exemption is claimed.[7] College teachers feel that their particular version of American history, or the physical sciences, or American and European literature, is indispensable; hence they "take no chances" when considering students for exemption, even though the students have what anyone else would regard as adequate basic knowledge in these fields.

It is not so commonly recognized that there is also great duplication of effort in grades 7-8-9. Grade 7 is traditionally devoted to a review of what has been taught up to that point, so that students who have a cumulative debit in their reading, writing, and arithmetic skills and in their knowledge of social studies and science may have a chance to catch up. A large part of grade 8 is devoted to a foretaste of what high school will be like. Students commonly have a half year of baby algebra, some introductory work in foreign languages, and work in composition and literature that is intended to anticipate the work of grade 9. The primary consideration is what the ninth grade teachers will think of those students; hence the eighth grade teachers cover as much of the work of grade 9 as possible. This is called "easing the transition." Ninth grade teachers regularly despise and ignore this special preparation, partly because some students from the "sending districts" have not had it, partly because it is superficial, designed to create a good impression rather than yield genuine mastery, and partly because all teachers tend to scorn the teaching of any part of their subjects in a lower school—just as college teachers reject all that has been taught in the humanities, social studies, and science in high school. If a student protests, they can point to tests that show he has not mastered this material, but tests at any point in education would show that most students have not mastered the material just covered, at least from the standpoint of the teacher who proposes to teach it over again.

The result is not merely loss of time but loss of momentum and interest. This is well illustrated in the case of my own son [Diederich repeats the algebra anecdote that is in the previous chapter] The same thing will happen again between grades 11-12 and grades 13-14. He has just had an excellent two year course in American history under a gifted teacher who uses nothing but college texts and whose research papers often call for reference to 20 or 30 books. His college will probably refuse to believe that he knows anything about American history, and will prove it if need be by asking him some questions that only a quiz champion could answer without special preparation. Then he will be required to loaf through a baby course in the same subject, with the result that he will lose all interest in American history and hope never to have to go through it again. He has already been through it two or three times. He still does not "know" it, but who ever does?[8]

Robert Maynard Hutchins did a great deal to overcome the duplication between grades 11-12 and grades 13-14 by combining them at the University of Chicago into a single cohesive four year unit. There was real continuity from grade to grade. He also installed an extensive program of placement tests which purported to take account of anything the student had learned previously. I do not believe they were entirely successful for that purpose because they were built out of portions of comprehensive examinations for University of Chicago courses. Hence it did not avail a student if he had just had a thorough course in the standard variety of American history; he had to face an examination designed for a course that might have more appropriately been called "Great Debates in American History," for which the usual high school course affords little preparation. Granted that this was a valuable course, but is it not possible that a student who had just taken a more orthodox approach to American history might have had enough for purposes of citizenship? Or that exemption from this course and admission to a more advanced course in World History might have been more profitable? However that may be, entering students for the most part could not pass the Social Sciences Placement Test, and hence had to take American history over again from a slightly different point of view.

The same thing happened in the natural sciences. Those who had just had an orthodox course in biology had to take an examination designed for a biology course that was unified around just three problems: the circulation of the blood, evolution, and heredity, including all the steps and crucial experiments that led to the present state of knowledge. Most biology teachers would regard it not as a course in biology but as a course in scientific method. Again, it was an extremely valuable course, but is it not possible that an orthodox course in grade 10 might be enough? Students who had just finished an orthodox biology course in high school could not pass the placement test.[9]

Apart from this failure to latch on to what the student already knew in a more traditional fashion than Chicago would accept, the University of Chicago bandwagon failed to attract a procession for two main reasons. Parents would not send their children away to college in grade 11, when they still had two years of free public education ahead of them in their own communities, so that most students entered in grade 13 and hence suffered all the repetition of introductory work of which I have been complaining. Graduate schools in other institutions, for the most part, refused to recognize the Chicago A.B. as the equivalent of a full-fledged A.B., regardless of the evidence on standardized tests that Chicago sophomores knew more than the average senior in other colleges.

Since the labor of constructing an integrated eight year program in each field will be great, including the production of many new teaching materials and tests, I recommend that no teacher have more than two classes a day to teach, although occasionally he might have to spend two additional periods observing or helping with his colleague's classes. I assume about two hours of preparation for each hour of teaching. One can be creative for two periods a day, but a daily round of four classes will soon reduce any teacher to doing what has always been done—teaching out of a standard textbook and following a standard syllabus.

A corollary is that classes will meet only twice a week: either on Tuesday and Thursday or on Wednesday and Friday. Monday morning will be devoted to a double period "core course" for all students on the theme, "How We Get the Things We Need"—from food, clothing and shelter up to higher needs such as freedom, justice, security, beauty, scientific knowledge, and education. Monday afternoon will usually be devoted to trips connected either with the core course or with any other course that needs them, to occasional short term electives, to educational movies, or to extra help on individual projects. If nothing else is scheduled on any given Monday, it may be devoted to study and library reading. If two periods a week seem inadequate, remember that it will be two periods a week for *eight years* in each of the major fields commonly included in liberal education, and that many colleges get along handsomely on two periods a week. Moreover, the two periods in English will be supplemented by two periods of library reading under supervision, and the two periods of science will be supplemented by two periods of laboratory work. Art, music, shop work, home economics, and the like will be scheduled outside the time allotted to academic subjects. The present plan does not contemplate any regular provision for full length electives; everybody will take English, social studies, science, mathematics, and foreign language for eight years, although a few students may be excused from any one of these subjects if it becomes perfectly clear that there is no further profit in it for them. Each class will be expected to make regular provision for the different interests and talents of its members. This can be done much more extensively than is commonly realized. In my Latin classes, for example, no student read exactly the same works as any other student.

A further corollary is that each student will have homework for only two subjects two nights a week and for three subjects on another two. Preparing for four "solid" subjects every night leads to a plethora of homework that students cannot possibly complete; hence they take refuge in neglect, bluffing, copying, and the like, which gives them a bad conscience and leaves them in a continuous state of tension. It seems impossible to restrain zealous teachers from assigning too much homework; hence we shall schedule only two or three solid subjects per day. The rest of the day, as the schedule shows, will be spent in low pressure, non-homework activities such as music, art, shop, laboratory work, home economics, library reading, student activities, and sports. There will be no homework for the core courses on Monday; hence there will be no homework Friday evening or over the weekend. It is my firm conviction, after seeing two children through high school and one through college, that the uncoordinated demands of four teachers per day pile up a fantastic amount of homework that can only be half done unless the student forgets about recreation and reading for pleasure and wears himself to the bone.[10]

It follows from what has been said that the present plan contemplates a period of education under the same roof comparable in length to the German *gymnasium*, the French *lycée*, and the English public school, and that, like them, it is intended only for superior students who will almost certainly go to college, and many to graduate and professional schools. This raises many questions of democracy in education and of selecting students at the tender age of 12 for so rigorous a program. As for democracy, the program will be free, local, and open to all classes—to anyone who can demonstrate his fitness for it by a series of the best intelligence tests and by his previous school record. There is no question that we can select students for such a program as well at age 12 as we can at age 16, when egalitarian "democracy" falters somewhat and we begin selecting students for college. If the program proves unsuitable for any student, or if he wants to learn a trade, he can transfer at any time to any other high school or college. Exceptional students from other schools who have a strong interest and background in liberal education can also transfer into the program at any time up to grade 13. Initially they may lose a year, but since the program ends with grade 14, they will still be a year ahead. These experimental schools would not be the only route to the professions or to public service, as the counterparts are in Europe. A student could get there equally well through the regular channels, two years later. Hence we do not believe that these schools would commit a student unalterably to a path in life at age 12, nor would they exclude anyone else from that path. They would simply offer exceptional opportunities to exceptional pupils, and I see nothing undemocratic in that.

The dangers in the European plan of education for superior students must be honestly faced, and then weighed against possible advantages. When connected with a highly structured class system and fortified by high tuition fees and other charges, it can be an undemocratic element in society, but I do not think that danger would attach to schools that were free, local, and open to any student of superior ability. There has been no such complaint against the Bronx High School of Science nor against other public schools for superior students in New York City. In a democratic society these students will remain democratic. We shall only put their talents to work two years earlier than normal, and save not only the two years but the loss of momentum and interest that comes of making superior students repeat the same work over and over again, for the sake of those who did not get it the first time.

As for the advantages of the European plan of education, unprejudiced observers agree that the products of the gymnasium, the lycée, and the public school are at least two years ahead of our students in the disciplines of liberal education, and that many attain a degree of cultivation that is rarely found in America. We must remember that our European cousins have been in this business of liberal education for a long time, and that their plan of having a long span of education between ages 12 and 20 on the same campus must have had a good deal to recommend it or it would not have been practiced in so many countries over so long a period of time. It certainly must have the effect of reducing duplication of effort and lost motion, for people on the same faculty will know what has been taught before, will be obliged to respect it, and will not ordinarily attempt to teach it over again. There is no need for us to emulate the excessive pressure upon students of the French and German schools. Their students probably know a great deal more than is good for them. We shall dispense knowledge at a rate that students can healthily absorb and leave a great deal of time in the daily schedule for non-bookish activities that are demonstrably good for students.[11]

After all the discussion of acceleration in recent years, it seems unnecessary to point out again that the span of graduate and professional training is already too long to permit superior students to establish a home and family and enter upon a career at a biologically reasonable age, and that we keep them at schoolboy tasks during what could be the most creative and productive period of their lives.[12] We have also heard more than enough about the interruption of two years imposed by military service and about the pressing need for high-level manpower. We are impressed at the moment by the need for keeping up with the Russians, for whom the period of basic education is ten years, followed by college or university training. Furthermore, the oncoming surge in enrollment is causing almost every community in the land to erect new high schools, and many to establish community colleges. The latter trend will probably accelerate after 1965 when the established colleges will find it almost impossible to accommodate all who desire higher education and are qualified for it. While they are building their new schools, some of these communities might as well relieve some of the pressure by erecting the simple and inexpensive building proposed in this report. It would take care of both high school and college training for superior students, and thereby leave more space in the regular junior highs, senior highs, and junior colleges. The junior high school made its way into the educational system, in part, for the same reasons. There were many theoretical arguments in its favor, but the practical reason was that the elementary schools were overcrowded, the high schools were overcrowded, and the problem was whether to build more elementary and high schools or to build junior highs that would take part of the load off both. The latter proved to be the more economical solution. In the same way, a new building that can take care of a sizable fraction of the students between 12 and 20 may leave enough room in the regular schools to get along for many years, and in addition provide college training for many students who might not be able to afford it outside the local community.

In its initial stages, the school should be subsidized by a foundation until it has time to work out a curriculum of demonstrated superiority for gifted students. Putting regular teachers into such buildings and having them teach a regular load of four or five classes a day would make it absolutely certain that no new, integrated, eight year curriculum would emerge. We must give these communities extra funds to enable them to hire gifted, creative teachers and scholars, permit them to teach only two classes a day, and bring in whatever consultants are necessary to work out a new curriculum that will go beyond anything that schools and colleges now provide in the basic fields of study. We want all these students to know mathematics to the point at which they can understand Einstein on the theory of relativity, science to the point at which they can follow new developments in nuclear physics, literature to the point at which they can appreciate the later works of Yeats and Eliot, and so on. The aid of a testing service with a strong research branch, such as ETS, should be enlisted in order to provide a continuous record of what was learned under various curricular and instructional arrangements. Heretofore the integration of school and college has been approached by having distinguished committees meet and recommend what the schools and colleges should do.[13] It will be a far different matter to have outstanding school and college teachers working together in pairs under the same roof, keeping in touch from day to day with what one another is doing, gradually working out an eight year program in which there is only the minimum repetition necessary for review, and being tested to find out which plans work better than others. The syllabi, materials, and tests prepared by and for these teachers should gradually be released as they prove their worth so that other schools may take advantage of a curriculum from which almost all non-essentials and dead wood have been eliminated, and which carries liberal education to a higher point than is commonly attained today.

ENDNOTES

1. "School and College" [1958] in Henry Chauncey Papers, Box 6, Folder 54, ETS Archives.
2. "The Colleges Undermine Themselves: An Indictment of the Admissions System" in *The Educational Record*, January 1933, v14, n1, 97.
3. *General Education in School and College* (Cambridge: Harvard University Press, 1952), 71. Funded by the Ford Foundation, the committee members who wrote this book examined students from Andover, Exeter and Lawrenceville who attended Harvard, Princeton, or Yale.
4. Arthur G. Powell, *Lessons from Privilege: The American Prep School Tradition* (Cambridge: Harvard University Press, 1996), Ch. 6.
5. Abraham Flexner, *The American College* (New York: The Century Company, 1908), 128.
6. Robert Orrill, "Grades 11-14: The Heartland or Wasteland of American Education?" in Michael C. Johanek, ed., *A Faithful Mirror: Reflections on the College Board and Education in America* (New York: College Entrance Examination Board, 2001), 81-101.
7. Sidney L. Pressey, *Educational Acceleration: Appraisals and Basic Problems* (Columbus: Ohio State University Press, 1949).
8. Diederich recalled that in his Holy Cross chemistry class, he repeated the same experiments he did in high schools. Diederich to Henry Chauncey, January 26, 1954 (Chauncey Papers, Box 6, Folder 54, ETS).
9. Described at length in Joseph J. Schwab, "The Natural Sciences" in *The Idea and Practice of General Education* (Chicago: University of Chicago Press, 1950, 1992), 239-265.
10. Abolishing or reducing homework appealed to many educators in the early 20th century; by the 1950s, recasting homework as projects with little or no book-work (visiting museums, for instance) was popular. See Brian Gill and Steven Schlossman, "'A Sin against Childhood': Progressive Education and the Crusade to Abolish Homework, 1897-1941" in *American Journal of Education*, November 1996, v105, n1, 27-66 and Gill and Schlossman, "The Lost Cause of Homework Reform" in *American Journal of Education*, November 2000, v109, n1, 27-62.

11. In 1994 Diederich revisited this point: "I sometimes think that students in the lycée and gymnasium are fantastically over-educated. At the most social and fun loving period of their lives, they are overloaded with material of little practical, intellectual or entertainment value to the detriment of their health, social skills, and even appetite for further learning. Why try to cram everything worth knowing into the years just before the scarce and coveted entrance to a [European] university? If their zest for learning is not killed by getting too much too early, it can be spread over a lifetime. These teachers' urge to unload everything that they know on a captive audience reminds me of a little boy who used to visit Marjory [a beloved friend] almost every day, and one day told her at length of an expected visit by an aunt and uncle with a very large family, which put his parents to wits' end to find beds for all of them. "Why are you telling me all this?" Marjory asked. He looked astonished and answered, "Why, if I didn't tell you, you wouldn't *know!*" Sometimes I wonder whether those teachers in the lycée or gymnasium have any better reason than this." Diederich to Siegmund Levarie, February 7, 1994 (Diederich Family Papers).
12. A young lawyer or doctor "can hardly begin to support himself before he is twenty-seven years old," Harvard President Charles Eliot lamented in 1888. "Some remedy is urgently demanded," he argued, and he did not have in mind what many professionals at that time did: they skipped college and went directly from high school to law or medical school. Charles William Eliot, *Educational Reform* (New York: Arno Press reprint, 1969), 152.
13. For an overview, see John A. Valentine, *The College Board and the School Curriculum* (New York: College Entrance Examination Board, 1987).

CHAPTER 13

CUTTING CLASS SIZE BY HALF
(1960)[1]

Too few teachers, many more students, not enough space: Diederich foresaw huge challenges for secondary and higher education in the 1960s. The post-war "baby boom" ensured that high schools enrollments would soar, and the percentage of graduates who entered college would continue to climb. The impending expansion would overwhelm English teachers, Diederich feared. They would lack the time to correct students papers even though good writing would be the key to survival in college. It would be impossible to reduce the average load to 100 students per English teacher, as James Conant recommended. Diederich recalled what Benjamin Willis, superintendent of the Chicago schools, had told him: "That would cost Chicago an additional two million a year. If I had two million, I couldn't get that many additional qualified teachers. And if I could get the teachers, I wouldn't have the classrooms to put them in."[2]

   The mothers who caused the problem should also solve it, Diederich liked to quip. College educated housewives could correct papers for ten hours each week. With a Ford Foundation grant, Diederich and ETS pioneered that "lay reader" initiative in 16 districts. So many women applied that only one in six was hired.
   In this paper, he relies on housewives to reorganize high school English. He splits the weekly schedule into four parts—free reading, self-correcting homework, analysis of papers, and discussion of literature. For three of the periods, students will be on their own, reading independently and using teaching machines to check their vocabulary, grammar, spelling, and punctuation. With the housewives over-

---

Paul Diederich and the Progressive American High School, pp. 155–162
Copyright © 2014 by Information Age Publishing
All rights of reproduction in any form reserved.

seeing those three periods, teachers would focus on the two periods devoted to books and papers (which the housewives would read and correct). Teachers would have to sharpen their skills to use the time wisely, Diederich acknowledged. His organizational changes would not guarantee better instruction, but they might take away the large class size excuse for dreary instruction.

Cutting Class Size by Half (1960)

The normal load of a high school English teacher is now about 170 students a day: five classes with more than thirty students in each class. That is not [just] a statistic: it is an expectation. Administrators can now count on the fact that English teachers in the larger high schools will take that number of students per day without actually lying down on the floor and screaming. By 1965 the load will almost certainly be 200 students a day. By that year the high school population will be half again as large as it was in 1958. When you consider how long it took to build the classrooms and provide the teachers we had in 1958, you can estimate the chances of getting half again as many by 1965.

Unless something drastic is done about it, these students will write, on the average, not more than four papers a year. It takes thirty-three hours to grade and correct 200 papers at the best rate that good teachers are able to maintain. If these teachers were foolish enough to assign a paper a week, they would have to read papers every school night from nine until midnight, plus nine hours on Saturday and nine hours on Sunday. Obviously teachers are not that foolish. Moreover, class discussion of books and student papers is almost impossible, since each student gets a chance to say something, on the average, about once every two days. What he says is usually a brief reply to a teacher's question. Arguments of students with one another are about as rare as they are in church.

College Pressures

At the same time, colleges are faced with the alternatives of either doubling both plant and staff by 1970 or rejecting a far greater proportion of those seeking higher education than they do now. Since the former is impossible, the latter is inevitable.[3] Unfortunately for English teachers, the easiest and most defensible way to get rid of any surplus that the colleges cannot accommodate is to reject or flunk out those who stand in the lower part of the distribution in verbal skills. Good tests of the verbal skills associated with reading and writing usually yield higher correlations with grade-point averages in college than any other tests thus far devised. The more selective colleges can give such tests for admission and reject those whose verbal skills are below par. Other colleges are following the lead of the University of Illinois in abolishing their remedial English courses, putting everyone into the regular course, and flunking out those who cannot meet its standards. By one device or another, at least a quarter and possibly a third of those seeking higher education will be rejected or flunked out on the ground that they cannot read or write at the level required by college work.

When parents are told that their children cannot have the opportunities that higher education affords because they are poor in English, they will descend on the School Board in large numbers and demand that something be done. The Board might well reply that the parents should have thought about this back in the forties when they were having children at such a reckless rate, but since Board members do not ordinarily take such a long view of causes and effects, they will probably storm into the high school and demand that the English teachers crack down. That stirs the adrenalin but solves no problems. "Cracking down" would accomplish nothing, but even if everyone's skill in reading and writing were suddenly doubled, the cutting point would simply move up. The lowest quarter or third in verbal skills would still not get a college education because the colleges will not have room for them.

All that high school English teachers can do in such a situation is to increase the chances that the *right* quarter or third are rejected—those who *cannot* learn to read or write at the levels that will be demanded by colleges rather than those who could have learned but whose overcrowded and badly taught English classes did not give them a reasonable chance.

At the same time, they must take steps to preserve their own sanity during the period of fantastic overcrowding that lies ahead. We do not care whether they crack down, but we do care whether they crack up. Teaching five classes a day with at least 40 students in each class is a load that would be regarded as cruel and inhuman even by a Roman galley slave. Unless drastic action is taken, about all that anyone will be able to do in high school English during the next ten years will be to try desperately to maintain order. Good teaching will be out of the question, except the little that can be done by the lecture method, either directly or on television. Unfortunately, no one has yet learned to read or write by attending lectures.

The Rutgers Plan

This was the problem that was faced and solved (in principle) by 63 English teachers who received Ford Foundation fellowships to attend a six week workshop on the present crisis in English during the 1959 summer session at Rutgers University. They evolved a plan whereby:

—No high school English teacher need ever meet more than 25 students at a time except by his own choice.

158 Cutting Class Size by Half (1960)

—Every high school English teacher may have one day a week completely free of class duties to see students who are either so far ahead or so far behind that they require individual attention.

—English classes will ordinarily meet two days a week; one for class discussion of books that have been read in common, the other for class discussion of student papers.

—Two days a week will be devoted to "free reading," probably in groups of over 200 students in temporary buildings designed for that purpose, directed by teams of specially qualified college-educated housewives who will be on duty not more than three hours a day at two to three dollars an hour.

—One day a week will be devoted to a test and follow-up of "self-correcting homework" (exercises that will tell the student whether he was right or wrong after each response). This will take care of drill on "fundamentals," and will probably be conducted in groups of 40 to 50 students by other specially qualified college-educated housewives("technicians") who will also be on part-time duty at two to three dollars an hour (This is the day on which the English teacher will be free to see students who need individual attention).

—A paper will ordinarily be assigned every two weeks, but three out of every four assignments will be graded and corrected by a reader (a third specially qualified college-educated housewife who will read the papers at home and receive about 25 cents per paper). The reader will read about 12 papers a year from each student while the teacher will read four and check enough of the others to keep in touch with the progress of the class.

[details about classroom space omitted]

Initiating the Plan

Each of the classes normally assigned to each teacher would simply be split into two sections, A and B, on any basis that the teacher fancied. Section A would have its class discussion of books and papers Mondays and Wednesdays while Section B would have its class discussion Tuesdays and Thursdays while Section A had "free reading." On Friday both sections would report to the "Skinner Room" (named after the inventor of "teaching machines") for a test on the self-correcting homework assigned for the week and for class discussion of items that gave trouble. On this day the English teacher would be free to see students who needed individual attention. Each teacher would have a different "conference day" so that the "Skinner Room" could be kept busy throughout the week, and the schedule of his sections would be changed accordingly. For example, if a teacher had his conference day on Wednesday, he could teach Section A Mondays and Thursdays, Section B Tuesdays and Fridays. If a student missed a test on account of a conference, he could make it up during any free period, since the same tests would be offered several times a day.

Incidentally, this separation of drill on "fundamentals" from class discussion of books and papers would permit students to work on different levels in "fundamentals" and in literature. A student who was studying Gertrude Stein in his literature class might still be assigned to a section that was drilling on subject and verb that fifth day of the week. After a session with Gertrude Stein, he might need it.

[Section on free reading omitted—duplicates the information in Chapter 8]

Self-Correcting Homework

The next great technological revolution in education is almost certain to be the adaptation of drill on "fundamentals" in all subjects to the kinds of "programmed exercises with immediate feedback" developed by Professor B.F. Skinner of Harvard. He uses an actual machine that presents questions, provides a space to write in answers, and then shows the student immediately whether he was right or wrong; and, if wrong, what was right. This is extremely effective.[4] Students cannot help learning the stuff once and for all, and teachers do not have to correct the papers. The only hitch is that both the machines and the exercises are expensive; they cannot be taken home for use with homework; and they do not lend themselves to class discussion. The basic idea, however, can be adapted to forms of exercises that can be run off on any ditto or mimeograph machine or printed in paperback booklets.[5] These can be used as homework with only a blank sheet of paper or cardboard to cover up the correct answer until the student has given his own. As the simplest possible example, take the following items on the word abstruse:

Directions: Cover everything below the sentence on which you are working with a sheet of paper. Mark each sentence R is it is right and W if it is wrong. The correct answer is on the line below:

1.	Nuclear physics is a very abstruse subject	
2.	His sermons were too abstruse for his poor parishioners to follow.	R
3.	He was the most abstruse specimen of humanity I have ever seen.	R
4.	Abstruse subjects are not appropriate for elementary schools.	W
5.	I do not think he was wicked; he was only abstruse.	R
6.	He had read only an abstruse, not the original article.	W

7.	His explanation of space-curvature was too abstruse for me.	W
8.	He could explain an abstruse theory in very simple terms.	R
9.	*Abstruse:* 1—mathematical; 2—degenerate; 3—shortened account	R
	4—hard to understand 5—hard to believe	
	Now write a sentence of your own using this word correctly	4

You may wonder why the student does not cheat—that is, merely copy the correct answers without bothering to read the sentences. He will get no credit for his score on the exercise and will not even be asked to turn it in. Instead, after he has studied about twenty words in this fashion, he will report to the "Skinner Room" for a test in which each word is used correctly or incorrectly in a single sentence that has not appeared in the exercise. He will mark these sentences R or W with no right answers anywhere in sight. Then students will trade papers and score them while the "technician" reads the correct answers aloud. These scores will count in the record and affect the student's grade. Whenever a student marks an answer "wrong" he will hold up his hand. The "technician" will count and record the number of hands opposite each item in her copy of the test. When the scoring is finished, she will lead a discussion of items that more than 10% of the students missed—chiefly by calling on students to defend their answers and on other students to reply. After that, she will introduce the material that is to be studied as homework in this fashion in the following week.

It should be obvious that this sort of test and follow-up of work on programmed exercises can be handled by any college-educated housewife who has been tested for thorough knowledge of English fundamentals and interviewed to make sure that she is fanatical about them. It would be hard to devise an easier teaching assignment for a beginner. If a school insists, this work may be handled by teachers, but that would keep them from having one day a week free of class duties to see students who require individual attention. When every teacher is responsible for the development in English of about 200 students, the true professionals will insist on that one day a week to catch those who have strayed from the flock—especially those who have strayed ahead.

It is sad but true, however, that many English teachers do not know anything but the fundamentals and would not know what to do with the conference day if they had it. In such cases, it might be wise for the school to have them attend to the drill on fundamentals and to have some of the housewives (especially former teachers) see the students who need special help. In extreme cases, a teacher might be assigned full-time to drill on fundamentals and have no other teaching duties. It should be understood, however, that this work carries the status of "technician" rather than that of "teacher." Unfortunately, that is the true status of far too many English teachers today.

Class Discussion of Books and Papers

Oddly enough, the one feature of the Rutgers Plan that is least certain to work well is the two days a week that are to be devoted to class discussion of books and student papers. Most high school English teachers handle these two basic professional tasks very badly, if they ever get around to them at all. The typical class period in English is devoted to some point of grammar that has been taught over and over again, and that could be handled far better in half the time by a nonprofessional with the aid of self-correcting exercises programmed by experts.

When teachers finally get around to books, most of them are fairly competent with the introduction and footnotes—anything that critics, editors, and historians have said *about* the book—but they have few thought-provoking questions to ask about what the book itself says. What is going on in the first paragraph? Was that a good place to start? At what other points might the author have started? Why do you think he chose this one? Does the first paragraph suggest in any way what the whole book is about? What do you know at the end of the first paragraph that you need to know at any later point? Such questions as these are rarely asked. More often, teachers fish for their pet clichés.

When it comes to the discussion of student papers, about all that the average teacher can think of doing is to have some of the students read their papers aloud and ask others to comment and criticize. That is a foolish and impossible demand. Few experienced teachers could pick out the good and bad things in a paper after hearing it read aloud once. Students can only hazard a few generalities. What ought to be done is to ditto copies of three or four papers (without names) of different levels of merit on each assignment. Distribute them well in advance of the discussion and have students study them as homework, grade them, and insert accolades, corrections, and suggestions for improvement between lines and in the margins. Then, when they come to class, the students can take up each paper line by line or paragraph by paragraph and decide what, if anything, needs to be done about it.

The Rutgers Plan will enforce attention to these two primary tasks of the professional English teacher. It will leave him with too little time to do anything else (except his conferences once a week with students who need special help), and it will brand much of what he has been doing as "technicians' work." It is hoped that the other features of the plan will not become the focus of attention. They are intended chiefly to clear the less difficult tasks out of his way and to give the professional teacher small enough groups so that he can really increase competence in reading and writing.

Some of the other subjects can be properly taught to huge classes, but not English. Students have to argue with one another over what a passage means, or how a paper can be improved. The teacher has to act chiefly as catalyst and moderator. If he can do that successfully, more of his students will get into college and stay there. Of those who have been drilled five days a week in large classes on subject and verb, a larger fraction will not.

ENDNOTES

1. "The Rutgers Plan for Cutting Class Size in Two" in *The English Journal*, v49, n4, April 1960, 229-236.
2. Diederich to Levarie, December 16, 1987 (Diederich Family Papers).
3. Diederich's predictions were too pessimistic. The prosperity of the late 1950s and 1960s paid for more schools and teachers, especially in the rapidly growing suburbs. The expansion of state universities, branch campuses, and community colleges kept pace with rising enrollments in higher education.
4. Many students found the use of Skinner's machines repetitive and monotonous, with brighter students convinced they were designed for the weakest learners. Martha Casas, "The History Surrounding the Use of Skinnerian Teaching Machines and Programmed Instruction, 1960-1970" (unpublished EdD thesis, Harvard Graduate School of Education, 1997), 142.
5. Diederich designed a smaller, cheaper, and (by eliminating electrical wires) safer version of Skinner's teaching machine. He claimed that a good machine would reduce the amount of "drudgery" in English classes—in his own unannounced classroom visits, he saw 60% of instruction devoted to the drill and review that a machine could do more efficiently. "The Diederich Scorekeeper" [December 22, 1954] in Green File, ETS Archives.

CHAPTER 14

REORGANIZING THE EDUCATIONAL TESTING SERVICE

(1970)[1]

Diederich worked at ETS from 1949 to 1976, and for most of those years he was a researcher rather than an administrator. Much of his work was in the assessment of proficiency in English, but he was usually free to explore whatever topics interested him, especially when an external grant underwrote the expense (more than half of the ETS research funds came from government, foundation, and other external contracts in the 1950s and 1960s). Diederich took part in studies of basic skills, programmed instruction, minority students, newspapers in the curriculum, part time "lay readers" of English papers (his pride and joy), vocabulary books, and other topics. As an ETS Executive Vice President later said, it was rare to hear anyone say "you can't do that."[2]

The freedom that let Diederich undertake a wide range of projects also let the other researchers pay little attention to life in schools. Almost all had PhDs in psychometrics (the niche within psychology for the quantitative study of testing). They made far fewer presentations at AERA (the major annual conference for College of Education faculty) than at psychology conferences. One colleague told Diederich that he had no idea there was a national organization of high school principals.[3]

Elsewhere in ETS the connections with schools were stronger. A small Evaluation and Advisory Services unit (which Diederich directed for one year) coached schools on the use and abuse of tests. Advisory committees for ETS' major client, The College Board, included teachers who could reject items on the tests prepared by ETS. And President Chauncey kept in close touch with many educators; his annual reports thoughtfully discussed recent trends in American and international education. But among the researchers Diederich felt "lonely," he wrote in 1955. At that time he wanted ETS to examine the short and long term effects of education ("How do you measure citizenship? How do you measure the spirit and methods of scientific inquiry?"). He estimated that psychometrics and government contracts each took 30% of the ETS research effort, with another 30% for personality, guidance, and business projects. With only 10% for education, it was no wonder that "our researchers look slightly nauseated whenever the word education is mentioned."[4]

The reorganization sketched below might have let Diederich exert more influence on high schools (as well as schools doing the same to ETS). He thought it was unlikely to be adopted. But as ETS doubled in size every five years in the 1960s and 1970s, it took on various projects in and near schools. The annual report in 1976, the year Diederich retired after three extensions beyond the normal retirement age of 65, listed work on compensatory education, Head Start, desegregation, vocational guidance, and school finance.[5] There had been a surge of interest in program evaluation and policy analysis, and in the 1980s, ETS created a new division solely for services to elementary and secondary education. ETS widened its focus from the groups that underwrote testing programs to an unprecedented concern with the institutions that used the test results as well as the individuals who had educational and career choices to make.[6]

Reorganizing the Educational Testing Service (1970)

ETS is still in what I call the "Thurstone stage" rather than the "Tyler stage" of organization: namely, it is dominated by mathematical psychologists with only lukewarm interest in what is going on in schools—although the situation has improved in recent years.[7] When I first came to ETS in 1949, it seemed to me that the Research Division was interested only in the development of statistical procedures and was composed of individuals who were attracted to testing mainly by the mathematical problems it presents. Similar invasions by mathematicians had occurred in genetics, agricultural experiments, and should have occurred in meteorology. Now this interest in the mathematics of testing is concentrated chiefly in the Psychometrics Group of the Division of Psychological Studies, although everyone else in this Division is distinguished more by statistical competence than by acquaintance with what is going on in schools

Let me recall a few instances of this unconcern to sort out the dimensions of the problem. When I first came to ETS, I assumed that I should hang around the Humanities group in Test Development, find out what their testing problems were, and try to solve them by experimental studies. The head of that group was particularly receptive because he was a personal friend, and I had been on his doctoral committee at the University of Chicago. But after several exploratory conversations, I could see that he was getting restless, and he finally asked, "What project and job shall I charge this to?" Only then did I realize that there was no project and job to which I could charge it. I would have to make a formal research proposal, usually to the College Board, without much prior consultation or examination of data, and then wait a year or more to get it approved.

I finally thought of one thing I could do for this group, and it had a fairly typical result. At that time I was an avid proponent of "extended context" as a way of increasing the validity of both reading and writing tests (passages of at least 1,500 words). I had carried this idea about as far as it could go in my examinations at the University of Chicago and in the tests I developed for the United States Armed Forces Institute. To get on a new tack, I asked myself: What is the opposite of a long passage? The answer was obvious: a single sentence. So I selected 200 rich, meaty sentences from *Bartlett's Quotations* and similar sources and got about 50 student interpretations of each sentence from college freshmen writing courses. From these I selected one good and four poor interpretations of each sentence and tried them out in the experimental sections of the SAT Verbal. The answer finally came from Statistical Analysis that they were almost exactly as good as but no better than the kinds of reading comprehension passages then in use. Since it was a strict rule that no new item-type would be adopted unless it had proved superior to the one in use, those items were discarded and have never since been used. I still regret this because, in certain testing situations, they would afford greater flexibility than the usual reading comprehension passages: one could set a wide variety of reading problems in minimal testing time.

From that day to this I have yielded to no one in my admiration for the splendid statistical analyses of our tests that [ETS colleague] Frances Swineford makes. I have frequently told her and others that she is the only one who keeps us honest. But I also lament the fact that there is no parallel review of the *content* of our tests: the importance of what is tested, its representativeness of the content that is most widely taught, its coverage of the intellectual skills that are supposed to be developed by each discipline—something comparable to the test reviews in the Mental Measurements Yearbooks.[8] I suppose that something of this sort is done in the meetings of our test committees, but there is nothing on paper to prove that anyone has ever looked critically at our tests as measures of the supposed outcomes of instruction. This could not be done by a single person like Frances Swineford. It would have to be done by an expert in each field: a scientist would have to review the science tests, a historian the history tests, etc.

Another illustrative anecdote: I needed to use the "Interest Index" of the Eight Year Study in the form revised by John French and called AIM—Academic Interest Measures—in one of my studies, but I found that it took a long time to get it scored, cost $1.15 per student, and the 24 scores were written on each answer sheet without labels and in an order that made them very inconvenient to use. Since I had a large hand in the development of this instrument, I got permission to retype the items in an order that made all responses to a given field of study (such as English) lie in two lines across a multilithed answer sheet. Then it could be both scored and interpreted by each student in about 10 minutes with the help of a "Scoring Aid" that was simply a strip of paper one-third the length of a page. If you put the top edge of this slip just under the line marked A, the bottom edge would lie just above the line marked M. Each student could then count (in his head) the numbers written in these two lines (since there were only 16 numbers and they were either 0, 1, or 2). The sum would be entered in a blank labeled A+M___; right next to this was the abbreviation of the subject (like Eng___), and in this blank the student wrote H (high), M (middle), or L (low) after comparing his sum with a simplified table to norms for boys and girls of that grade, printed on the same sheet. In these norms M was the mean; H was one standard deviation above; L was one standard deviation below; the student wrote whichever was nearest his sum.

Now the point of this anecdote is this: I showed my revision and simplified scoring procedure to the person in charge of research on this instrument, and his response was fairly typical. He did a little study to find out whether my arrangement of items (in which each field was represented in every twelfth item) gave rise to less "halo effect"[9] than the current arrangement (in which each field is represented in every fourth item). He found no difference and hence no reason to change—despite the fact that the current arrangement could not be scored in my fashion without a perforated scoring key that would be difficult to cut out and expensive to manufacture. He said, "Well, suppose it does cost the school $1.15 to get it scored; it doesn't cost me anything." He also said that if teachers found it hard to understand the scores in the order in which they were presented, they must be pretty dim, because he found no such difficulty.

I use this anecdote to illustrate not only insensitivity to what teachers will put up with but a lack of knowledge of the development of other interest measures. The Strong Interest Inventory [a popular test of career interests] only became practicable for widespread use after a way was found to score it on the newly developed IBM scoring machine. Even then, it took so many passes through the machine that the cost at first was $1.50 per student. Even so, that was regarded as a breakthrough, because the previous cost of hand-scoring by clerks was out of sight.

In my study, students in grade 11 usually finished marking their responses to the Interest Index within 30 minutes; then they could score their own answer sheet and interpret each score as High, Middle or Low (differently for boys than for girls) within the remaining 10 minutes of the class period. There was no delay of three weeks in receiving the raw scores; there was no extra charge; and there was not the difficulty of interpreting each score by referring to complicated tables printed in a manual, of which only the teacher had a copy. Yet the investigator could shrug off these advantages because they made no difference to *him*. Since that person is no longer at ETS, I feel safe in relating this anecdote ... [ETS researcher] Marty Katz, who has inherited this instrument, frequently recommends my procedure...

So far as I know, this is our only instrument in the affective domain that has been widely used. For some years now we have had a group interested in the development of measures of personality and social behavior, thus far with no pay-off in usable instruments. To my way of thinking, the attention of this group has been misdirected. They have been looking for personal and social characteristics that do not change—like the Myers-Briggs "types."[10] They have given little if any attention to aspects of personality and character that schools would like to develop, such as the following:

Self-direction, initiative

Industry, perseverance, thoroughness

Honesty, responsibility

Orderliness, system, neatness

Good judgment, decisiveness

Ability to lead and follow

Ability to work and play with others without friction

Habit of completing assignments satisfactorily and on time

In the domain of mental health, how about these:

Security: self-confidence, pride, independence, flexibility, cheerfulness

Affection: gives and takes affection freely, shows good will to others

For the life of me, I cannot see why measures of such characteristics as these are beneath the notice of psychologists. I suppose that, because they are subject to change, they do not lend themselves to the formulation of psychological laws. But it still seems odd to me that, while teachers and counselors are interested chiefly in personal and social characteristics that can change, our group is interested only in those they cannot change. Couldn't we consider something along the lines of the Hartshorne-May studies of honesty [that demonstrated that honesty in one setting—among friends, for instance—did not predict honesty with teachers or parents]? That whole line of development seems to have broken off sharply, and I can't imagine why.

When one leader of this group was asked, "What suggests problems for you to work on?" his reply was, "The literature."[11] That is a fine way to start a vicious circle. As an alternative, I would suggest, "School objectives." Whenever I make that suggestion, the psychologists in the group act as though I had farted.

Now let me take another tack. Long before the National Assessment [of Educational Progress, the first federal snapshot of student achievement] was started [in 1966], I was bemoaning the fact that, although every year we collect information on what students can do and can't do in almost all subjects that are taught in schools and colleges, and although we record this information on our massive collection of item-cards, we never issue reports to the profession with such titles as "What is Wrong with English" or "What Students Don't Know about Music." We routinely collect more information of this sort every year than the National Assessment is likely to gather in the next decade, but we never summarize it and report it. Why not? It seems to me a lame excuse that none of our samples is completely representative of the nation as a whole (the College Board population is definitely a select population). But what of that? It is still a definable population and includes several definable subgroups. Teachers, administrators, and school boards would be interested in what students like these can do and can't do at the point of admission to college.

I have been daydreaming about how I would restructure ETS if I had a completely free hand and a lot of empty space in our new building. I'd start with a suggestion I made when we first moved into Thurstone Hall [in 1962] and we had to divide the space between Test Development and Research. To me the answer was obvious: put a testmaker in one office, a researcher in the next, and so on. Sally Matlack [administrative assistant to the Director of Research] said that this would not work because testmakers have to talk with one another a great deal in the course of developing a test, and this would bother the researchers. I wanted the researchers to overhear some of this conversation and, if possible, contribute to it, but in deference to the general will I now suggest leaving one office in ten vacant, fitted up as a conference room, to be used for all conversations that might disturb others.

On a deeper level, I'd like to amalgamate Research and Test Development into a single new division, the Measurement Division, with as many departments as there are in schools and colleges. The head of each department should be a recognized master of that discipline with special interest and competence in testing. He should have a passion for the diffusion of knowledge of his subject among the general population, tempered by an ability to come to grips with the question, "How much of it is enough for the average citizen who does not intend to specialize in it? What parts of it are most important for such a person?" [PD discusses internal candidates for those new departments] Our present group in Personality and Social Behavior might merge with our Department of Guidance and Counseling (since that is where their measures would most often be used) or they might be important enough to have a department of their own. Our present group in Psychometrics—Fred Lord and Co.— would be in a different division altogether—the Division of Data Analysis. Our group in Human Learning and Cognition (to which I belong) should be disbanded; its members should be reassigned to other departments. It is a fictitious entity, created only by the fact that such a subject is taught in graduate departments of psychology. It has very little connection with any kind of learning that goes on in schools. Three members share an interest in psycholinguistics—the light that is thrown on mental processes by language acquisition. They might go into either Languages and Linguistics or into a Department of Psychology.

Each department should include at least one person with a primary interest in research in testing and test results in that branch of learning. Often he would head the department, but not necessarily. He should work closely with two or more testmakers—the sorts of people we have in Test Development. Ultimately at least one person in each department should spend part or all of his time on the development of instructional materials (as our Early Education Group does now). Some of these materials might be adapted to programmed or computer-assisted instruction; others to workbooks; still others (and most commonly) to booklets of "Homework Assignments" in each field. I have in hand a series of booklets of this sort that will be published as manuals to accompany the twenty Cooperative Literature Tests (on the twenty literary works that are most frequently taught in grades 9-12). This came about because I had about 3,200 items left over after selecting the 80 best items on each work for the two published forms of the test. The other items, while not good enough for the test or not suitable for other reasons, would make excellent material for study as homework and later discussion in class—arguments by students with one another over the items on which there was a substantial difference of opinion. It is because there is so much wastage of this sort in testing, and because test items are so closely related to instructional items, that I think the production of instructional materials should become a regular part of our work.

Now I come to a very thorny problem. How many of the Cooperative Literature Tests do I honestly expect to sell? Barely enough to keep them in our catalogue. How many of the homework booklets will be distributed? We could not give them away. We shall have to force them upon the attention of teachers by publishing them in the guise of test manuals that will be sent free with every consignment of those tests.

Why am I so pessimistic? Because I was chiefly responsible for the development of our Newspaper Tests, sponsored by the American Newspaper Publishers Association Foundation and the National Council for the Social Studies. These tests were directed to a very large audience: for the past 13 years the newspaper publishers have supported a program called "Newspaper in the Classroom" that, at last count, involved 322 newspapers, 17,000 schools, 50,000 teachers, over three million students, and about 68 million copies of newspapers distributed annually (most of them free or sold for three or four cents apiece). The newspaper publishers have poured about 48 million dollars into this program with no hope of any immediate return. The four tests (two for junior, two for senior high schools) based on simulated newspapers were as neat a job of test building as you will ever see. Every item used in the published forms showed an advantage of newspaper classes over control classes that had approximately equal scores on reading comprehension tests. The tests were very extensively publicized. There was a leading article in *ETS Developments* (May 1969) that reached our clientele of about 65,000 test users; there was another article in *Social Education* that reached the 22,500 members of the National Council for the Social Studies. The Foundation sent out flyers explaining the tests and their uses [...] copies of the tests and the Handbook explaining their development and use were given to everyone who attended the workshops and institutes on the use of newspapers in the classroom during the summer of 1969.

Then, last May, I asked for a report on sales of these tests during their first year in circulation. There were exactly twelve orders. As [the Roman poet] Horace once said, "Parturiunt montes, nascitur ridiculus mus"—The mountains are in labor, a ridiculous mouse is born.

I should have been prepared for this because ETS has had similar luck in the past. Soon after I came to ETS, Cooperative Tests [one of the organizations that merged in 1947 to form ETS] inherited the evaluation instruments of the Eight Year Study, which are still cited as models of imaginative and resourceful test development on hard-to-measure objectives. We gave them an attractive new format, cut them down to 40 minute forms that could be administered within single class periods, established new norms, and gave them lavish publicity. After five years, we had sold 3,000 copies of the

Interest Index, 2,000 copies of the Interpretation of Data Test, and hardly any copies of anything else. The same sort of thing happened when we inherited the tests developed by the United States Armed Forces Institute and by the Cooperative Study of Evaluation in General Education (Grades 13-14). Apparently teachers and administrators will not buy tests that cover anything less than a full year's work in a subject; they shy away from tests measuring a single large objective within a field of study (like Interpreting Data), and tests measuring outcomes of units within courses or minor elements in course (such as most of the "Newspaper in the Classroom" programs).

It was finally decided that whenever we inherited copyright to such measures, it would be cheaper for us to give them away than to attempt to sell them. Hence we established the Office of Special Tests, which furnishes single copies of such instruments with the right to reproduce them for experimental use. Teachers who are interested in objectives or units that are the least bit off the beaten track usually want to produce their own measures. All we can sell on a large enough scale to justify the cost of publication are tests of what I call the "least common denominator" of all teaching of the standard subjects.

Is there any way out of this discouraging situation? There may be. When I developed four programmed workbooks on vocabulary (as a by-product of an experimental study), I first offered them to ETS for publication. This offer was batted around for about two years, and the Trustees finally turned it down—on the ground that ETS should not get involved in the publication of instructional materials. It was suggested that I offer them to a commercial test publisher, with all royalties payable to ETS research funds, since I had developed these workbooks on ETS time. I chose Harcourt, Brace & World, since it has the best line of English textbooks and was doing more at the time about programmed instruction than any other publisher. They were accepted, and they have since been paying ETS about $40,000 a year in royalties. If we had published them, we would have sold about 100 copies and then quit.

What makes this difference? The commercial publishers have a large staff of aggressive and active Field Representatives who are vulgarly called "salesmen." If you want to get any worthy educational product into widespread use—particularly a test, or test-related instructional materials—somebody has got to sell it. It has to be sold by people who get into the schools and talk turkey to principals and department heads, who give away copies of what they are selling and hang around persistently until they get an order. They have to be supported by advertising and by exhibits in national meetings of professional associations, but these are of no avail without the salesmen.[12]

The Cooperative Literature Tests, the booklets of homework assignments, the Newspaper Tests, and other products of my own that I want to get into widespread use ... we can sell some of these because they are related to our monopolies: tests for admission to secondary schools, colleges, and graduate schools. But all the rest will have to be sold by salesmen, no matter how we disguise their function by such honorific titles as "Field Representatives." Moreover, we have to get into advertising on quite a large scale. As I see it, there is nothing unethical about bringing a worthy educational product rather forcibly to the attention of the potential user. If we don't, we must resign ourselves to the fact that such products will simply not be used. They have to compete with the products of commercial textbook publishers who have no such compunctions.

If this prospect is too distasteful for us (or to our Board of Trustees) the only alternative I see is to turn over such products to commercial publishers, with royalties payable to ETS. But if we want to promote them ourselves, and thereby retain more complete control over them, we must be prepared for a major expansion of what I think of as our Division of Dissemination. It would include our present information, advisory, and instructional services, our exhibits at conventions, our publications, our regional offices, and ultimately about a tenfold expansion of our Field Representatives. We ought also to lure away one of the most successful Sales Managers from the commercial publishers to manage those representatives and give them a more realistic conception of what they are for. Their job is to sell tests and test-related instructional materials. We must also consider an annual advertising budget of something like $100,000. Ten years from now, this amount may seem ridiculously low.

I am allowing myself to daydream in this unorthodox fashion because there is such a slight chance that any of these ideas will be adopted. That is the difference between a pampered researcher and a man with executive responsibilities; the latter has to contend with vested interests, traditional policies, legal restrictions, the expectations of our present clientele, and other forces that resist change. If by some particularly vindictive Act of God the whole Officers' Division was wiped out and I was summoned to fill the breach until replacements could be found, I would hope to carry out not more than one percent of these recommendations.

If you wonder how I could find the time to write such an infernally long memo, the answer is that I have been waiting for data on the Literature Tests to get back from the computer, and I had finally run out of things to do. That should not be overlooked as a primary source of creative ideas in the present Research Division: Waiting for the Computer.

In another memo Diederich wrote in 1970, he continued these reflections by commenting on the omissions in an internal report on the new services ETS might offer in the 1970s:

I did not find in this report the sort of intimate and detailed knowledge of what is going on in the schools and has gone on in the recent past that uncovers desperate problems or promising possibilities. I have in mind the sort of practical acquaintance with what is already being done in the better schools that Dr. Conant showed in his various reports. I regarded his reports as conservative-with-good-reasons: he did not want to recommend anything that he has not seen successfully carried out; hence his reports were deliberately limited, as one title suggests, to "The American High School Today"—NOT to "The American High School Tomorrow." We get more of that in people like Lloyd Trump and his followers. As to what has gone on in the recent past, I think of Lawrence Cremin's admirable history of the progressive education movement that reached a peak in the 1930s and was then knocked in the head by World War II, with most of its possibilities unrealized. The 1940s, as I see them, were just a dead loss; the 1950s brought back an emphasis on scholastic achievement that was under-emphasized by the progressives, and carried out some long-overdue curriculum revisions in the areas of science, mathematics, and foreign languages. In the past decade, we have seen a resurgence of interest in innovation and experimentation, mainly directed by administrators and hence directed at what I and many teachers think of as externals that have not yet paid off in better learning and in many ways have hampered it: such things as flexible schedules, team teaching, ungraded schools, paraprofessionals, programmed instruction, multi-media instruction, flexible architectural arrangements, and the like. Even so, I think many of these innovations opened up possibilities of improvement that may bear fruit in the next decade. For example, we are still hampered by the tradition that a "subject" is something that has to have five class meetings per week—a tradition that grew up *in this country only* as a result of the Carnegie Report of 1905—never for valid or compelling reasons and now completely outmoded. We could knock this tradition in the head by taking advantage of the possibilities opened up by flexible scheduling and by the dissatisfaction with the traditional time allocations expressed by influential committees of the very accrediting agencies that enforce such standards.

People like Conant, Trump, and Cremin know a great deal about what is going on and has recently been going on in schools, and they have strong opinions about which of these practices make no sense whatever and which of them, while still carried out imperfectly, present possibilities of improvement that we [ETS] ought to get behind and facilitate by the assistance of our testing know-how.

There are three types of people whose knowledge of what is going on in education leaves something to be desired:

—The woolly-headed, Dewey-eyed "educator" who thinks that all problems will be solved if you just get interdisciplinary teams of teachers together an hour a day to gabble and thereafter leave it up to the students to do whatever they damn please—in other words, to invent, implement, and carry out an educational program by making all decisions that they refuse to make for fear that they may make mistakes. If these "educators" had their way, no textbook would ever get written until some particular student expressed a need for that particular textbook. The fact that it would then take about five years to get it to him never enters their calculations.

—The hard-headed "subject matter specialist" who may be caricatured as thinking about education from the standpoint of what a Ph.D. in his field ideally would learn at each stage of his education. These fellows produce the textbooks and hence have a great deal more influence on what is actually done in class than the "educators," but they put in a great deal that only a future scholar in that field needs to know—not what the average citizen need to know. They also produce an impossible load of homework, and they are always competing with other subjects for more time and crowding out much more educative work in art, music, shop, home economics, physical education, and the like.

—The psychologist, who cheerfully admits that he has no idea what is going on in schools and does not propose to learn because it is sure to be awful; who, in our time, tends to believe that education will not improve until computer-assisted programmed instruction in many media makes it possible for each student to go his own way at his own pace in learning whatever he happens to want to learn at any moment. He tends to rely on experiments with something like 68 frames, carried out in 14.2 minutes with 95% success; he never gets around to figuring out what would happen if you extended this to 10,000 frames for each subject over the whole year. I have seen what happens. By Christmas at least the better students are so bored that they could scream. Here is the major assumption I want to challenge: individualized instruction is the answer (possibly supplemented here and there by interaction tasks to learn how to get along with others). I believe that an able teacher can get a response from a class that he could never get by teaching the same things to 25 individuals one at a time. The mutual stimulation, by-play, teacher's explanations and corrections, rivalry, and cooperative effort all give *momentum* to the work of a class that soon grinds to a halt if each student has to go it alone. True, some adjustment to individual needs, interests, and rates of learning has to be made, but it can be made without reducing everything done in school to the level of a solo performance. There may be a place for solos, but there is also a place for the symphony orchestra—and that is what a good teacher is able to get from a class that he could not get from individuals.

It is obvious that I would not want any of those three characters (whose faults I have exaggerated to make my point quickly) to determine the educational needs of the 1970s. There are plenty of practical school men around whose judgment is sound. We typically have such people on our committees; I wish we could have more of them on our permanent staff. Theoretically our test development people ought to have this practical acquaintance with the work of the schools, but we catch them so young and work them so hard that they do not have a chance to get around and see what is going on in strong schools in many parts of the country.

I have something like this broad acquaintance myself in the field of the humanities at the high school and junior college level. I have often argued with Bill Turnbull [President of ETS from 1970 to 1981] that if we could get similar people with my degree of awareness in science, math, social studies and practical arts, we could save the soul of ETS and possibly transform American education. Bill's reply always is: "Who?" Then I am stumped. Unfortunately the people who know most what is going on in schools do not know enough or care enough about testing to want to make a career at ETS. So I do not know whom to suggest, but I still sense the need for those people at ETS.

So many of the mistakes of the past are cropping up again today. For example, there are outfits that take pride in their lists of thousands of "behavioral objectives," apparently unaware of the fact that Bobbitt, Charters, and their followers produced lists just as long and just as behavioral during the 1920s, and they fell of their own weight. The weird combinations of subjects in "core courses" or "integrated courses" tried and found wanting during the 1930s are with us again in 1970. The fine and practical arts, vocational education, and physical education are still crowded into odd bits and pieces of time left over from the demands of the Big Five college preparatory subjects in the flexible schedules of today as they were in the old curricular organizations of the 1930s. The chief aim of Guidance still appears to be that of persuading about 20% more students to head for college than really want to go, but then persuading them to be realistic about which colleges they can enter. School testing, record-keeping, and reporting practices seem to me to have undergone no improvement whatsoever since 1935, when I first began visiting the thirty schools of the Eight Year Study. I could write—in fact, have written—whole chapters on what is wrong with them: chiefly that they take more time and cause more anxiety and heartache on both the giving and the receiving end than they are worth. They are still the responsibility of individual teachers, who have never done and never will do anything intelligent about them, rather than the responsibility of departments, who have power to initiate and sustain change. On the other hand, in 1657, just 300 years before Skinner published his first paper on programmed instruction, Comenius brought out a really good programmed textbook, the *Orbis Pictus*—a Latin Primer, the first illustrated textbook for children—that exemplified many good ideas Skinner never thought of (notably its strong appeal to children's interests) and was probably the most successful textbook in publishing history. It lasted over 200 years and was translated into 20 languages in Comenius' lifetime, including Russian, Arabic, Mongolian and Turkish. Why don't we remember?

ENDNOTES

1. "Developing Educational Awareness within ETS" in Folder 649, William Turnbull Papers (ETS Archives).
2. Robert Solomon Oral History (ETS Archives), 3-7.
3. Diederich to Morris Finder, September 23, 1994 and February 27, 1995 (Finder Papers, Box 1, University of Chicago Archives); Henry Dyer Oral History (ETS Archives), 12.
4. "Memorandum for Mr. Dyer" November 17, 1955 in "Research and Development Planning Board" folder, Box 17, Series 6 A/B (ETS Archives).
5. *1976 Annual Report*, 5-11.
6. Len Swanson Oral History (ETS Archives), 18-19.
7. Diederich refers to his former colleague and neighbor Leon L. Thurstone, an eminent professor of psychology at the University of Chicago from 1924 to 1952, best known for his quantitative studies of "primary mental abilities" (seven facets of intelligence). Thurstone preceded Tyler as the chief examiner at Chicago (1931-38). Neither man ever worked at ETS.
8. A widely used compilation of brief reviews of hundreds of tests, overseen for many years at Rutgers University by Oscar Buros, Diederich's former colleague on the Eight Year Study.
9. In this case, a strong interest in English would incline the student to rate highly all items connected with English. In general, the tendency to let positive (or negative) reactions to a person or thing sway the evaluation of its particulars.
10. A personality test derived from the ideas of Carl Jung. For a snapshot of Henry Chauncey's longstanding fascination with the Myers-Briggs, see Nicholas Lemann, *The Big Test* (New York: Farrar, Straus and Giroux, 1999), 91-92. For my misgivings about that book, see Robert L. Hampel, "Books by Journalists on American Education" in *History of Education Quarterly*, v41, n1, Spring 2001, 95-100.
11. Diederich had in mind Samuel Messick, a former head of research for whom an ETS building is named. Paul Diederich to Morris Finder, September 23, 1994 (Finder Papers, Box 1, University of Chicago Archives)

12. As one example of the reluctance to sell, ETS through the 1960s had a rule against hospitality suites and cocktail parties at national conferences. Aside from a few public relations staff, the marketing efforts were miniscule, featuring short movies and pamphlets about testing. Benjamin Shimberg Oral History (ETS Archives), 44-51. Another staff member recalled a memo in which he used the word customer. It came back with "a very stern lecture about how no, we don't have customers. We are not a business. We have clients." Michael Zieky Oral History (ETS Archives)

EPILOGUE

Remembering (October 3, 1996)

From a letter to Siegmund Levarie (Diederich Family Papers, Princeton, NJ)

I became annoyed and somewhat alarmed when I found that I could not remember what I did yesterday—in the sense of something I accomplished. If it was as distinctive as cutting the grass, I could usually remember that, but not something more routine like pruning. Recently, this forgetting extended to recalling during the afternoon what I had done during the morning. Then I recognized it as a problem and invented a way of investigating it.

I decided to keep a record of what I did from hour to hour each day on a 3 by 5 index card. I might have called this record a diary, but since a diary, like that of Samuel Pepys, usually has extensive accounts of external events, thoughts, feelings, reading, etc., and I wanted to concentrate on *what I did*, I decided to call it "Doings." I had a tin box of index cards of various colors, so I opened this and set it beside my radio at arm's length from the chair in which I read. Then I would lay one card each day on the shelf within easy reach and leave a pen beside it. For something to write on I chose the slim 6 by 9 volume, *A New Introduction to Greek*. I resolved to write on this card what I had done as soon as I finished doing it.

The first day's record had three revealing entries:

9–11 Nap   1:40–3:40 Nap   7:30–9:30 Nap

At first glance this seemed absurd, but after thinking it over, I decided that it was not atypical. My official time for sleep is 9 P.M. to 5 A.M., which is 8 hours. But I nearly always have a period of wakefulness, beginning around 1 A.M., in which I get out of bed and read or ruminate, and this often lasts as long as two hours.

After I wake up at 5 A.M., I do various chores until about 9 A.M. when I suddenly feel very sleepy. I have learned not to fight this, so I go back to bed and usually sleep about 2 hours, counting it as a continuation of my night's sleep—not really a nap. The same thing happens again after lunch, and then I sleep about two hours and regard it as my nap. It used to be one hour, but with advancing age it has gradually extended to two.

Then, after dinner, there is often a game I want to watch that starts at 8 P.M. and ends about 11. If I watched from the beginning, I would get so sleepy by 9 P.M. that I could not follow the action. I would rather pick it up about 9:30 so that I could see how it came out. Hence I often go to bed soon after watching the news on TV from 6 P.M. to 7 P.M. and sleep about two hours. Then I am wide awake for the latter part of the game.

This program makes a good deal of sense, but what does it suggest about my life expectancy? It gives me a total of 12 hours of sleep out of 24 and 12 hours of activity. Is this healthy? I have learned to trust my body and so believe it is. But does it also indicate that my shift from time to eternity is near at hand? Probably it does, but it does not frighten me. Long ago I outgrew my fear of death along with my belief in heaven, hell, and judgment. I am grateful for my brief glimpse of the wonders of creation.

In retirement, Diederich consulted occasionally, wrote a few articles, and after his wife of 45 years died in 1982, he devoted most of his time to reading. He filled three to five page single-spaced letters with his ruminations on ancient Greek literature, philosophy, music, Biblical passages, and any issue musicologist Siegmund Levarie, his closest friend, mentioned in their weekly correspondence. Diederich occasionally read new books on education—for instance, Ernest Boyer's High School *(1985) prompted Diederich to send Boyer his favorite curricular proposal, the course on how we get the things we need—but Diederich preferred to reread landmark works in the humanities (for instance, he found in Cicero the same sort of enumeration of essential values that he had espoused as the ultimate purpose of education). One thing did not change—he continued to make what he called "little ingenuities." When he was 86 he found a drill bit—a rasp—that scrapped the inside of his pipe more effectively than a pocket knife. At 87 Diederich disconnected the bag on his riding mower to let the clippings fly: it took half as much time to collect them a day later when they were dry. In the following year, he pried the staples from two match books, glued the books back-to-back on a piece of plywood, cut off the matches to make a pile of 40, and then no longer struggled to light up. "My distinctive gift is the simplification of everything," Diederich wrote in 1994, three years before his death at 91.*

MORE DIEDERICH

The readers who knew Diederich best during his lifetime were English teachers. During his quarter century at ETS he focused his research on the assessment of what students learn and teachers do in English classrooms. He emphasized what many educators call "formative" assessment—how can tests provide diagnostic information rather than rank and sort students. Many of Diederich's papers were collected in an anthology, *Measuring Growth in English* (National Council of Teachers of English, 1974), published in his honor by the professional association whose meetings he often attended. For his brief flirtation with teaching machines, see "Self-correcting homework in English" in *Proceedings of the 1959 Invitational Conference on Testing Problems* (ETS, 1959). "College Educated Housewives as Lay Readers" (NASSP Bulletin, April 1963) praised the part-time employment of bright women to correct English papers.

Diederich described his work as an examiner at the University of Chicago in "Teaching English with Test Exercises" (*The School Review*, February 1947) and, in the same journal, "The Effects of Independent Comprehensive Examinations" (November, 1947) as well as "The Abolition of Subject Requirement for Admission to College" (September 1949).

Diederich and his ETS colleague Sydell Carlton published several workbooks. Harcourt, Brace, & World issued the two volume *Vocabulary for College* in 1964 and 1965, which at its peak yielded annual royalties of $40,000 for ETS.

In addition to English, I have not included articles that reveal the more quantitative side of Diederich's mind. There are several publications on statistics (*Short-Cut Statistics for Teacher-Made Tests*, ETS, 1960), science ("Learning to do science" in *Educational Horizons*, November 1972), program evaluation ("Measuring The Effects of Newspapers in the Classroom" in *Social Education*, February 1970), and test construction (technical reports circulated within ETS and available in the ETS Archives).

Diederich preferred to write articles rather than books; even his dissertation (published in 1939 as *The Frequency of Latin Words and their Endings* University of Chicago Press) was short. A book on which he was the third author (Heaton, Camp, & Diederich, *Professional Education for Experienced Teachers: The Program of the Summer Workshop*, University of Chicago Press 1940) is of enduring interest for its description of intensive professional development that went beyond imparting particular techniques to include the artistic, emotional, and physical growth of teachers.

Anyone interested in more Diederich might consider exploring where he worked. For the Ohio State years, Robert W. Butche, *Images of Excellence: The Ohio State University School* (New York: Peter Lang, 2000) is full of valuable details (such as the charge to the founding Director "that three-fourths of the teachers shall be men, since it is well known the American secondary schools are over-feminized"). The spirit of the school pervades the book created by the class of 1938 (*Were We Guinea Pigs?* New York: Henry Holt, 1938). For the Eight Year Study, the 800 page book of snapshots Diederich helped compile is indispensable (*Thirty Schools Tell Their Stories*, New York: Harper & Brothers, 1943), as is the best scholarly work on the topic (Craig Kridel and Robert V. Bullough, Jr., *Stories of the Eight Year Study: Reexamining Secondary Education in America*, Albany NY: State University of New York Press, 2007). For the University of Chicago in the 1940s, there are excellent biographies of its President by Harry Ashmore (*Unseasonable Truths: The Life of Robert Maynard Hutchins*, Boston: Little Brown, 1989) and Mary Ann Dzuback (*Robert M. Hutchins: Portrait of an Educator* Chicago: University of Chicago Press, 1991). The curriculum and the examinations Diederich helped to create are thoroughly described in F. Champion Ward, ed., *The Idea and Practice of General Education: An Account of the College of the University of Chicago* (Chicago: University of Chicago Press, 1950). There is not much reliable scholarship on the history of the Educational Testing Service; Nicholas Lemann's chapters in *The Big Test* (New York: Farrar, Straus, & Giroux, 1999) are astonishingly snide. Norbert Elliot's new biography of the founding President of ETS is far more balanced: *Henry Chauncey: A Life* (New York: Peter Lang, 2014).

ABOUT THE AUTHOR

Bob Hampel graduated with honors from Yale University and received his Ph.D. in history from Cornell University. In 1981, his research interests shifted from 19th century American politics to 20th century education when he joined Theodore Sizer's "A Study of High Schools," a four year appraisal of American secondary education. For the project he wrote *The Last Little Citadel: American High Schools since 1940* (Houghton Mifflin, 1986).

Since 1985, Hampel has taught education history and policy at the University of Delaware, where he won three awards for outstanding teaching and twice served as Interim Director of the School of Education. In Delaware, Hampel has been a Public Service Fellow for the Governor, a trustee of the Sanford School, and a consultant to the Delaware Department of Education. Outside Delaware, he served from 2002 to 2011 as the Secretary/Treasurer of the national History of Education Society.

Coauthor of *Kids and School Reform* (Jossey-Bass, 1997) and several dozen articles, Hampel is now writing a history of what he calls "shortcuts to learning," various ways Americans have tried to make education both faster and easier.

INDEX

Bettelheim, Bruno, 37

Chauncey, Henry, 101, 110, 164
Comenius, John Amos, 37, 176
Computer-assisted instruction, 174
Conant, James Bryant, 101-107, 173
Cooperative housing, 33-34

Diederich, Paul B.
  childhood, xi, 53-54, 60
  Educational Testing Service, researcher at (1949-1976), 163-177
  ethical beliefs, 78-86, 119-121
  family, xi, 60, 130
  mechanical aptitude, xi, 20, 37, 132, 180
  musical aptitude, xiii, 60, 65
  Ph.D. dissertation (1939), xi, 88-99
  prose style, xv, 64, 103
  religious views, xiv, 81
  research on English composition, xviii, 163, 181
  social and political philosophy, xiv, 65-70, 78-86
  teaching methods, Ohio State University School (1932-1935), xvi, 4-5, 7, 45-49, 54, 59, 89-99
  teaching methods, University of Chicago (1942-1948), 59, 133-134
  undergraduate education (1924-1928), xiii, 18
  University of Chicago, examiner at (1942-1948), 43-44, 49, 112, 181
  vocabulary workbooks, 171
Douglas, Senator Paul, 34-35

Educational Testing Service
  Academic Interest Measures, 166
  Cooperative Literature Tests, 169-170
  Myers-Briggs test, 167
  newspaper tests, 170
  personality tests, 110, 121, 167-168
  relations with schools, 164-167, 173, 175
  reorganization of, 164, 168-169
  sales representatives, 171-172
Eight Year Study (1932-1940)
  accomplishments of, 2
  Beaver Country Day School, 22
  Dalton School, 29, 31, 48
  Denver, Colorado, 29, 31
  Des Moines, Iowa, 8-9
  evaluation staff of, 118, 122

Francis Parker School, 47-48
George School, 56
guidance, xvi, 109, 175
Horace Mann School, 15, 45
Los Angeles, 31
Oakland University High School, 52
Ohio State University School, xvi, 1-2, 21, 45-47, 89-99, 109, 136
psychoanalysts and, 4, 36
Smith, Eugene R., 7, 37
sports, 19, 21
summer workshops (1937-1939), 39-40, 117
Zachry, Caroline, 4
Eliot, Charles W., 10, 154
European schools, 150-151, 154

Harvard University, xviii, 54, 65, 71, 105
Havighurst, Robert, 40, 90
High School (United States)
    Advanced Placement, 102, 137, 145
    Carnegie units, 7-8
    class size, Rutgers Plan for reducing, 157-162
    college courses, overlap with, 146-148
    core courses, xvi, 30-32, 45-46, 57, 63, 106, 140, 149, 174
    counselors, 24-30, 113-126
    daily schedule, 3, 56-57, 103-106, 141-143, 149, 155, 158-159
    electives, 10-14
    English teachers, 50-51, 53, 155-162
    foreign languages, 14-15, 47-48, 57-58, 102
    free reading, 52-59
    grades 7 to 10, high school as, 137-144
    graduation, 9, 19
    gym class, 11, 19-24
    homework, 142, 150, 159-160

    housewives as teachers' aides, 158-160
    lack of activity in, 15, 103-104
    Latin, 45-49, 90-99
    libraries, 54, 143
    marks, 4-6
    pressure on students, 10, 12, 55, 103-104
    social promotion, 6-7
    talented students, 54, 101-105, 138-139, 147, 150-152
    vocational courses, 13, 16-19
Holmes, Henry, xiii, 145
Hutchins, Robert M., xii, 43-44, 72, 148

Kohler, Wolfgang, 30

Levarie, Siegmund, ix, 60, 179-180

McKeon, Richard, 43, 77
McNeill, William, 44

National Association of Secondary School Principals, 45
National Education Association, 42
National Lampoon, 110

Ohio State University School, xvi, 1-2, 21, 45-47, 89-99, 109, 136

Plato, 71
Powell, Arthur G., x, 63
Princeton, New Jersey, schools in, 138
Professional development, 39-42
Progressive Education
    administrative progressivism, xiv
    Committee of Ten, 7
    core courses, xvi, 30-32, 45-46, 57, 63, 106, 140, 149, 174
    counselors, 24-30, 113-126
    midwestern values, 63
    teaching methods, 15, 39, 129-136

Richards, I. A.
    Basic English xi, 71, 75
    literary criticism 49-50
    philosophy courses in high schools 32, 72-75

Skinner, B. F., xi, 158-159, 162
Spaulding, Francis, xiii

Thorndike, Edward, 38, 111
Thurstone, Leon L., 164, 176
Turnbull, William, 175

Tyler, Ralph xii, 35, 49, 72, 77, 109, 115, 127, 138

University of Chicago
    Board of Examiners, xii, 43-44, 49, 124, 165, 181
    Laboratory School, 10, 59, 125

Waples, Douglas, 49
Willis, Benjamin, 155

CPSIA information can be obtained at www.ICGtesting.com
Printed in the USA
BVOW07*0840090514

352455BV00027B/115/P